314-5
8

MEDIA CENTER MANAGEMENT

A Practical Guide

Studies in Media Management

_____

BROADCAST MANAGEMENT
Radio-Television
First Edition by Ward L. Quaal and Leo A. Martin
Second Edition, Revised and Enlarged
by Ward L. Quaal and James A. Brown

CLASSROOM TELEVISION
New Frontiers in ITV
by George N. Gordon

CASE STUDIES IN BROADCAST MANAGEMENT
Second Edition, Revised and Enlarged
by Howard W. Coleman

THE MOVIE BUSINESS
American Film Industry Practice
Edited by A. William Bluem and Jason E. Squire

THE CHANGING MAGAZINE
Trends in Readership and Management
by Roland E. Wolseley

FILM LIBRARY TECHNIQUES
Principles of Administration
by Helen P. Harrison

THE FILM INDUSTRIES
Practical Business/Legal Problems
in Production, Distribution and Exhibition
Second Edition, Revised and Enlarged
by Michael F. Mayer

AMERICAN NEWSPAPERS IN THE 1980s
Revised and Reset
by Ernest C. Hynds

MEDIA CENTER MANAGEMENT:
A Practical Guide
by William T. Schmid

Media Center Management

A PRACTICAL GUIDE

by William T. Schmid

COMMUNICATION ARTS BOOKS

HASTINGS HOUSE · PUBLISHERS
New York 10016

Library of Congress Cataloging in Publication Data

Schmid, William T   Media center management.

(Communication arts books) (Studies in media management)
    Bibliography: p.
    Includes index.
    1. Audio-visual library service.   2. Instructional materials centers.   I. Title.
Z717.S35   028.7   80-14803
ISBN 0-8038-4730-0
ISBN 0-8038-4731-9 (pbk.)

Published simultaneously in Canada by
Copp Clark Ltd., Toronto

Printed in the United States of America

CONTENTS

Preface   xi

1   MEDIA CENTER ORGANIZATION   1

Typical Media Centers   1
Environmental Influences   3
Clients—Management—Staff—Politics—Facilities—
Equipment—Budget
Three Organizational Approaches   7
Independent Decentralized Organization—Centralized
Organization—Hybrid Organization: Centralization with
Decentralization
Management Tips   18
Develop Accountability—Guarantee Consistency—Analyze
Staff Volume—Establish Growth Projections—Do Not
Overcommit—Determine Accurate Turnaround Time—
Standardize Operational Procedures

2   PERSONNEL   26

Personnel Selection   26
Advertising for Positions—Screening Applications—

v

Interviewing—Hiring
Orientation and Training   30
Orientation Programs—Professional Training
Performance Review   34
Termination   35

3 DESIGNING SERVICE FORMS   37

Hints on Service Form Design   37
Internal and External Information—Essential
Information—Easy Use—Logical Sequencing—Staff
Recommendations—Prototype—Final Revisions—
Completion Time—Additional Suggestions

4 OBTAINING USEFUL UTILIZATION DATA   50

Key Utilization Concepts   50
Decide What to Count—Obtain Key Data—Select Time
Frame for Comparison—How Utilization Can Work for
You

5 COST ACCOUNTING   62

Cost Accounting Productions   63
Determining Costs—Tabulating Costs—Making
Comparisons
Cost Accounting Equipment   84
Determining Costs—Depreciation—Cost Effectiveness

6 INSTRUCTIONAL MATERIALS SELECTION AND
   PURCHASING PROCEDURES   96

Instructional Development Considerations   97
Instructional Development Model—Instructional   97
Development—Theory and Practice—Learn
Instrutional Development Through Practice
The Selection Process   103
Media Selection Considerations—Acquisition Procedures
Cataloguing .   109

7 EQUIPMENT SELECTION AND PURCHASING
   PROCEDURES   111

   Cautions Regarding Equipment Selection   111
   Plea for Media Center Equipment Review—Creeping
   Complexity—Instructional Development—Theory and Practice
   Equipment Selection   115
   Determine Equipment Function—Select Equipment to Fit
   Function—Evaluate Equipment
   Equipment Purchase   134
   Bid Procedures—Two Types of Requisitions—Requisition
   Writing Tips—Selecting a Good Dealer—Evaluating
   Sales—Equipment Check-in Procedure—Inventory
   Procedure—Distribution or Circulation Coding

8 PROMOTING MEDIA CENTER SERVICES   148

   Public Relations   148
   Brochures—Exhibits—Staff Speakers' Bureau—Tours—
   News Releases—Awards—Letters of
   Commendation and Appreciation—Newsletters—Evaluation
   Forms—Client Feedback Sessions—Extra Effort
   Political Relations   153
   Provide Reliable Service—Learn the Real Organization
   Chart—Determine Motivation—Plan Initial Contact—Solicit
   Client Participation

9 DEVELOPING CONSTRUCTIVE CLIENT
   RELATIONSHIP   156

   Requirements for Media Center Director   157
   Recognize the Instructor as the Content Specialist—Stress
   Instructor's Sources of Control—Adjust to Different
   Personalities—Treat Ideas with Sensitivity—Eliminate
   Technological Fears—Keep Technology in its Place—Talk
   in Understandable Terms—Be Tolerant of Limited
   Technical Knowledge—Be Realistic About Instructional
   Design—Develop a Sample Portfolio
   Requirements for the Instructor   161

Be Prepared to Make Commitments—Recognize the Media
Director as the Media Specialist—Establish Objectives—
Use Only Essential Content—Be Prepared for the
Production—Measure Effectiveness
Common Requirements for the Media Director and
Instructor   166
Keep an Open Mind—Learn to Compromise

10 COMPLAINTS: HANDLING THEM EFFECTIVELY   169

Client—Management Perspectives   169
Handling Complaints   171
Be Courteous—Be Concerned—Put Yourself in Client's
Shoes—Take Responsibility—Be in Control—Get the
Facts—Act Quickly—Learn from Your Mistakes—
Anticipate Possible Problems

RESOURCE SECTION 1: SERVICE FORMS   177

Graphic Production Forms   179
Television Production Forms   186
Audio Production Forms   197
Media Distribution Forms   204
Learning Resource Center Forms   213

RESOURCE SECTION 2: A SELECTED BIBLIOGRAPHY
(annotated)   216

Management Skills   216
Library Skills   219
Instructional Development   221
Materials Evaluation and Utilization   221
Equipment Evaluation and Utilization   223
Production   224
Computer Technology   225
Associations and Organizations   225

Index   227

PREFACE

THIS TEXT has three major objectives: (1) to provide techniques that have *practical* application for the management of media center programs; (2) to present management concepts that have *broad* relevance for people working in a wide variety of media support services; and (3) to serve as a practical supplemental text for students taking courses in the management of media center programs. For purposes of this book, a media center is defined as a department that facilitates education, training and promotion through the production of media materials (i.e. slides, overhead transparencies, filmstrips, videotapes, 16mm films, etc.) and delivery of support services (i.e. circulation of audiovisual equipment, playback of video programs, cataloguing and accession of resources through library services, etc.). Emphasis is not on theory but rather the practical, sometimes frustrating, realities of managing a media center. The perspective is general, having application for people working in media programs in education, business and industry, libraries, medicine, government, the military, and museums. People in any media program, large or small, should find techniques in this book useful. Most everyone in instructional technology, from production assistant to media director, has some management responsibilities. Students using this book as a text will receive a very realistic view of media center management. Neophytes just entering the educational media field along with experienced professionals should be able to use suggestions in this book.

Media Center Management: A Practical Guide, is not a "how to" book on media production or equipment operation, but rather a publication presenting basic principles that can be used to manage a variety of media center services. This book takes a no-nonsense approach, discussing media center management the way it is, not the way we would like it to be. Emphasis is placed on how to function effectively in the real world, rather than the ideal world. You might consider this publication a survival manual on how to get through the day with limited need for aspirin and tranquilizers!

Terminology is generalized, to ensure broad application. The reader should concentrate on the principles and techniques employed, rather than specific terminology. For example, "client" is used to represent a variety of people who use media center services such as teachers, students, content specialists, trainers, and producers. "Students" and "trainees" are used synonymously. The emphasis is always to concentrate on management techniques with wide application rather than terminology unique to a particular media center program.

Chapter 1 looks at the various factors which influence the organization of a media center. The advantages and disadvantages of the various organization structures are discussed. Chapter 2 covers the important job of personnel selection and training. People, not equipment and facilities, are your most important resource. Major areas include personnel selection, orientation and training, performance review, and termination procedures. "When in doubt, create another form," is a phrase that all too often leads to numerous unproductive service forms. Chapter 3 suggests some useful tips on how to design effective service forms that do not quickly become obsolete. The survival of a media center can depend on the ability to document the value of service programs. Chapter 4 shows how to obtain, and constructively use utilization data that will substantiate the success of programs and provide the needed rationale for increased financial support. Cost accounting techniques for media programs and equipment are covered in Chapter 5. The sections in Chapter 5 on how to measure cost effectiveness should be valuable as more and more organizations question the financial investment in media programs. Selection and purchasing procedures for instructional materials are discussed in Chapter 6. Chapter 7 presents a step-by-step approach to the appropriate selection and purchase of media equipment. The skillful art of learning to toot your own horn without becoming a nuisance is presented in Chapter 8. In many organizations, media centers are considered overhead and expendable if budget cuts are necessary. Closely linked with survival and any chance for growth is the ability to effectively promote the instructional and cost effective services of a media center. Chapter 9 suggests ways in which media professionals and clients can work together to develop effective media programs and materials. The practical approach used throughout this book is especially evident in Chapter 10 which presents some tips on how to handle complaints effectively. At some point media center services will not please everyone and it is imperative that you be able to solve problems quickly and equitably.

Two resource sections are also provided. Resource Section 1 has examples of service forms which can be used as is, or altered to fit specific media center needs. A selected bibliography (annotated) in Resource Section 2, lists some additional sources of information related to media center management.

No one writes a book alone. The author is grateful to a number of people who, through their comments and ideas, helped shape this book. I express my appreciation to Pat Fewell, Jerrold Kemp, Jim Lied, Forrest Wisely, Sharon Richardson and Dave Russell. Laura DiMascio, and other members of the Media Services Graphic Production Unit at Illinois State University, did a tremendous job creating visual material for this book. Thanks to the editorial staff of my publisher who helped me through this publication, my first book. A special heartfelt thank you to Richard B. Lewis, who suggested I write this book, and spent tireless hours editing much of the copy. Dick, with his warm sincere personality, has started many of us down the frustrating, agonizing, lonely road to publication, filled with delays, setbacks, and continual rewrites, and yet we all still love him. A genuine debt of gratitude to my secretary, Pat Helme, who typed draft after draft, but more importantly kept prodding with that incessant question, "How's the book coming?" Through the pushing and encouragement of Dick Lewis and Pat Helme, you now have, hopefully, a useful addition to your library. Without their assistance this book would not have been written. With friends like this, all things are possible. Thank you.

MEDIA CENTER MANAGEMENT

A Practical Guide

CHAPTER 1

Media Center Organization

$\mathbf{F}$OR PURPOSES of this book, a media center is defined as a department that facilitates education, training and promotion through the production of media materials (i.e. slides, overhead transparencies, filmstrips, videotapes, 16mm films, etc.) and delivery of support services (i.e. circulation of audiovisual equipment, playback of video programs, cataloging and accession of resources through library services, etc.).

This chapter provides some basic organizational concepts for media centers that primarily support instructional and informational needs. Today media centers are found in many areas: education, business and industry, libraries, medicine, government, the military, and museums. Some media centers are small with limited production capability while others provide a full range of support. This chapter gives you an understanding of basic forces influencing media centers, advantages and disadvantages of various organizational arrangements, and a better idea of what positive structural changes are possible within your own environment. Many principles presented can be applied in specific areas such as television, audio production, graphics, photography, audiovisual equipment circulation, library services, printing, and learning resource centers. These concepts have application in large centers with many departments or small centers having only one full-time position.

TYPICAL MEDIA CENTERS

Many people are overly concerned with titles and labels. A look at two very different media centers, one in education and another in industry, can de-

1

Fig. 1-1

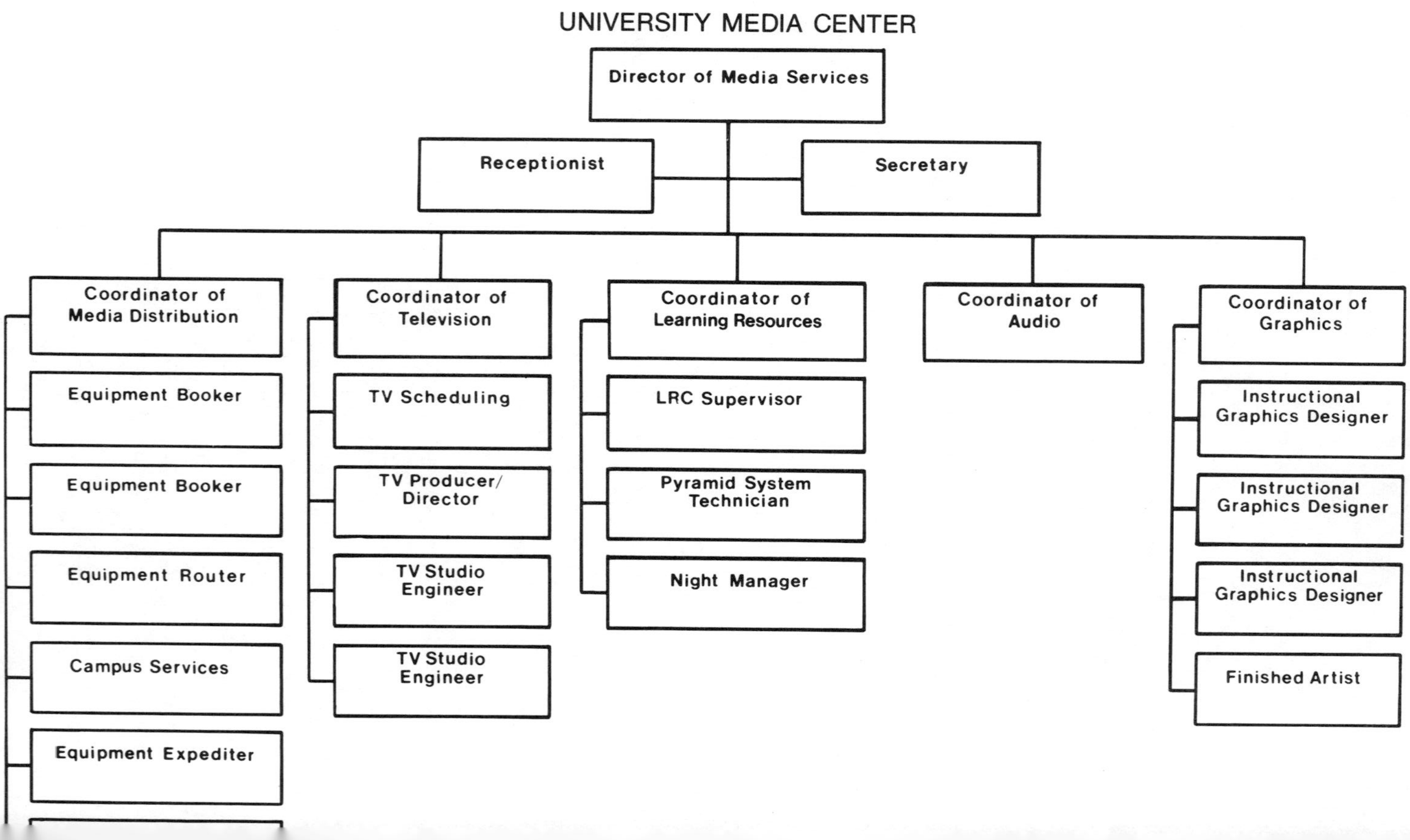

UNIVERSITY MEDIA CENTER

2

termine if there are any similarities. Figure 1-1 shows what a university media center might look like with the following major operating units: coordinator of distribution, in charge of circulating audiovisual equipment and materials; coordinator of television, in charge of producing instructional videotapes and 16mm films; coordinator of learning resources, in charge of cataloging and providing playback facilities for packaged presentations such as tape/slide programs; coordinator of audio, in charge of producing all instructional audiotapes which become a part of tape/slide programs; and, coordinator of graphics, in charge of producing all original art work and photography.

Figure 1-2 shows what the organizational chart for a corporate media center might look like. Major responsibilities are divided between production and development with the following operating units: chief photographer, in charge of all still and cinematography; art director, in charge of producing all original art work; media director, in charge of all videotape and multimedia productions; and, superintendent of AV services, in charge of the circulation of all audiovisual equipment along with playback facilities for packaged programs.

Although the titles are different, the functions are similar. In the university media center, photographic functions are handled in two areas. The coordinator of television does all cinematography while the coordinator of graphics does all still photography. In the corporate media center, all photography is done through the chief photographer's department. Other examples could be shown but the major point is to identify functions and functional relationships rather than terminology.

One additional word on terminology. As stated in the Preface, the intent of this book is to have broad application for media centers in education, business and industry, libraries, medicine, government, the military, and museums. Each area has its own set of "buzz words" and labels. To use labels from each area would be confusing and awkward. Therefore, "client" stands for anyone seeking service from a media center. A client may be a teacher, content specialist, student, trainer, instructional developer, librarian, trainee, or customer. Certainly the list could be longer. So, again, this is an additional plea to think in terms of *functions,* not *labels.*

ENVIRONMENTAL INFLUENCES

Any media center is the product of its environment. For this reason, no two media centers are organized exactly the same way. Most factors making up this environment are subtle. Figure 1-3 shows an operational environment consisting of clients, management, staff, politics, facilities, equipment, and budget. Arrows indicate all these have a direct influence on how media centers are organized. No matter what type of organization the media center serves, these influences quickly establish boundaries of growth.

Clients

People who use a media center, whether they be students, instructors, administrators, or employees, basically are concerned about convenient, reliable

Fig. 1-2

CORPORATE MEDIA CENTER

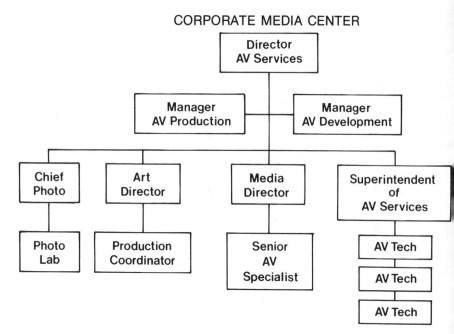

service. Anything less, clients consider an inconvenience and not worth the trouble. Human nature indicates we all patronize services which are easiest to use. Client needs represent a real and appropriate influence on the very organizational foundation of a media center. Any media director who does not recognize and work effectively with client needs will not have a successful operation.

Management

The media manager's own concerns have a direct influence on media center structure. Any manager should strive for convenient, reliable service, but this starts with a well conceived organizational chart showing direct lines of accountability. The growth of informal procedures between clients and media staff might be a first indication of deficiencies in the formal organizational structure and necessitate cause for change in that formal structure.

A basic requirement of any media center organizational structure must be to facilitate the efficient utilization of personnel, equipment, materials, and space. Without staff and facilities, a media center cannot function. Since there never seems to be enough staff and facilities, it is imperative they be used wisely.

The ideal media center organizational structure should also provide for lateral and vertical staff advancement. If there are chances for professional development, any new employee coming into a media center is likely to be more enthusiastic and encouraged to perform effectively. Large media centers with many positions have a built-in advantage for advancement. However, the small center should be organized to allow at least for staff development on a variety of projects.

Staff

Politics

Management

Facilities

Equipment

Clients

Budget

Media Center

Support from upper administrative levels makes all things possible while a lack of such support makes all things impossible. With the very survival of a media center hanging in the balance, upper level administrators have a direct influence on organizational structure. These administrators usually have no background in instructional technology, so media center managers must continually tutor them regarding advantages and disadvantages of educational media. Without such continuing education techniques administrators often have simplistic answers to complex problems of media center operations. For example, many administrators view media centers as pure overhead, a cost that could easily be eliminated during a period of tight budgets. Media center managers in any organization must document the positive cost-effective contribution of their operation.

Staff

No single factor has more direct influence on a media center than staff. Personnel considerations are two dimensional: the number of staff members and, more important, staff talent. Most people fall into the easy trap of defining media capability in terms of equipment, facilities, and budget. Without talented staff, none of these can be fully developed. A talented staff can take mediocre equipment, facilities, and budget and provide valuable services, but the reverse is not necessarily true. A mediocre staff will not be saved automatically by superior equipment, facilities, and budget. A talented staff is equally important both for the well endowed or struggling media center. Chapter 2 will cover personnel in more depth since staff has such a direct influence on service quality.

Politics

Many people do not think of politics as a major influential force in media center management. Political factors pertain to the power of individuals and groups that make decisions. Some of this decision-making is formal, following the organizational structure of the school, company, or organization.

Political factors may be present in the educational setting where state and national politicians can make or break the cause of educational media. On the local level politics may also be a factor of the bureaucratic power structure in every school system, library, or business. Who reports to whom, and with how much clout, can have an effect on operations. Consequently, the media center director is always better off reporting high up in the administrative structure. In education the media center should be directly linked with the instructional process and the success of students, while in business the center should contribute directly to profitable performance.

Much of the decision-making process can take place on an informal, subtle level, not nearly as visible but equally effective. Decisions should be made on the basis of an objective review yielding key facts. However, other factors also enter because decision-making is a human enterprise, subject to all the human drives of pressure, greed, advancement, power, prestige, patronage, and influence.

The media director should be aware of informal lines of influence which can have much influence on the fate of a media center. Such behind-the-scenes realities as who likes whom, who gets invited to the right cocktail parties, who can influence and who has the real power to make decisions, must be recognized and dealt with effectively. A media center director, for instance, may report to a vice president in charge of corporate communications who is just a figurehead with little real power. On the other hand, a junior executive in finance who is a strong proponent of media and also a close personal friend of the president, could have much influence. In the game of politics, media managers must learn to recognize the teams and play the game accordingly. The subtle nuances of political power can be a tremendous force in shaping the media center organizational structure.

Facilities

Staff and equipment must be housed in adequate facilities. There is a direct relationship between good facilities and the ability of the media center to meet service demands. A major challenge for media managers is to make upper level administrators aware of the unique architectural requirements that influence service capability. Electrical, air conditioning, acoustical, and work-flow relationships represent just a few of the many design considerations which must be properly addressed to ensure a smooth efficient operation.

Equipment

Equipment capability has a direct influence on service effectiveness. There is probably no other topic that has more glamour appeal than equipment. Few people in media can resist the temptation of new equipment which promises increased capability—which, however, is only available for a price. Equipment technology has advanced much faster than our ability to develop effective programs. The major challenge is to make the perfect match of the right equipment for the right purpose (this will be fully addressed in Chapter 6, "Equipment Selection and Purchasing Procedures").

Budget

Another obvious factor having a direct influence on operations is budget. There is probably no single area of greater concern for a manager than budget. Many managers feel that budget, not personnel or facilities, makes all things possible, as a good, realistic budget can attract talented staff and equip them with the tools to turn out superior products and services. Because of the obvious importance of budget, Chapter 4, "Obtaining Useful Utilization Data," and Chapter 5, "Cost Accounting," will deal with budget acquisition and controls.

THREE ORGANIZATIONAL APPROACHES

All organizational models in this section include a wide variety of services. There seems to be a growing management philosophy that diverse media services have much in common. Hopefully this is a healthy departure from the days when, for example, librarians and audiovisual people stayed in their own camps. People were either "print" or "non-print." Some even felt print was better than non-print and others supported the reverse. This gave instructional technology its very own version of the crusades! Now there seems to be some healthy cross-fertilization of interests. Media professionals from different support services are realizing the client is the most important common denominator. Clients do not care about format nearly as much as content and results. There is no "best medium," only the best medium for a particular application. Certainly such a philosophy is not yet universally practiced but there has been much progress.

Independent Decentralized Organization

One classic organizational approach is to have autonomous services, each with its own clientele. Figure 1-4 shows a variety of independent services. Although titles for these services vary, the overall concept is representative. A word of explanation is appropriate for learning resources which could also be called a learning resource center or learning resource laboratory. Regardless of title, this area usually houses instructional programs along with media equipment for lesson playback, preview, and production. Each department in Figure 1-4 has its own facilities, staff, and budget. Arrows represent the typical direction of service. A photographic unit might serve television, printing, and graphic departments along with regular clients such as teachers or instructional developers. Broken arrows indicate typical informal relationships between service areas. Informal relationships mean there is no direct responsibility to provide service to other media support areas. In many cases, there might be a charge for services. For example, in Figure 1-4, if television production does not have sufficient budget it could not retain photographic services. Solid arrows indicate that clients must go to each area for service. Bold arrows indicate those service areas typically having the highest client volume.

There are several good reasons why independent media departments (which usually represent spin-offs from related operations) have developed over the years. Service centers in education often evolved from academic programs, such as a television service from the communications department, or an audiovisual service from the education department, or a learning resource center from a library studies program. Industrial television services many times developed out of public relations, training, or advertising departments. As these media areas grew they often broke away from the fostering department and became separate entities.

Personalized service and convenient location probably sum up the advantages of independent service departments. Since these service areas are usually small, the client feels there is more personalized service. Most independent areas grow out of a concentrated need and thus remain conveniently close to this need. Being logistically close to the client's work location is probably the single most important advantage of the independent media service area.

There are some inherent disadvantages with independent media departments. Users must go from one department to the next to coordinate a multifaceted media project such as a slide/tape program. The broken arrows in Figure 1-4 illustrates a lack of formal interdependence between services. Instead of cooperation there may be competition. The television service may produce a

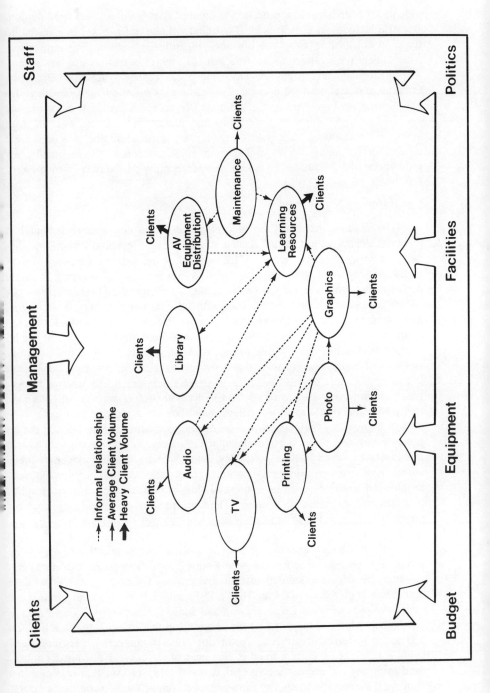

Staff

Politics

Management

Facilities

Clients

Budget

Equipment

Clients → Maintenance → Clients

AV Equipment Distribution → Clients

Learning Resources → Clients

Library → Clients

Graphics → Clients

Photo → Clients

Audio → Clients

TV → Clients

Printing → Clients

- - → Informal relationship
→ Average Client Volume
➡ Heavy Client Volume

9

videotape which more appropriately should have been a slide presentation. Because budgets are closely related to client volume, television has a vested interest in not turning away any business, regardless of appropriate application. Independent media departments foster duplication of personnel and equipment. Television may have a graphic artist and photographer along with supporting drawing and darkroom equipment. The same expertise and facilities may also exist in the photographic and graphic service areas. A multiplicity of graphic and darkroom facilities might be justified in certain instances but, in most cases, is impractical. The small organizational structure in an independent media service area can restrict personnel advancement. Professional staff growth can also be limited by a lack of interaction with a variety of media professionals.

Centralized Organization

The opposite extreme from decentralized media departments is found in the total centralization of all related media areas. Decentralization was discussed first since many media services started as independent functions. Eventually, in certain cases, management saw advantages for merging separate departments into a centralized media center. In Figure 1-5, broken arrows between media areas have been replaced with solid arrows indicating a strong formal interdependence through centralization. In this model autonomous management of separate areas has been replaced with one manager over all media operations. For example, in this arrangement, photo is charged with the responsibility and budgeted to provide direct support to printing, graphics, audio, and television. Outside clients may have to pay for services, or an internal budget based on projected volume may be available. Although clients can still work directly with individual services, at least now they are all in one location.

In many cases the maximum centralization shown in Figure 1-5 will not be possible because of local environmental influences. A good compromise in a move toward centralization would be consolidation of all production areas where there is a large similar commitment to specialized staff, equipment, materials, and space. Such areas could include graphics, television, photography, maintenance, printing, and audio. The construction or remodeling cost for production areas is usually much higher then for other facilities in a media center.

Efficient design and use of floor space are additional advantages of the physically centralized center. A good floor plan can recognize important relationships between service departments and provide for proper work flow. Several media center floor plans are shown in Figures 1-6 to 1-9, to illustrate these relationships. In Figure 1-6, television and audio production are located next to each other. This is done to foster the relationship that exists between television and audio in terms of projects, production talent, engineering personnel, and some equipment. A current trend is also evident in Figure 1-6. Master control, used primarily for engineering functions, was a relatively small area in comparison with the television studio. Now, master control tends to be much larger, accommodating editing and tape duplication. This trend has been caused by rapid development of small electronic field production equipment for produc-

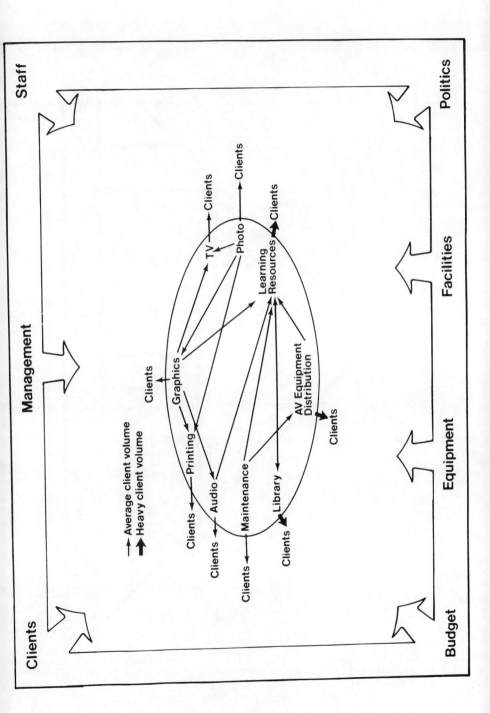

Fig. 1-6

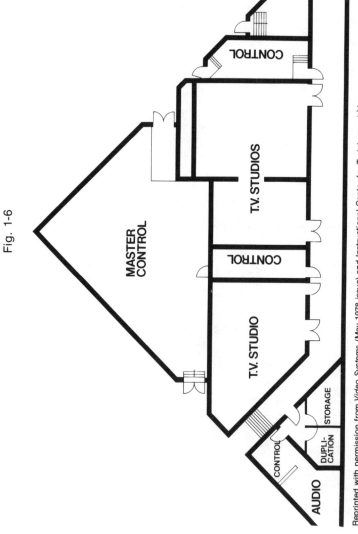

MASTER CONTROL

T.V. STUDIOS

CONTROL

T.V. STUDIO

CONTROL

AUDIO

CONTROL

DUPLI-CATION

STORAGE

Reprinted with permission from *Video Systems* (May 1978 issue) and Instructional Center for Training and Management Development at Xerox Corporation.

Fig. 1-7

Proposed media center floor plan reprinted with permission from Media Services at Illinois State University.

tions outside the studio and simultaneous acceptance of the ¾″ and ½″ video-cassette formats for editing and duplication. Technological developments can cause sudden changes in space requirements, so be flexible when planning facilities.

Figure 1-7 goes even further with television, audio, graphics, and film all located close together. This takes advantage of the support role graphics has with audio for tape/slide programs, with television for slides and camera cards, and with film for animation flats. Audio has support roles with film and television for specialized sound tracks. The floor plan allows for maximum utilization of facilities. The television studio can double as a large recording studio for audio and an interior shooting studio for film. Figure 1-8 shows how a good floor plan can maintain important relationships between different service areas. The learning resource center is the hub, housing program preview, audiovisual equipment practice stations, and individualized lesson playback areas. The equipment pool, along with circulating audiovisual equipment, provides immediate backup during equipment breakdowns in the learning re-

13

Fig. 1-8

Proposed media center floor plan reprinted with permission from Media Services at Illinois State University.

source center. This is especially important in programs where students are on a tight schedule to complete a certain number of mediated course modules. Special short-duration equipment setups can be easily handled with the equipment pool next door. Repair and first-line maintenance support the equipment pool and playback equipment located in the learning resource center.

Figure 1-9 provides for maximum cooperation between production and service areas. Television, audio, and film are all located close together in one corner of the floor. The equipment pool for circulation of audiovisual equipment is across the hall. However, this floor plan goes even further by placing three major meeting rooms with projection booth facilities on the same floor. Attractive and functional meeting rooms are strategically located close to the equipment pool. Therefore, this floor design fosters desirable cooperation among media support areas while providing meetings with a full complement of those same services. The close proximity of support services to meeting rooms is also a very realistic design for those last minute emergencies during meetings.

AV Technical Services

Control

TV Studio

Dressing Rooms

Pre-view

Prop Storage

Distribution

Media Library

Meeting Room

Projection Booth

AV Services

Audio Studios

Control

Film Editg

Film Library

Broadcast Services

Dressing Rooms

Pre-view

Storage and Display Preparation

Equipment Pool

Conference Services

Projection Booth

Meeting

Rooms

Meeting Rooms

Projection Booth

Reprinted with permission from the Public Relations Department at Sears, Roebuck and Company

Time for a media management axiom: *last minute audiovisual emergencies at meetings have been, currently are, and ever shall be, a fact of life. Amen!* The positive service dynamics implicit in these floor plans are only possible through a centralized media organization.

Physical consolidation also promotes maximum utilization of resources. One center brings together personnel with a wide variety of media competence. This can stimulate interdependence and a teamwork approach in which the most appropriate medium is selected and used to accomplish a particular task. Individual personalities can either make or break teamwork potential, but at least the centralized media center provides opportunities for such positive dynamics. This teamwork philosophy also provides media staff with professional growth opportunities through wide exposure to a variety of media approaches. By sheer size, the centralized media center allows for lateral and vertical promotional opportunities. Look back at Figures 1-1 and 1-2, and see the numerous promotional opportunities inherent in the organizational structure of a large media center. In Figure 1-1, someone could start as an artist with several promotional options: (1) coordinator of graphics; (2) coordinator of some related area such as television or audio; and, (3) director of the center. Media people often branch out from their original interest and large centralized centers facilitate this growth. Clients also benefit since the centralized approach provides one-stop, convenient service, no matter how complex the program.

The major advantages of a centralized media center seem to correct most of the disadvantages of decentralization. A stronger feeling of interdependence among media service departments is nurtured by consolidating these areas administratively and physically. Administrative consolidation provides overall budget control, eliminates some of the budget competition which can hinder objective media utilization, and fosters coordinated development. This last point is crucial since no organization can afford to have independent media departments going off in separate directions with little coordination towards common goals. The fractionalized, uncoordinated growth of separate media areas results in unnecessary duplication of personnel, equipment, materials, and space, along with ineffective use of limited budgets. The centralized media center allows for the efficient use of these resources.

Despite all the advantages, the centralized structure is not without some disadvantages. The consolidated center may be labeled impersonal and because of a centralized location may eliminate easy "next-door" type of service. Client convenience is directly proportional to how much a service will be used, and cannot be ignored in the media center organizational structure.

Hybrid Organization: Centralization with Decentralization

Since there are inherent advantages and disadvantages in both decentralized and centralized media organizations, it is possible to apply the positive aspects of each to achieve the best of both worlds. All media departments can be centralized for overall control and efficient use of resources, while establishing decentralized satellite centers close to specific client needs. Figure 1-10 is exactly like Figure 1-5 except for the addition of satellite centers. Decentralization through satellite centers is used for library materials, audiovisual

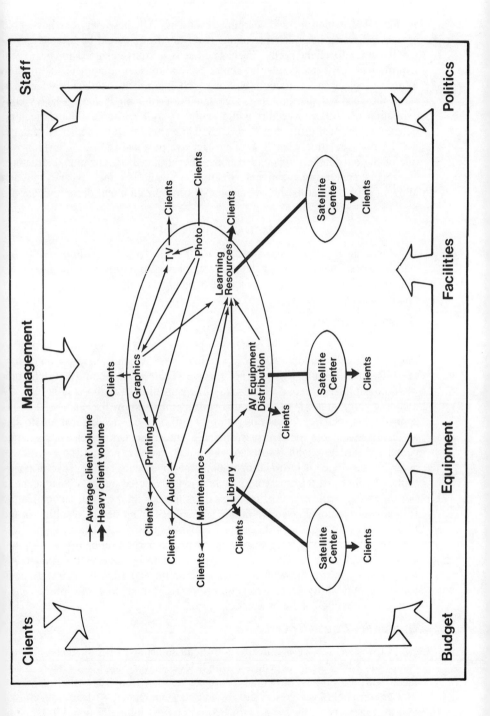

17

equipment distribution, and learning resources. All these services have bold arrows indicating heavy client volume and, therefore, should be located conveniently close to client needs. Each satellite is custom designed to meet local requirements. A typical satellite center for audiovisual equipment distribution might be located in a classroom building with equipment specifically selected to serve the needs of that building. One satellite center might have a heavy concentration of 16mm projectors while another may have more slide projectors, depending on local instructional need. Satellite centers offer another advantage, usually being relatively small so clients receive personalized service which was one of the only major advantages of the decentralized organizational structure. No media center organizational structure is ideal, but this hybrid approach allows for incorporating the advantages of centralization and decentralization.

MANAGEMENT TIPS

Once an organizational structure has been selected that fits local needs, certain operational guidelines should be employed to ensure maximum service. The tips below are proven management techniques that can be used in any media center.

Develop Accountability

In order for any media center to operate smoothly, the entire work load must be logically subdivided into operating units. A manager who cannot successfully delegate authority will not survive. There must be an exact definition of responsibilities for two reasons: (1) to ensure that each job is done quickly and efficiently; and, (2) to ensure that staff members know the range of their responsibilities. Such a division of authority will only be successful if employees are held accountable for their performance. The organizational chart of a media center should show who reports to whom and, more important, how the work actually gets done. If informal operational arrangements evolve, several possibilities might exist: (1) someone is taking on additional duties; (2) someone is not doing the required work, forcing others to take up the load; and/or (3) the formal organizational structure no longer satisfies client needs, resulting in the use of make-shift solutions. Under any circumstances, well planned lines of accountability must exist for management to quickly isolate problems or acknowledge accomplishments. Correction or praise should be done with dispatch. All too often the media manager is quick to criticize and slow to praise. Judicial use of accountability keeps everyone on the right track so confusion and inefficient use of time can be avoided.

Guarantee Consistency

Consistent service is crucial yet difficult to achieve. People using a media center must be able to depend on a high level of service. Most clients, when faced with the options of sporadic service, ranging from very good to mediocre, or consistent average service, would choose the latter. At least with consistent average service they can plan accordingly and know the job will be completed on the date promised within quality standards. Achieving consisten

Fig. 1-11

STAFF PRODUCTIVITY FORMULA

ıula	$\dfrac{\text{Annual Service Volume}}{\text{Total Staff}}$ = Average Volume per Staff Member
nple hic uction	$\dfrac{\text{9000 Units of Finished Artwork}}{\text{3 Artists}}$ = 3000 Units per Artist
nple a Equipment ibution	$\dfrac{\text{12000 Requests for Media Equipment}}{\text{2 Staff Members}}$ = 6000 Requests per Staff Member

service is difficult when considering the number of variables at work. Variables include fluctuations in budget, productivity of personnel, objectives of the organization, operating costs, and service volume. A continual balancing act is required between all factors influencing productivity to maintain a dependable level of service. The manager must plan ahead and project the correct mix of the above variables to ensure consistent service. Some techniques for maintaining consistent service will be covered in this chapter since with consistency comes increased service volume while inconsistency will result in a decline in patronage.

Analyze Staff Volume

The quantity and quality of staff directly affects media center services. Variety of staff talent can heavily influence productivity, especially in production areas such as television, audio, and graphics. One artist may work slowly yet turn out high quality work while another produces rapidly but quality may suffer. Carrying variety even further, the pace and quality of each artist may also be heavily influenced by the type of assignment. Artists, just like other production people, usually have certain things they can do very well. Some managers will assign jobs based on what a person can do best while other managers believe in giving production people a variety of assignments to broaden their experience. With either approach, an average production volume per position must emerge, in order to project future personnel requirements.

The easiest way to determine staff productivity is to take the total service volume in a given time frame and divide by the number of staff. Figure 1-11 shows this basic formula and how it can be applied in two very different operations. In each case, annual output for the area is divided by total number of staff to derive the average volume per staff member. If a graphics area turned out 9,000 units of finished art work in a year with a staff of three artists, the average staff load is 3,000 units of art work per year. A unit is defined as a single piece of art work such as a slide or overhead transparency. True, this average does not take into account individual staff differences, or the complexity of each task, but at least it provides a starting point for estimating average staff productivity. The same approach can work for other areas such as distribution of media equipment. In media equipment distribution, 12,000 requests divided by two staff members yields an average staff load of 6,000 requests per year. Once the average yearly production load per staff member has been established, a media manager can start to make intelligent decisions about staff requirements for special assignments or projected future volume.

Establish Growth Projections

Being able to determine how much production or service volume a staff member generates per year is a key to other valuable management information. However, service quality should not be totally sacrificed for increased productivity. An appropriate balance must be maintained between output and quality.

A manager must know the average service volume each staff member can generate to make accurate growth projections. This involves a two-step process: (1) determining the factors which will influence future volume; and, (2) dividing projected volume by average staff output to determine personnel requirements. There are several sources of information that can help when estimating future service volume: (1) the average increase in media center productivity experienced over several representative years; and (2) expected growth of the institution the media center serves. In education, a projected increased enrollment could have a major impact on a media center. Introduction of a new product in business may require media center support for the development of sales training packages. A new state law requiring additional training for nurses may necessitate increased program acquisitions and playback facilities for the media center in a hospital. The reverse is also true where a decline in service needs might result in media center cutbacks. The media manager must be kept informed of all pertinent developments in the organization which rely on media support.

Once volume levels are projected, staff needs can be estimated. In Figure 1-12, graphic production has estimated an annual growth of 20 percent so the units of finished art work will jump from 9,000 the first year to 10,800 the second year. Dividing 3,000 units of finished art work per artist into 10,800 results in 3.6 positions. Since the .6 is not a full position, graphics decides to wait a year before adding a position. By not adding the position, the turnaround time—total time required between submission and completion of a service request—jumps from five to eight days. Service requests for graphics that used to take an average of five days to complete now take eight. To guarantee consistent service, it is better to increase staff when the need first becomes apparent rather than when the maximum staff load is reached. But then, who in a media center works under ideal circumstances? So, during the third year, the projected volume has jumped to 12,960 and is divided by 3,000 units per artist to substantiate the need for at least one additional artist. Notice that with the additional artist the turnaround time drops back to five days. This approach to matching required staff with projected demand can be used for most operating units in a media center. The same approach is used in Figure 1-12 for media equipment distribution, charged with the responsibility to supply audiovisual equipment. The only differences are type of work, average volume per staff member, and turnaround time. In Figure 1-12, media equipment distribution can tolerate only a one-day turnaround time. People usually desire very quick ser

			1 yr	2 yr	3 yr	4 yr	5 yr
Graphic Production	Output	Units per Year Projected 20% Increase	9,000	10,800	12,960	15,552	18,662
		Turnaround Time[a] [days]	5	8	5	5	5
	Staff	Existing	3	3	3	4	5
		New	0	[.6]	1.3	1.1	1.2
		Total	3	3	4	5	6
Media Equipment Distribution	Output	Orders Processed Projected 25% Increase	12,000	15,000	18,750	23,437	29,296
		Turnaround Time [days]	1	2	1	2.5	1.5
	Staff	Existing	2	2	2	3	3
		New	0	[.5]	1.1	[.9]	1.8
		Total	2	2	3	3	4

[a] Total time required between submission and completion of a service request.

vice because they do not plan ahead when ordering audiovisual equipment. Ideally it would be nice to have a turnaround time of several hours for any service; however, this book is not about the ideal but, rather, what is cost effective and realistic. Having a large staff of artists available to complete all requests on an immediate basis is convenient but not cost effective. Therefore, each media center operating unit must establish an acceptable balance between work volume and turnaround time. Figure 1-12 also shows the strong relationship between available staff, service volume, and turnaround time, given an adequate operating budget and staff working at maximum efficiency. As service volume goes up and staff size remains the same, turnaround time increases. When staff is increased to keep pace with volume, turnaround time drops. This relationship must be kept in mind when projecting future service volume and staff.

Do Not Overcommit

Most people in the media field enjoy providing service. They should be able to empathize with people's needs. Add to this premise a clientele that desires more services than are possible, and overcommitment can become the short term cure for a long term illness. Overcommitment starts out as a one-time exception to usual policies to help a client in dire need. No harm done? Wrong. A basic axiom of media management: *the exception quickly becomes the rule.* All of a sudden the media manager who made an exception for one particular case is now bombarded by other requests for the "new service." When the manager explains it was a one-time exception, there are quick retorts of special treatment for certain favorites. If the manager does not yield to the pressure, clients always go to that reliable standby, nasty phone calls followed by even stronger letters to everyone in a position of authority. If the manager succumbs to the pressure the center quickly starts trying to provide an added service without proper provisions. The result is poor, inconsistent service with the very same clients complaining. Another media management axiom: *you can't please all the people all the time and some people you can't please at all!* The moral of the story is not to overcommit in the zeal to help a client. Such action usually means the manager will win the battle but lose the war. Overcommitment, in the long run, becomes more of a disservice to clients because of an inability to deliver services on a dependable basis.

Certainly, there will be times when exceptions represent the only logical method for solving a problem. Just remember to weigh heavily the consequences of initiating exceptions to well developed policies before making a decision. The refined art of knowing when exceptions are appropriate is a management skill that usually comes only with experience.

A postscript is also required on the overcommitment problem. There must be a good understandable reason why a request cannot be filled. Just saying, "It has always been our policy," or "We have never done it," is not fair to the client. Chances of adverse client reaction drop considerably when reasons are given for not being able to honor the request. Sincerity and courtesy can also help, along with giving options for filling the request which do fall within the capability of the center.

Determine Accurate Turnaround Time

As noted earlier, turnaround time is the total time required between submission and completion of a service request. The relationship of turnaround time to other factors that effect productivity was discussed in connection with Figure 1-12. Turnaround time can fluctuate radically, depending on available staff and service volume. The only point to be made here is to establish a realistic turnaround time that satisfies the needs of most clients and the operational capability of the center. A realistic turnaround time for clients will vary with the service unit. For graphics, three to five days might be required, while audiovisual equipment distribution might be able to fill a request within several hours. If the turnaround time does not meet the schedules and deadlines of most clients, a more realistic time frame for completing service requests must be established. Conversely, a turnaround time which is acceptable for clients but causes chaos within the center is also unsatisfactory. A balance must be established between client needs and what is realistically possible. These two factors should establish an accurate turnaround time which then must be maintained. Once such validity has been established, clients will develop their planning around this time frame. A manager must do everything possible to guarantee a stated turnaround time to build credibility for the center.

Standardize Operational Procedures

A media manager maintains a constant balancing act with such variables as adequate staff, sufficient budget, desirable turnaround time, and fluctuations in service volume. When service volume and turnaround time increase, the usual answer is more staff and budget. *A better solution is increased efficiency.* The only way to achieve optimum efficiency is to standardize all possible operational procedures. Standardizing operational procedures means establishing the simplest set of procedures to accomplish a specific task with the least expenditure of personnel time, equipment, and materials. The simpler the procedure, the easier it is for personnel to learn, resulting in fewer errors. Mistakes and confusion quickly convert to increased personnel time. Standardization means establishing set procedures for certain types of routine jobs to save time. Assembly line concepts should be employed whenever possible. Developing service forms that get the job done is a very important part of standardization and will be covered in Chapter 3, ''Designing Service Forms.'' Keeping personnel, equipment, and materials expenditures to a minimum can release these same valuable resources for increased volume.

Every effort should be made to standardize all routine requests. There are probably days when a manager feels there is no such thing as a routine request! But, objectively, routine requests probably make up 80–90 percent of the total service volume. Figure 1-13 shows the impact of standardization using a hypothetical example. Moving from center to right, using standardized procedures, 80 percent of the routine requests can be efficiently processed in 40 percent of the available staff time, a conversion factor of one-half. This allows for special requests that are different from the norm, requiring additional staff time. An arbitrary conversion factor of 3 is used for special requests, resulting in 60 percent of the staff time. The ability to make time for special requests is very important since usually positive client feedback is not for satisfactory delivery of expected services, but for completion of special, out of the ordinary requests. This is human nature. People who request an advertised service cannot be expected to be overly laudatory when they receive these services. If an airline flies a passenger from Chicago to New York on time, without incident, there is no cause for celebration since this is what the airline is paid to do. Indeed, management might be alarmed if a passenger writes a complimentary letter about going from Chicago to New York *safely* on their airline! But, if the airline exerts extra effort to ensure a passenger makes a connecting flight there might be cause for enthusiastic praise.

Please note that special requests are different from exceptions leading to overcommitment mentioned earlier. *Special requests* are within the capability of the media center whereas *exceptions* require inordinate measures beyond normal procedures for completion. A special request might require a wide angle lens on a slide projector instead of the standard lens. An exception might involve changing the standard lenses for wide angle lenses on 50 projectors in 15 locations with a day of notice! The latter request might only be accomplished through extensive personnel overtime and renting 45 wide angle lenses and, therefore, is not a service within the capability of the center.

Moving from center to left in Figure 1-13, the repercussions of not standardizing the routine can be seen. Here, 80 percent of the regular requests take 80 percent of the available staff time, using one as a conversion factor. Sufficient time for special requests is not created through standardizing routine jobs. The only way to create additional time for special requests is to consider overtime for personnel or hiring additional staff. Each approach can unnecessarily increase the budget. Efficient standardized operating procedures can create the additional time required for special projects without a commensurate budget increase.

Although many examples of standardization will appear in this book, here are some tips for improved efficiency:

1. group similar requests for processing;
2. use assembly line techniques;
3. keep all processing steps close together;
4. design service forms which are easy to use;
5. keep alternatives to a minimum;
6. use compatible equipment.

SUMMARY

When considering the organizational structure for a single service department or a large media center, one must be aware of the influential impact of the local environment. Clients, management, staff, politics, facilities, equipment, and budget all have a direct influence on the organization of the media center. A realistic view of the environment will help determine what organizational op-

Fig. 1-13

ANDARDIZED VERSUS NON-STANDARDIZED OPERATING PROCEDURES

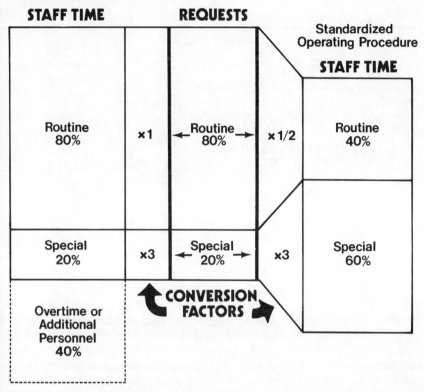

tions are possible. Decentralized media departments make possible personalized services, conveniently close to client needs, but lack management control and wise use of space, equipment, materials, and staff. Centralized organization establishes proper management control and cost effective use of facilities but may lack personalized service, close to client needs. A hybrid approach can combine the advantages of centralized control with satellite centers to provide services close to clients. A well conceived media center reflects as much as possible the surrounding environmental needs. Desirable qualities for any media center organization should include accountability, consistent service, reliable turnaround time, and standardized procedures for efficient use of staff.

CHAPTER 2

Personnel

THE PROPER SELECTION and training of personnel can have more impact— positive or negative—on a media center than any other management consideration. Media practitioners often become enamored with the glitter of technology and facilities to the exclusion of personnel. A media management axiom: *people make it happen.* The likelihood for a successful operation is directly proportional to staff capability. In this chapter, tips on how to hire personnel will be presented first followed by suggestions on staff development.

PERSONNEL SELECTION

Any number of personnel books cover this subject in much more detail. Since few media managers have time to wade through endless sources covering the age-old topic of personnel, a brief discussion of some basic techniques is provided here.

Advertising for Positions

If it is a manager's market, limited advertising may bring a flood of applications. In an applicant's market, there may be more openings than people available. Regardless of market, a media manager must accurately describe the position. In a tight market where there are few applicants for a position, sometimes the manager might tend to over-emphasize the positive aspects of the position. Any publicity about the position should be specific and accurate so as not to waste the applicant's or interviewer's time.

Once the job description and ad are written, several avenues of publicity are available. Placing the ad in trade journals can be effective, especially for a specific position. Professional organizations may have a full-time placement office, run a personnel section in their newsletter, or operate a job center at their national convention. Consult Resource Section 2: A Selected Bibliography for professional associations and trade publications you might contact to list openings or seek candidates. This is not a definitive list but a good start. Position openings can also be sent to trade schools, community or junior colleges, and universities. The local newspaper should be considered, especially in a large city. Personal contacts can be a valuable source for qualified candidates. Get to know key instructors or placement officers in educational institutions and professional associations. A few quick phone calls may develop an enticing list of qualified applicants. The media manager should also comply with all equal opportunity, affirmative action requirements. Most organizations, as general policy, use the following statement in any position announcement: "equal opportunity-affirmative action employer."

Screening Applications

There is nothing a manager hates more than reading through a large pile of resumés. There is only one thing worse and that is having no one respond to a position opening. With a large response, however, all the resumés start to sound the same. If the advertisement accurately described the position, many resumés probably sound like the ideal candidate, making the selection process difficult. The best way to weed out is to list essential qualifications; those resumés meeting such essentials are kept. The next step involves ranking the remaining resumés on a scale from excellent to poor, or one through five.

During the ranking process, two considerations should be kept in mind. Applicants who either call before applying to find out more about the position or use a follow-up call to find out the status of the position are exhibiting that extra effort and interest which are very positive characteristics. Often this additional effort continues to be evident in the way they approach their job. Excessive calling can be a nuisance but the applicant who tactfully calls regarding a position might be worth remembering. Another plus is the applicant who sends a personal letter highlighting his or her qualifications which uniquely fit the position. A cover letter is, many times, more important than a resumé. Anyone can send a blind resumé to openings, but a personal letter shows an additional time commitment and often a genuine interest in the vacancy.

Once the applicants have been ranked one through five, an additional ranking step is used. All the "ones" are ranked with the most desirable canadidate being contacted first. This step can be done by mail or phone and should verify the candidate's continued interest and availability. Checking on current eligibility is important since several weeks can pass between the time the position is first advertised and initial screening is completed. Another step often overlooked is checking with previous employers and references; it is best to contact previous employers and references before the invitation for an interview. Both sources can be very revealing, particularly if in the negative. Finding this out ahead of time can save the expense of the interview. Any response from a previous employer or reference must be carefully weighed in light of what the manager wants. A previous employer might be highly critical of a past employee because he or she was too aggressive when, in fact, that is just the personality trait you want. If the "ones" do not result in interested available candidates, the manager moves on to the "twos" and so on until an active list of applicants is developed.

Interviewing

The interview should give the candidate a chance to: (1) become more fully acquainted with the manager; (2) meet other staff, especially those who would work closely with the candidate; (3) see the media center; (4) understand in more depth the requirements of the position; and (5) express in greater detail qualities the candidate brings to the position.

Perhaps the worst way a manager can start an interview is to say, "Tell me about yourself." Many candidates will launch off into a "this is my life" routine covering all their education, experience, and hobbies in the hopes of hitting the specific information the manager wants. There is some real value in a few minutes of casual conversation covering anything but the position opening. Most candidates come into an interview a little nervous and this gives them a chance to settle down and talk in a relaxed manner. Once the candidate seems at ease the manager should start with a full description of the position. With the requirements of the position fully outlined, the manager can ask what education and experience uniquely qualifies the candidate for the position. Now the applicant no longer has to use the scatter-gun approach but can confidently speak to specifics. If the position advertisement was well written and the screening process conducted properly, the applicant should be able to describe his/her qualifications with ease and confidence. Although the media manager should get some new information, the valuable part of the personal interview should be a better determination of the applicant's personality. Certainly a clear understanding of an individual's total personality is seldom discernable in a letter, application, or resumé. Yet, a good personality is very important, especially in a media center where service is the major function.

Problem-solving questions the candidate would face in the position should be a part of the interview. The manager might not agree with all answers and disagreements should be stated openly to give the candidate a chance to provide a defense and display how he or she would handle stress. Staff who might work with the candidate should also be given a chance to ask questions. Periods of heavy questioning and discussion should be followed by periods of relaxation such as touring facilities or having lunch. This keeps the candidate from becoming exhausted and provides a more relaxed environment so the manager can get a true assessment of personality and qualifications.

Hiring

After all candidates have been interviewed, the manager should review several things before making a decision. Staff reaction to the candidate should be ascertained, especially from people who would work closely with the candidate. If the staff is not positive regarding the applicant's qualifications and personality, serious trouble could develop.

The manager should assume the applicant's perspective and judge whether or not the position represents a good professional move. A combination of salary, professional opportunities and geographic location should be attractive for the applicant. If the opening does not offer advantages in any of these areas, it would be best not to hire the candidate. Hiring a person for an opening that has few advantages over his/her current position might be a short term solution to a long term problem. A person hired under such circumstances might not stay long, forcing the manager to start the interview process again.

A manager wants someone who has the right professional qualifications and a winning personality. Realistically, this represents a rare find. The game of trade-offs begins. If the applicant has basic required skills, the most important concern should be personality. Most managers will probably select the applicant they like best as a person. This is an important consideration if they must work closely with the applicant. Media centers are primarily service oriented. Staff must be able to deal effectively with different client personalities. Just as important is the ability to work well with other staff members when the pressure of deadlines can sometimes push patience to the limit. Usually a person with a good positive personality can develop additional professional skill on the job. However, an applicant with extensive creative and technological ability may not necessarily have a winning personality. Indeed, some highly creative people may tend to be temperamental with clients and staff. An individual with a difficult disposition will probably upset clients and create internal staff tension. Chances of changing the temperamental attitude are remote. Therefore, personality should be the most important consideration. Another axiom of media management: *you can teach technology but you cannot teach personality.* Although psychologists will argue personality is a learned response which can be altered, there is little time for such behavior modification in the real world of media center management.

The manager should be able to make the best choice after reviewing staff reaction and the applicant's own motivation, professional qualifications, and personality. One final caution is warranted. The manager may not be very happy with the final candidates but makes an unenthusiastic selection figuring, "I've got to get someone and anyone is better than no one." Such an approach may come back to haunt the manager. A combination of poor professional qualifications and poor personality may, in the long run, take more of the manager's time in discipline, problem solving, and training than leaving the position vacant until a better field of candidates can be found. A more prudent approach might be, "I've got to get someone, but right now, no one is better than just anyone." Such a policy is even more valid if cross-training techniques have been developed, a concept covered later in this chapter. Cross-training allows other staff to pick up some of the load caused by a vacancy. If the staff understands the ramifications of hiring someone less than adequate, they will probably accept the added work load in order to buy additional time for a better field of candidates.

ORIENTATION AND TRAINING

Once hired, a person will probably go through some training. Depending on entry level capability, very rigorous formalized training programs might be required. Other less demanding training might include a quick orientation on how things are done at a particular center. This section will not present specific training programs since often training must be custom-designed to specific requirements of the center. More appropriately, this section will briefly describe different approaches to orientation and training programs.

Orientation Programs

Orientation programs can bring back memories of boring speeches having nothing to do with the initial anxieties of a new job. In this section, two kinds of orientation programs are discussed. The first will cover the typical goal of helping the employee adjust to a new job. A second program covers the broader challenge of providing all employees with a better working knowledge of the entire media center.

Specific Orientation Program. Any new staff member, regardless of the level of education and experience, will have to make some adjustments in a new job. Orientation is important because it can make a lasting impression and set a precedent for attitude, professionalism, and required standards. A very informal orientation, or no program at all, where a new employee is just dropped into a position, quickly establishes undesirable impressions. The new employee may feel the same sloppy approach can be used in the actual work. If the orientation program is well planned, with an emphasis on required standards and professionalism, the new staff member should adopt the same attitude. An *esprit de corps* can become just as contagious as unmotivated poor performance, and a thoughtful personalized orientation program can do much to nurture the former. New staff orientation programs should do the following:

1. inform employee about routine personnel matters such as vacation, sick leave, payroll, health insurance, and life insurance;
2. state performance standards and performance review procedures;
3. indicate dress code;
4. review types of training which will be initiated;
5. provide sources to answer questions;
6. establish an atmosphere which encourages questions;
7. eliminate new job anxiety;
8. explain probationary period and grievance procedures.

General Orientation Program. Many staff orientation programs deal only with the specific area where the individual will be working. These programs are needed, but tend to ignore the broader responsibility of providing the employee with a good working knowledge of the entire center. There is a need to understand the overall program as well as a specific area where the new employee works. In a small center there may be little need for a general orientation program because the staff probably has multiple responsibilities. This is especially true in K-12 building level programs where the media center director may also be the entire staff! In small centers, staff work closely together and have a good understanding of how their jobs relate to total output. Therefore, this discussion will tend to have more relevance for larger media centers.

A manager of a large media center usually has responsibility for a number of diverse activities such as television, audio, graphics, learning resources, audiovisual equipment circulation, printing, photography, and equipment repair. In such a center numerous disciplines work together to provide programs and services. Staff members in a particular area can quickly become engrossed in their responsibilities and lose sight of the total media center program. They forget how important their job is and how it relates with other operations within the center. However, to the client, any member of a media center represents that entire center and should be able to provide intelligent answers or at least accurately direct someone to the appropriate source.

A good general orientation program should have three objectives: (1) provide staff with a comprehension of how their jobs fit in the entire operation; (2) provide staff with an understanding of the total media center in order to answer client questions; and, (3) provide staff with an opportunity to have some fun while involved in the program. The third objective may sound frivolous, but a staff orientation program that is enjoyed increases the probability of developing an enthusiastic and informed staff.

The major problem in organizing an orientation program is to coordinate the flow of staff through each operating unit of the center. If there is a predictable slow period during the operating year, even a few days, this will provide sufficient time to circulate the staff through all areas. Each staff member should be circulated through every department for a "workshop" in which they learn about the area, obtain hands-on experience where applicable, and receive answers to questions. Workshop groups should consist of people who might not normally work together so they can get acquainted. The emphasis in each workshop should be on enjoyment and practical information.

If the workshops are designed properly, each staff member should have a much better knowledge of other media center operations. Staff should also have a better idea of the overall impact of the center and how their jobs contribute, in a positive way, to that impact. Clients benefit by receiving accurate information from any staff member. Thus, a high degree of professionalism is visible to anyone using the media center. Developing professionalism should always be a primary objective of any orientation program.

Professional Training

The higher the position, the more training and experience required. Most media people come to a position with some formal professional training. Yet the media field keeps changing, forcing staff to learn new techniques. In order to keep staff up to date on new technologies, several approaches to the training problem will be covered, moving from inexpensive to expensive.

Beginning Training. Media managers are sometimes forced to hire people in certain positions with no specialized media education or experience. A typing clerk may be hired to schedule audiovisual equipment. The personnel department would argue that scheduling equipment is basically a clerical job. But the position also requires a working knowledge of audiovisual equipment and a person hired as a typing clerk probably has none. When people request audiovisual equipment they expect the individual booking the request to be able to answer any technical questions. The inability to answer questions looks unprofessional. Large organizations and certainly government civil service systems may end up having to use some personnel classifications or job titles that are inaccurate for certain media positions. These organizations usually have a complex classification system using titles like AV Technician-I, Typing Clerk-II, or Delivery-I. Such a system forces the personnel department to use the closest existing classification rather than endure the bureaucratic nightmare of trying to write a new position description. This system perpetuates the need for training by using inaccurate classifications which attract people who fit the classification but not all the requirements of the actual job.

Any training program should use an instructional design approach: determine entry level skills; specify needs; establish objectives; design a program to meet those objectives; evaluate the program to make sure the objectives are met; revise; and, implement. Such an approach guarantees the training program is covering only what is essential for the staff member to function satisfactorily. The use of only essential training content is crucial since it is easy to get off the subject and teach the new employee more than is required. Remember, priorities must be established with possibly a phased training program. Using the audiovisual equipment scheduling position as an example, a phased program could consist of three steps. The first step would be to quickly develop a new employee to a point where he/she could meet basic requirements of the position, such as recognizing different pieces of equipment by name and completing required paper work. A second phase would include knowing how to operate each piece of equipment. A third phase would be learning what type of equipment to use in a particular situation and being able to advise clients.

Once objectives are established, a combination of commercially prepared instructional packages and tests can be used to start the program. Although possibly expensive, commercially prepared packages that meet objectives, can be far less costly than developing your own training programs.

Most training material should be self-paced, involving little direct instruction time by other staff. As the training program develops, additional custom-designed materials might be added to fit unique local needs. Certification tests can also be incorporated on a regular basis to make sure staff members are not forgetting crucial information. Another media axiom: *use it or lose it*. People will forget skills and information they do not use regularly. Distribution of audiovisual equipment is a good example of an area where the schedulers might not operate the equipment very often yet be asked operational questions. Periodic certification tests on equipment identification, operation, and application can help them be prepared to answer questions with confidence.

The media manager should argue strenuously for accurate position classifications and minimum qualifications which preclude the need for basic training. When the local organization or bureaucracy does not permit accurate position classifications, a basic training program must be developed.

Mid-level Training. Many staff members already have basic training and may be experienced when hired. The objective is to build on established knowledge and refine procedures and techniques. Principles of instructional design mentioned under "Beginning Training" should still be employed. A concern again is what additional training is really required to meet observable, measurable objectives. Often staff request additional training using the general justification that, "It will broaden my knowledge of media and, after all, more education can't hurt." However, education for the sake of education does not stand up under the tough scrutiny of instructional design principles. Another favorite is to learn a new technology and, "stay current in the field." Sounds noble enough except if the media center does not have the new technology, why go to the expense of providing the training? The real reason staff members are often sent to workshops and institutes is not for the education but probably for morale. A workshop with limited benefits is a very expensive morale-building technique. A manager has every right to expect a measurable payoff from a mid-level training program.

There are several ways to save money on mid-level training programs. Assigned readings from leading journals and books in the field with follow-up discussion can be a very inexpensive mid-level training program. Since much of the additional knowledge desired covers enhancement of already acquired skills, the assigned reading approach can be a very inexpensive way to fill the void. Preview commercially produced training programs before purchase. Get opinions from others who have acquired these training programs. Workshops, seminars, and institutes can be evaluated in much the same way by asking participants what they thought of them. Workshop instructors are usually listed in advance publicity and can be contacted for a better idea of material covered. Once a workshop has been selected the person attending can be given the responsibility of obtaining as much information as possible in order to teach other staff members. This establishes a level of accountability and enlarges the return on the original investment.

Advanced Training. Usually the staff member requiring advanced training is being groomed for a promotion or additional responsibilities. Major technological innovations in the media field may require advanced specialized training. Also, try and make sure the individual receiving expensive advanced training has a good career track record and plans to stay with the media center for a while. Managers can expend funds training people who, by virtue of the additional knowledge and skill, are able to accept a new position elsewhere. Such training may involve seminars, correspondence courses or period of time at a technical school or university. In each case, the instruction is expensive and the media manager must make sure return on the investment is worth the expenditure. The very same rules of instructional design and evaluation by others who have taken the advanced training should be used before commiting funds.

Cross-training. Cross-training refers to training staff members in areas that are not their usual responsibility. A person who primarily schedules rental films may also be trained to schedule equipment. Since both jobs require scheduling skills the cross-training activity does not place an unusual burden on the employee. Commercial artists working in a graphic production area can learn to operate television cameras. Many television directors will state that basic camera operating skills are quickly learned, but teaching a sense of composition becomes a constant battle. The director is always saying "tilt up a little," "frame up the shot," or the ever popular "pan left—no, your other left," instead of concentrating on more important aspects of the production. Graphic artists have already developed a sense of composition, making television camera operation a natural for cross-training. Managers should always look for common areas of knowledge or skill where cross-training programs can be easily implemented.

Cross-training has several advantages. The most important, from a management perspective, is that cross-training helps ensure consistent service, a desirable objective discussed in Chapter 1. When people are on vacation or sick, cross-training provides the necessary backup to guarantee continued trouble-free service. Just as a coach uses substitute players to keep a game moving, a media manager must have a well developed "bench" to ensure uninterrupted service. Employees receive additional variety in their work. Learning new skills through additional experience grooms employees for future promotional opportunities. Cross-training can exist at any level. However, most cross-training efforts should be done in areas having the most direct impact on daily client needs.

PERFORMANCE REVIEW

Once an individual is on the staff, performance reviews should be a regular part of the personnel program. Reviews are necessary to let the employee know areas of strength along with areas needing improvement.

Although it is very easy to praise, managers many times do not offer positive feedback as often as they should. If things are going well, there is the tendency to take excellent performance for granted. A concerted effort should be made to praise good work. A quick phone call to acknowledge a job well done can be a real morale booster. In a large media center, the manager probably does not have extensive daily contact with the entire staff. An impromptu visit to compliment exceptional performance can be very effective. Conscious efforts to praise good performance can help build staff morale and pride.

The only thing worse than not giving praise is not providing constructive criticism. Usually media managers shy away from criticism because of possibly offending the employee. There is more anxiety connected with criticism than with giving praise. If the manager continues to come up with excuses for not confronting the employee, small problems can escalate into large problems. In a major confrontation the employee might rightfully complain there was no indication of a problem. An employee has every right to be informed when there is a need to correct procedures or personality problems. A manager who wishes not to address such problems squarely should consider the alternatives: correct a minor problem where the chance of severe employee reaction is slight, or correct a major problem which may cause negative over-reaction by both manager and employee. The consequence of error, or the impact the problem could have on media center operations, will also increase if the original problem is allowed to fester and grow. It is always best to correct small problems where the consequence of error is minimal. Managers must remember they have every right to expect a certain level of staff performance and personnel not meeting those standards should be informed. If such a procedure is not used the manager will be spending too much time solving large problems. The manager should be able to handle most corrective actions by suggesting realistic solutions and obtaining ideas from the employee. A positive atmosphere can be created if the employee is also given responsibility for suggesting ways that performance can be improved. Using a constructive, teamwork approach, with the manager and employee both working to improve the employee's performance, can go far to defuse a touchy situation. The employee should be given a chance to take corrective action.

TERMINATION

If ample opportunity has been provided for correction and the employee has not cooperated or is unable to change, then suggested reassignment or termination should come as no surprise. A termination is never enjoyable for the manager or employee. In cases where the employee is not interested in improving performance or has been involved in numerous disciplinary actions, the termination may be clear cut and necessary. The difficult case is where the employee has tried hard but does not have the innate talent to master the job. This usually represents an incorrect match of employee and position. The manager must stress that this mismatch does not mean the employee is a failure but rather is in a position calling for talents he/she does not possess. We have all at some time wanted to do something but simply lacked the required talent. Realizing this can help the employee understand the need for reassignment or even termination. In such cases it might be possible to offer the option of letting the employee resign rather than having a termination notice on the employment record. If the individual is a good conscientious employee every effort should be made for reassignment within the organization rather than termination. Under any circumstances, the employee must realize the manager cannot keep someone who is not suited to fulfill the requirements of the position. Keeping incompetent staff in order to sidestep the anxiety connected with termination or reassignment will: (1) involve more management time in the long run by constantly having to solve problems that would never occur with a qualified employee in the position; and, (2) more importantly, lead to a visible erosion of service standards. Neither of these eventualities is worth the tradeoff of facing poor performance squarely with positive corrective action. Managers must be able to prove the employee was notified of problems, provided with suggestions for improvement and given ample time to make the required changes before any termination action is taken. Even when the only alternative is termination, the manager can use the occasion to suggest other more appropriate career opportunities outside the media center.

SUMMARY

A competent staff is the single most important resource of a media center. Selection procedures should include: (1) an accurate description of the position; (2) a screening process to elicit highly motivated, qualified candidates; (3) interview techniques allowing the candidate to describe unique qualifications for the position; and (4) hiring practices that do not over-emphasize professional skills to the detriment of important personality qualities. Once hired, specific orientation programs should establish performance standards, provide answers to questions and relieve some of the anxiety connected with a new job. General orientation programs can help employees understand the entire media center operation. This knowledge can result in an added degree of professionalism and a sense of importance for each staff member. Beginning, mid-level and advanced training programs can be considered as well as cross-training. Any training program must meet instructional objectives and be worth the time and expense involved. Performance reviews should be a regular part of the personnel program. Managers should offer constructive criticism in a problem-solving teamwork approach with the employee. Most large problems start as small ones and that is when problems should be corrected. Reassignment or termination should stress an incorrect match of talent and job requirements rather than employee failure.

CHAPTER 3

Designing Service Forms

DESIGNING SERVICE forms is an inescapable part of the media manager's duties. The old adage, "when in doubt create another form," certainly rings true with media centers. Sooner or later everyone figures that a new form will solve an organizational, production, or procedural problem. Although managers may despise forms and the ever increasing need for new ones, properly designed forms are essential for several reasons. Much of the standardization required for an efficient cost-effective operation mentioned in Chapter 1 is accomplished through well designed forms. Information from forms can be used for decisions regarding budget, equipment, personnel, and facilities. Properly designed forms generate important management information for media centers. Poorly designed forms provide inaccurate information leading to poor decisions.

HINTS ON SERVICE FORM DESIGN

The following steps can be used when designing any kind of service form. Using this sequence of steps should result in effective forms at less expense with fewer revisions.

Internal and External Information

Divide the form into internal and external information to make sure all data are covered. Internal information refers to data used only by media center staff. This information should usually be expressed in media shorthand such as

"VTR" for videotape recorder, "PB" for television playback, and "TAT" for turnaround time. Figure 3-1 shows a graphic production form with much internal information expressed in media shorthand such as "STM" for Strathmore, "CD" for cardstock, and "CP" for colored paper. Media shorthand increases efficiency by allowing more information to be included in less space. The internal information should supply all data required to complete the production or service request. External information covers a description of the client such as name, department and phone number. Figure 3-1 shows typical external information. If there are questions, including all necessary external information can save staff time. Plenty of space should be left for the phone number because often the client can be reached at several numbers. By using the concept of internal and external information, the media manager has a better chance of making sure all relevant information is included.

Essential Information

Include only essential information when designing a service form. Essential content can be defined as the least amount of information necessary to complete the request. A form that tries to accommodate every eventuality will be cumbersome and inefficient. The "what if" syndrome can go on forever regarding forms and there is no way to totally anticipate future needs. A form which can handle 95–98% of the requests should be considered satisfactory. When deciding on essential information, remember a form needs to accomplish only two objectives: expedite the request and obtain utilization data. These are the *only* two things a form must do, everything else is nonessential.

Easy Use

Forms must be easy to use. Including only essential material goes a long way in satisfying the easy use requirement. Forms should be easy to read. Managers who have prime responsibility for designing forms must remember their creations will be read all day by staff, and possible eye strain should be a consideration. A typical cause of eye strain is not allowing sufficient space to write information. Figure 3-2 shows a classic example of a form which is hard to read and does not provide enough writing space. Such a form will take longer to complete and can easily generate incorrect information. Usually squeezing information into a small space is done to cut costs by printing smaller forms. The resulting trade-offs of confusion and misinformation are usually not worth the savings. If forms must be completed while using a phone, the form should be large enough for easy use. Possibly a clipboard could be mounted on the desk to keep the form stationary when being completed. Some scheduling areas have gone to telephone headsets, leaving both hands free to complete forms.

Logical Sequencing

Information should be arranged in a logical sequence. This might mean moving from top to bottom or left to right when completing the form. Sequence might also be determined by the way the client asks for or provides information. Another organizational technique would be to arrange information from most often to least often used. If content is arranged in a linear fashion the

Fig. 3-1

/hite copy-
Graphics Production
ellow copy-Client

Graphics Production
Unit 436-6651

Production Request

Date in:	Requested:	Completed:	Accepted by:	Job #:

TAT: ________

Artist: ______________

Requested by: ______________

Department: ______________

Phone: ______________

Description or Directions:

		Mat. Used	End Prod.			Mat. Used	End Prod.
Drawing	STM			Film	35mm		
	CD _T.V. _8Ply _14Ply				35mm B&W _Line _Cont.		
	CP				4x5		
	TP				8x10 _S.K. _Kodak		
	AL			Paper	5x7		
	_2x2 _Overhead				8x10 _S.K. _Kodak		
					11x14		

We are interested in knowing how you liked the service and/or materials provided by Media Services. If you have comments, please indicate below.

Quality of materials

☐ very good ☐ good ☐ average ☐ poor ☐ very poor

Send to:
Director of Media Services
436-7691

Comments:

Fig. 3-2

SLIDE PRODUCTION REQUEST

| Date in: 7/9/79 | Completed: 7/10/79 | Job Number |
| Requested: 5m¹¹ | Picked up: 7/11/79 | M.S. 362 | P.S. |

Description or directions: *Two graphs each on separate slides. Use full color and fill entire screen.*

Materials used: *2 16×18 color sheets paper, Miscellaneous zipatone, presstype, tape, Film - 40 frame*

Authorization *gs.* **Cost** *Processing Fee - $4.85*

staff member is not jumping all over the form looking for the correct space to write information. Filing considerations can also affect the sequence of information. Key accessing information such as order number, social security number, or client name, should be positioned at the top for easy filing and retrieval. If different forms must be cross-referenced the key access information should be located in the same place on each form so unnecessary time is not spent scanning the entire form. Little inconveniences caused by illogical sequencing of information can represent hundreds of wasted staff hours.

Staff Recommendations

Many managers have had service forms designed, printed and implemented with no advice from staff and reaction eventually comes in the form of wrath for the creator of a form that does not work. Staff advice is a valuable resource media managers should use for two reasons: (1) because managers are often removed from daily operational activities, staff members may have better insights on what will work in practice; and (2) staff members like the opportunity to contribute ideas that will affect their work. When planning a form, the manager can ask personnel to suggest what should be included. A rough draft can be developed for further staff reaction and revision. Staff who must work with a form have a vested interest in making sure it is satisfactory. They will be quick to spot nuances in form design such as sequence of information, size of type, and appropriate abbreviations, which a manager may not notice. This is not to say the manager should have minimal involvement. Indeed, the manager, being removed from the line function, can provide fresh objectivity the staff may not possess because of being too close to the operation. A joint effort that capitalizes on the experience of staff and management usually results in a practical and efficient form.

Prototype

Another classic mistake made by managers is to design a new multi-layer pressure-sensitive form and run off thousands of copies, only to realize after two days of use that a critical piece of information was not included. The options are not pleasant. The manager might consider misplacing 100,000 8-part pressure-sensitive forms! The forms have to be discarded or staff must modify each form when used. Both procedures represent a financial loss, one in wasted materials and the other in wasted time. The best way to avoid such a loss is to develop a prototype form and run a small quantity using the cheapest duplication method available. A short run on Ditto is infinitely cheaper than a long run of camera-ready art work on a printing press. If multiple copies are needed, use carbon paper during the short test period. When possible, have the staff try the prototype in regular operational procedures since the crucial test for any form is actual use. A manager can spend days second-guessing possible problems. Often in a few minutes of actual use problems with a form will become obvious. If actual use of a prototype is not possible, consider simulations. Some managers might not want to test a prototype form in actual operations for fear of jeopardizing services. With a simulation, staff members can try completing the form under circumstances approximating actual operational conditions. The simulation can be realistic by limiting the time for completion, filling out the form while on the phone, or trying to keep up with an impatient client who is a very fast talker. Through actual use or simulations, many form design problems can be rectified before final printing.

Final Revisions

Usually a prototype form needs only to be used for several weeks to determine how well the form will work. A case study will most easily demonstrate the form design process. Using the above design considerations of internal and external information, essential content, easy use, logical sequencing, and staff recommendations, the manager might develop a prototype such as shown in Figure 3-3 which is a form for scheduling audiovisual equipment. Based on staff suggestions and design considerations, Figure 3-3 should represent the very best prototype that can be developed. This prototype is tested through actual use, or simulation of actual use, for a long enough period to experience an average variety of requests for audiovisual equipment.

After the test period the manager should run a spot check looking for any consistent trends in how forms were completed. A typical completed form is shown in Figure 3-4. At first glance, the form might appear satisfactory. However, the manager should look for three symptoms signaling need for revisions: information not provided; additional information in the margin; and poorly organized information. One or more of these symptoms should be evident with some consistency on a number of forms before making revisions.

Figure 3-5 shows a typical example of all three symptoms. Although this form did facilitate satisfactory completion of the request there are some problems. Information that was not completed has been circled with a bold line. In most cases the staff did not need this information to successfully execute the

Fig. 3-3

MEDIA DISTRIBUTION
(Equipment & Materials)

White-office   Pink-return
Yellow-delivery Gold-client

Name _____ Dept. _____ Phone: Office _____ Home _____
Home Address _____
Order Taken: Time _____ Date _____
Bldg. _____ Room _____ Use Date _____
Return Date _____   Course Title _____
Students Served _____   Not Filled ☐ Code _____

Equipment

Materials

Fig. 3-4

MEDIA DISTRIBUTION
(Equipment & Materials)

Will drop at STV 250 Satellite

White-office   Pink-return
Yellow-delivery Gold-client

Use time: 7:00
Return time: 8:00

Name _BURNS, DON_ Dept. _Political Science_ Phone: Office_438-234/_Home _____
Home Address _____
Order Taken: Time _____ Date _____
Bldg. _STV_____ Room _231_ Use Date _5/21/80_   *booked by JWB?*   *Section?*
Return Date _5/30/80_ Course Title _American Government_
Students Served _25_   Not Filled ☐ Code _____

Equipment   _OH- 16mm_

Materials   _16mm films:_
            Introduction to the Senate
            Beginning of a Law
                 John Smith will operate

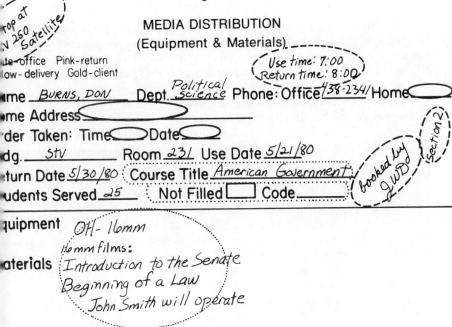

Fig. 3-5

MEDIA DISTRIBUTION
(Equipment & Materials)

Top at V 250 Satellite

te-office   Pink-return
ow-delivery   Gold-client

Use time: 7:00
Return time: 8:00

me _BURNS, DON_   Dept. _Political Science_   Phone: Office _438-234_ / Home

me Address

der Taken: Time   Date

dg. _Stv_   Room _231_   Use Date _5/21/80_

turn Date _5/30/80_   Course Title _American Government_

booked by JWD

Section 2

udents Served _25_   Not Filled   Code

quipment   _OH- 16mm_

aterials   _16 mm films:_
Introduction to the Senate
Beginning of a Law
John Smith will operate

request. These requested data can be eliminated from the final version of the form. Additional information not originally designed into the prototype has been circled with a dashed line. Staff members needed this information although not originally designed into the form. Information staff members added to complete the request should be included on the final form. Poorly organized data have been circled with a dotted line. There are several courses entitled "American Government" so it would be better to revise the form to ask for course number. A course number is more accurate and faster to write than a course title. There is no reason to mark the "not filled" box and then put in a code number signifying the reason the request could not be filled. By writing in the code number both operations are accomplished. The whole area where equipment and materials are listed should be reworked because of numerous chances for error. In the equipment section, specific types were to be written out such as "overhead projector" and "16mm projector." Under the pressure of time abbreviations were used such as "OH" and "16mm." Other abbreviations were created under the pressure of time such as "OP" for opaque projector. Depending on the legibility, "OP" for opaque projection, could be confused with "OH" for overhead, resulting in filling the order with the wrong equipment. In this case the client wanted an overhead projector and a 16mm projector, but "OH-16mm" was read as "overhead projector #16mm." Some people might also think there were three 16mm films: "Introduction to the Senate," "The Beginning of a Law," and "John Smith Will Operate." Actually, "John Smith Will Operate," is not a film title but the person assigned to operate the 16mm projector! Scheduling people could look for weeks and conclude "John Smith Will Operate" is lost. John Smith is not lost. He is still in a classroom trying to thread a 16mm film on an overhead projector which does not say much for John and even less for the form creating the problem in the first place! The above analysis indicates a need for revision. Since a prototype was used, expense can be kept to a minimum.

Figure 3-6 shows the final form with all the revisions. Nonessential information has been dropped. Critical information added to the prototype by staff members during the test period has been included. Poorly organized information has been reworked. All basic pieces of equipment have been printed on the form to eliminate confusion over hard-to-read abbreviations and hand writing. Equipment is listed from top to bottom going from most often to least often requested. A special "materials" section has been included providing "shelf no." to clarify program titles and "operator" to eliminate confusion concerning a projectionist. Flexibility is also incorporated for non-routine requests by having a space for special instructions under "notes" and some spaces labeled "other" to list seldom used equipment. Leave some extra space on the form for unexpected additional information. Just about the time you think all conceivable possibilities have been covered there will be a surprise! Leaving some room for the unexpected situation will eliminate need for costly redesign. Figure 3-7 shows how the same request might look on the revised form.

The revised form in Figure 3-6 is a good practical example of the concept of maximum efficiency through standardization, first discussed in Chapter 1. All information that would be needed for routine requests is printed on the form. The final version is also a four-part pressure-sensitive no-carbon form. When writing the original information the goal should always be to complete as many steps as possible simultaneously. When the order is taken the file copy, circulation copy, delivery copy, and pick-up copy are all completed simultaneously by filling out the original. All design considerations for service forms should have the common objective of efficiency through standardization of terms and procedures.

Completion Time

A stopwatch can be used to note the time required to complete forms. This is especially important in a high-volume service such as the equipment distribution case study in Figures 3-3 to 3-7. Staff time required to complete a form is crucial since clients do not want to spend a great deal of time on the phone or in person ordering items. Time spent completing a form also has a direct relationship with request volume. The manager should not let staff know when they are being timed in completing a form so that realistic data can be obtained. Timing different employees completing a form over a period of several days can yield some interesting results. The form shown in Figure 3-3 took an average of five minutes to complete while the revised form in Figure 3-6 took only two minutes. When the audiovisual equipment distribution area processes about 60,000 requests a year, a savings of three minutes per request represents a tremendous ability to handle additional volume without the usual need for additional personnel. Well designed service forms accommodating increased volume, can be much less expensive than acquiring additional staff.

Fig. 3-6

MEDIA DISTRIBUTION

Name _____ Dept. _____ Phone _____ Stud. Served _____
Del./P.U. Pt. _____ Use Date _____ Time _____ Bldg. _____ Room _____
Course _____ Sec. _____ Return Date _____ Time _____ N.F. Code _____

Quan.	Equipment	Dist. Code	Quan.	Equipment	Dist. Code	Quan.	Equipment	Dist. Code
	16mm			Filmstrip			Dual 8m	
	OH			CART			Screen, Prt	
	S 8 So			Rec Play MS			Tpe Rcr MS	
	CRSL			Cass S Sync			TV 1/2 RR	
	CASS			VCR 3/4			R 8 LOOP	
	Monitor MC			TV RR Ens			OTHER	
	Fm strp cass			Fm strp R/P			OTHER	
	S8 LOOP			3 1/2 x 4			OTHER	
	TV VCR Ens			Opaque			OTHER	

Materials

Shelf No.

Notes

Booked by _____
Operator _____

45

Fig. 3-7

MEDIA DISTRIBUTION

Name __BURNS, DON__ Dept. __Political Science__ Phone __438-2341__ Stud. Served __25__

Del./P.U. Pt. __Stu Sat. 250__ Use Date __5/21/80__ Time __7:00__ Bldg. __Stu__ Room __231__

Course __320__ Sec. __2__ Return Date __5/30/80__ Time __8:00__ N.F. Code _____

Quan.	Equipment	Dist. Code	Quan.	Equipment	Dist. Code	Quan.	Equipment	Dist. Code
1	16mm	5		Filmstrip			Dual 8m	
1	OH	8		CART			Screen, Prt	
	S 8 So			Rec Play MS			Tpe Rcr MS	
	CRSL			Cass S Sync			TV 1/2 RR	
	CASS			VCR 3/4			R 8 LOOP	
	Monitor MC			TV RR Ens			OTHER	
	Fm strp cass			Fm strp R/P			OTHER	
	S8 LOOP			3 1/2 x 4			OTHER	
	TV VCR Ens			Opaque			OTHER	

Materials
Introduction to the Senate
Beginning of a Law

Shelf No.
16mm - 40
16mm - 65

Notes _Will come from Center and drop at Stu Sat 250_

Booked by __JWD__
Operator __John Smith__

46

Fig. 3-8

№ 9146

MEDIA DISTRIBUTION

Name _____ Dept. _____ Phone _____ Stud. Served _____

Del./P.U. Pt. _____ Use Date _____ Time _____ Bldg. _____ Room _____

Course _____ Sec. _____ Return Date _____ Time _____ N.F. Code _____

Quan.	Equipment	Type	Dist. Code	Quan.	Equipment	Type	Dist. Code	Quan.	Equipment	Type	Dist. Code
	16mm				Filmstrip	005			Dual 8m	015	
	OH	008			CART	010			Screen, Prt	021	
	S 8 So	017			Rec Play MS				Tpe Rcr MS		
	CRSL	025			Cass S Sync				TV 1/2 RR	083	
	CASS	035			VCR 3/4	081			R 8 LOOP	102	
	Monitor MC				TV RR Ens	122			OTHER		
	Fm strp cass	132			Fm strp R/P	133			OTHER		
	S8 LOOP	141			3 1/2 x 4	145			OTHER		
	TV VCR Ens	178			Opaque	007			OTHER		

Materials

Shelf No.	Notes

Booked by _____
Operator _____

47

Fig. 3-9

CONVERSION TABLE FOR REGULAR AND MILITARY TIME

Regular Time	Military Time
1:00 a.m.	1:00
2:00	2:00
3:00	3:00
4:00	4:00
5:00	5:00
6:00	6:00
7:00	7:00
8:00	8:00
9:00	9:00
10:00	10:00
11:00	11:00
12:00 p.m.	12:00
1:00	13:00
2:00	14:00
3:00	15:00
4:00	16:00
5:00	17:00
6:00	18:00
7:00	19:00
8:00	20:00
9:00	21:00
10:00	22:00
11:00	23:00
12:00	24:00

Additional Suggestions

A high volume service area might find computer tabulation of utilization data cost-effective. Again, to use the case study shown in Figures 3-3 to 3-7, only slight form modifications need to be made for computer tabulation. The form in Figure 3-8 is much like Figure 3-6 with these changes: (1) each form has a preprinted transaction number in the upper righthand corner; and (2) numerical codes are used for most standard equipment types such as 008 for an overhead projector. Those equipment types without a printed number indicate more than one type is available. For example, the 16mm projector might be 050 for self-thread or 051 for manual thread. The correct type code is written when taking the order.

Use of military time might also be applicable in this case study. In Figure 3-4 there could have been some confusion whether the "use" and "return time" were a.m. or p.m. You can see from the conversion table in Figure 3-9 that military time eliminates all confusion over a.m. or p.m. Confusion is reduced as long as people remember the conversion! Handy conversion tables should be provided for any new staff not familiar with military time. Use of military time might be worth consideration for a media center with a long operating day such as from 7:00 a.m. to 11:00 p.m. or, if you prefer, 7:00 to 23:00 hours!

SUMMARY

Well designed production and service forms are a key requirement for an efficient media center. A media manager must know how to develop effective service forms. A form must accurately record utilization data and efficiently expedite requests. All information required to measure the effectiveness of a media center and to formulate justification for increased staff, facilities and budget is usually first recorded on some type of service form. How efficiently a media center functions is also heavily dependent on how the service forms are designed. A prototype for a new form should be used first so revisions can be made at minimal expense. Staff using the form should be given the opportunity for reactions and suggestions. The final form should be easy to use and contain only essential information germane to facilitating routine requests while allowing for flexibility to accommodate special cases.

CHAPTER 4

Obtaining Useful Utilization Data

U TILIZATION DATA show how much a media center is used. Hence, this chapter could also be called "The Numbers Game and How to Play It." Few people will jump to this chapter because of an insatiable interest in utilization techniques. There is nothing exciting about the boring topic of tabulating and using utilization data until the media manager realizes that good utilization information can justify the rationale for increased budgets, personnel, facilities, and equipment. Utilization data can range from simple to complex, depending on the needs of the media center. In this chapter the treatment will deal with basics and is geared toward practical application. Although specific examples will be cited the concepts should have general application in any media production or service area.

KEY UTILIZATION CONCEPTS

As with any "numbers game" there are many ways to say the same thing with numbers. Depending on the approach used regarding a given set of numbers, the results can be accurate, misleading, or hopelessly complex. Since there are many ways to present numerical information, some basic decisions have to be made regarding utilization data, forming the concepts discussed below.

Decide What to Count

A fundamental concern for the manager is to decide what will be counted for utilization. The choices are many, covering categories such as students

erved, trainee contact hours, production requests filled, units of media produced, or total transactions processed. Amid the variety of possibilities the choice
becomes much easier if the manager selec*s categories most accurately reflect-
ng what actually happens in a media service area. Whatever is counted should
how the volume of work processed in the area since volume has a direct effect
on staff, facilities, and equipment. Ideally, utilization data should also show the
impact of the service on clientele. Selecting what to count that accurately
eflects productivity and successfully documents budget requests is the first and
most important decision a media manager must make when measuring utiliza-
ion.

Caution should be exercised to count only what is essential. Managers
often become carried away with tabulation and collect a great deal of seldom
used data. Often managers develop an unrealistic desire to be prepared for any
eventuality. The price paid for covering any eventuality results in large
amounts of staff time spent collecting and tabulating useless data. A basic
choice must be made between what the manager *must have* and what it would
be *nice to have*. The "nice to have" category is where the manager has
trouble. Many times the manager says, "It sure would be nice to have some
data on this topic." The next logical question should be, "What must I have to
accurately reflect the productivity of the area and make good arguments for
increased facilities, personnel, and equipment?" The "must haves" should
always take precedence over the "nice to haves." A manager's own track
record of what data really are used out of the total available can also help eliminate the "nice to haves."

Several utilization categories will be discussed, moving from simple to
complex. The utilization categories presented are requests filled, units produced, students or clients served, contact hours, and instructional effectiveness.

Requests Filled. The number of requests filled is an easy category to work
with and has wide application. Requests filled might be expressed in production
jobs for a photographic area, playbacks for a closed-circuit television cable system, or orders for audiovisual equipment. In some cases there is no possibility
of becoming more sophisticated. If a graphic production unit produces overhead transparencies for trainers who have permanent possession of the material,
there is little chance of obtaining accurate impact figures on how many trainees
were served by the material. If the same overhead transparencies were placed in
a learning resource center for check out by instructors, it would be very easy to
obtain the number of trainees served. The type of utilization possible depends
largely on cooperation from instructors, students, and upper management.

Units Produced. Another category of utilization that more accurately reflects volume is the number of units produced. A unit can be defined in different ways, depending on the service area. For television, a unit might be a
finished video-tape. Audiovisual equipment distribution might define units as
the number of pieces of media equipment requested in a single order. For
graphics, a finished piece of art work such as a slide could be a unit. Actual
jobs or requests completed can be misleading as the only measure of productivity for a media area since one job might involve 1,000 slides. There is also the
added problem of carry-over, referring to jobs not completed at the end of a

reporting period. Jobs are usually reported when completed. One month a graphics area may show only 25 completed jobs while in another month 85 completed jobs are reported. Explaining such erratic utilization figures to upper management can be embarrassing and unnecessary. A more accurate and reliable measure of volume is achieved through tabulating the number of completed units. One job may require producing 35 slides or units of artwork. At the end of the month 25 of the 35 units are completed and reported in the utilization data. Regardless of jobs in progress, the total number of units produced in a given reporting period will be more consistent.

Students or Trainees Served. A more accurate category of utilization is the number of students served. This utilization approach is more precise because it tabulates actual impact on clientele. Later we will see how students served forms the basis for estimating cost effectiveness in Chapter 5, "Cost Accounting." A student can be counted *each* time he or she is served by any aspect of a media service area. There are several different ways of expressing students or trainees served. A projector and screen may be requested for a class of 30 students. One media center might say the request served 30 students while another center might say the projector and screen each served 30 students for a total of 60 students served by the request. Another example might involve a television program transmitted over a cable system to five classrooms, each with 35 students, totaling 175 students served. The counting method selected should be defined so people understand the basis for data generated. A manager faced with many choices of how to express the same data should select the method that most accurately reflects volume and cost effectiveness. Care must also be taken to compare only data that is counted the same way.

Counting the number of students or trainees served should be used whenever possible. There is increased accuracy with students served since the number of requests filled can be misleading in terms of actual impact. One request might serve 20 students while another might serve 300. There is also the added public relations advantage of counting those served. Which sounds better, a distribution department that filled 15,000 requests for audiovisual equipment or served 375,000 students? The latter has more impact and is a more accurate statement of actual utilization.

Contact Hours. A very sophisticated utilization method is contact hours. Like students served, contact hours measures the impact a media department has on clients. However, contact hours represents a refinement of students served by tabulating the length of time a student was served, not just that the student was served. Anything less than an hour represents a fraction of the contact hour value. The contact hours measurement is used in the academic community to reflect the number of hours an instructor actually has direct contact with the class. While contact hours is more accurate it is also harder to obtain. Audiovisual equipment use tabulated on the basis of contact hours usually requires installing meters on all equipment. The differences between meter readings before and after use provides the contact hour value. Although the system sounds simple and more accurate, there are some words of caution. Meters must be installed properly to provide accurate data. On an audiotape recorder there could be a substantial difference in readings if a meter is connected to the ower switch instead of the record and playback buttons. Purchase, installation and maintenance of meters can be expensive and time consuming. Expensive meters could be eliminated if instructors estimated the time they actually used media equipment or programs in class. But this system is not realistic since most people would view such a requirement as an inconvenience. Control must be built into any system that will rely on contact hours. If media packages are checked out one at a time for student use in a learning resource center the time out and time returned must be noted to determine contact hours. A closed circuit television service also has built-in controls since the contact hour value is the program length. Contact hours is not advisable in areas where increased controls necessary to obtain the data result in decreased ease of use by the instructor and students.

Instructional Effectiveness. Ideally, documented data on increased instructional effectiveness or reduced instructional costs represent ultimate measurements of media center impact. Realistically, such information is extremely hard to obtain. Everyone gives conscientious lip service to the whole instructional design process but few practice what they preach. There is no question that people should be using the systematic design principles of determining behavioral objectives and being able to measure results when developing instructional materials. However, movement from theory to practice involves hard work. The hard work requirement is where most people balk and continue doing things the way they always have.

One way to implement the instructional design process is to establish a special group of people with instructional design training who would work directly with instructors and media production personnel. Another approach is to require that media personnel be able to effectively apply the basic steps used in the systematic development of educational materials which includes measurement of instructional effectiveness. Instructional design, leading to increased teaching effectiveness, is mentioned because the whole training field should be moving in this direction. However, from a practical perspective the widespread implementation of systematic design techniques will not happen without a continuing commitment from media practitioners.

Obtain Key Data

The major source for all utilization information will come from service forms. Little space is expended on forms in this section since the topic is covered in Chapter 3, "Designing Service Forms." The only point to stress here is that once decisions have been made on what to count, the manager must make sure the service forms are designed to obtain that information. Service forms represent the very foundation of any utilization system by providing the entry data on which all tabulation will be computed. If service forms do not obtain the required data, a worthwhile utilization system will not follow.

Select Time Frame for Comparison

Once the manager has decided what to count and designed forms which obtain this information a decision must be made on a time period for comparison. Many choices are available including daily, weekly, monthly, quarterly, or annual comparisons. The time frame selected should accurately show variance in work load. A change in work load involves two considerations: (1) the comparison of sequential time frames within a given year; and (2) the comparison of the same time frame for the previous year. If the time frame is too small or too large the fluctuations in work load will be hard to determine. A compromise must be reached where the time frame is large enough not to be cumbersome yet small enough to accurately show fluctuations. Most discussions and examples in this book use the month as the time frame simply because, for a number of different operations, this seems to accurately reflect changes in work load. However, the final decision regarding a time frame for comparison will depend on local considerations within each center.

General Trends. Once the proper time frame has been selected the manager can quickly determine changes in work load for different areas and, ultimately, after a sufficient data base has been established, project fluctuations. The establishment of general trends for heavy and light work volume can be a helpful planning guide for management.

Since audiovisual equipment distribution was used for the case study in Chapter 3, regarding development of service forms, the same area will be used in this chapter to maintain continuity. Utilization figures for media equipment are shown in Figure 4-1. Data is broken out on a monthly basis by equipment type. These data are taken from a typical university media center operating calendar where the fall semester runs from mid-August through mid-December, the spring semester from January through May, and the summer session from mid-June through mid-August. General trends quickly become evident. A screen pattern is superimposed to indicate general high volume trends in Figure 4-1. During the fall semester, October through December are generally the busiest months. Spring semester has a slightly different pattern in that the most active months are February through May. The start-up time or demand for services is much quicker in the spring than in the fall. Faculty on nine-month contracts who are away all summer take longer to get started with media requests than is evident after the Christmas break when they have only been gone for several weeks. July is the peak summer month since it falls in the middle of the summer session. Knowing the general trends for high volume helps management prepare for possible problems. Conversely, the utilization information in Figure 4-1 also shows the comparatively low months of August, September, January and June. These months can be used for projects which cannot be accomplished when utilization is high such as workshops, equipment inventory, staff development, remodeling and equipment installations. General utilization trends can help management prepare for high demand periods and indicate when slow periods might be used to undertake certain projects.

Surprises. General predictable utilization trends can sometimes lull the manager into a false sense of security. The manager must always analyze any general trend to see if there are any hidden exceptions within. In Figure 4-2, which is exactly like Figure 4-1, such an exception can be noted regarding 16mm and 8mm projectors. Use of 16mm projectors is starting to drop off going from 460 in April to 423 in May while 8mm projectors experience a

FISCAL YEAR (JULY-JUNE) OPERATING CALENDAR FOR EQUIPMENT DISTRIBUTION

	16mm Projectors	Filmstrip Projectors	Carousel Projectors	Tape Recorders	Overhead Projectors	8mm Projectors
July	229	55	60	98	109	18
Aug.	149	32	38	49	47	23
Sept.	199	65	84	78	338	19
Oct.	395	91	158	121	461	45
Nov.	362	97	162	129	397	34
Dec.	346	79	113	104	311	44
Jan.	227	60	135	90	327	67
Feb.	308	75	145	85	325	36
Mar.	458	83	187	148	476	50
Apr.	460	75	173	149	450	67
May	423	132	288	194	465	136
June	120	61	68	74	104	28

General High Volume Trends ▢

55

Fig. 4-2

FISCAL YEAR (JULY-JUNE) OPERATING CALENDAR FOR EQUIPMENT DISTRIBUTION

	16mm Projectors	Filmstrip Projectors	Carousel Projectors	Tape Recorders	Overhead Projectors	8mm Projectors
July	229	55	60	98	109	18
Aug.	149	32	38	49	47	23
Sept.	199	65	84	78	338	19
Oct.	395	91	158	121	461	45
Nov.	362	97	162	129	397	34
Dec.	346	79	113	104	311	44
Jan.	227	60	135	90	327	67
Feb.	308	75	145	85	325	36
Mar.	458	83	187	148	476	50
Apr.	460	75	173	149	450	67
May	423	132	288	194	465	136
June	120	61	68	74	104	28

large jump going from 67 in April to 136 in May. So, while the general trend indicates moderate growth in May, 16mm projectors are dropping and 8mm projectors are experiencing the biggest month of growth all year! An analysis of this strange quirk in the general trend indicates faculty are summarizing material for final examinations in May, involving little use of 16mm films. However, requests for 8mm projectors have more than doubled because students are finishing film projects due in May before final examinations. A totally prepared manager must look within general trends to eliminate any possible surprises.

How Utilization Can Work for You

Once the manager has decided what to count, developed forms for obtaining the information, and established a time frame showing variance in work load, the time has come to express this information in a way that best describes media center productivity. Utilization figures should support rationale for increased budget, personnel and facilities. A manager must be able to substantiate the positive role of the media center. Simply saying the media center is doing a good job, in a time of increasingly tight budgets, will not turn many influential heads. Numbers must be used to document media center productivity and instructional impact. There are several factors which should be incorporated to make utilization data effective.

Use Understandable Terms. Many managers express data using highly technical media terminology. Other media practitioners can understand the information but not the lay person reviewing the utilization. Some managers may think that if utilization is presented using media terminology, upper management will be duly impressed with the sophistication of the field and more inclined to grant budget requests. The media center manager must remember that often upper management has no background in media. Remember to express utilization in terms the reviewing audience will understand. Media managers should make life easier, not more difficult, for upper management.

Be Concise. Always use the least amount of information necessary to adequately express productivity or justify a request. Upper administrative officials are busy and appreciate utilization information that comes directly to the point.

Provide Options. When requesting additional budget, facilities or personnel, provide options. This gives administrators the feeling they made the decision and still have overall control. As a general rule, do not present ultimatums based on the calculated risk that if predicted consequences sound bad enough upper management will have no choice but to grant the request. A media manager left to explain why the organization did not fold as predicted when the additional graphic artists were not hired will be embarrassed and suffer a valuable loss of credibility.

Stress Common Goals. The data presented must relate directly to the main objectives of the organization and demonstrate how media are helping achieve those objectives. A media center in education will emphasize students served while a media center in business may stress increased profits through a better trained sales staff. Decreased patient-care costs may be a measurement used for a hospital media center. A public library media center will note high circulation figures for non-print materials and audiovisual equipment as an important part of community service. In all cases, the main mission of the organization is successfully integrated into the media center utilization. There must be a strong relationship between the media center and the primary mission of the institution, but many managers do not express utilization in such a way as to emphasize this positive support function. A media center will not last long unless it has a key role in helping the organization reach important goals.

Document Negative and Positive Utilization. Media managers are oriented, out of necessity, to emphasize positive aspects of their operation. Utilization in most media center reports expresses data in positive terms documenting accomplishments and growth. However, there is a corresponding need in crucial areas to document the negative aspects of the operation. On the surface, it does not seem to make sense to state what the media center failed to provide. Documenting failures seems to just add insult to injury. Media managers probably feel that upper level administrators reading negative reports might decide not to provide increased funding for a losing operation. Actually, documented evidence of service and production deficiencies, if properly presented, can have just the opposite effect, showing that the media manager is on top of problem areas and can justify corrective measures. Compare the manager who says, "I can just tell from the pressure that we need some additional video equipment," with the manager who says, "We need two additional videotape recorders because we could not fill 130 requests this year resulting in 1,300 students not being served." The second manager does not approach the problem from a vague "we need it" justification but, instead, has actual numbers to back up the request; he has learned to effectively play the numbers game.

Figure 4-3 shows how this negative information can be expressed. Note that the first two columns have the positive information covering requests filled and students served. The next three columns cover the negative data for requests not filled, students not served, and a request not filled code. The last column, for the requests not filled code, is crucial since it is important to know why the request could not be filled. No corrective action can be taken unless the cause can be verified. Documenting the cause for a problem may sound like a large task but in any media center area the reasons why something cannot be done usually fall into several major categories. Little time is needed to quickly determine these problem categories and assign a code to each. In Figure 4-3 all requests not filled are code "1" indicating the equipment is checked out and not available. The code "1" could indicate that additional equipment is needed to meet the demand. Had code "2" been used, additional part-time help for delivery would have been the answer. Code "3" would document a need for quicker repair services or possibly a better line of equipment not subject to frequent breakdowns Also, note in Figure 4-3 that most requests not filled are in the television category, substantiating the need for purchasing additional television equipment. If utilization is well organized the manager can quickly spot problem areas.

A logical question might be: "How do I document what I haven't been able to do when I haven't done it?" A justifiable question with a logical answer. In Figure 4-4, a typical equipment request form, shows a "N.F. Code" section for the not filled code. When a client calls requesting equipment the

MEDIA DISTRIBUTION
Monthly Report

Equipment Type	Requests Filled	Students Served	Requests Not Filled	Students Not Served	Requests Not Filled Code*
Filmstrips	103	1,579			
Films	133	4,774			
16mm Projectors	474	22,676			
Filmstrip Projectors	133	3,654			
Opaque Projectors	74	2,016			
Overhead Projectors	740	25,262			
8mm Projector (Dual)	118	1,934	1	41	1
Record Player (Monaural)	144	4,362			
Screens	76	3,974			
Slide Projectors	363	8,819			
Audio Reel-to-Reel Monaural Recorders	297	6,681	1	1	1
TV Cameras	4	49	3	30	1
TV VTR 3600	4	117	5	100	1
TV Monitors (black & white)	4	87	3	90	1
TV Systems Ensemble	7	38	2	40	1
Lantern Slide Projectors	22	1,028			
Rental Films	394	23,016			
TOTALS	3,090	110,066	15	302	

*Code for Requests Not Filled: 1 = Equipment checked out and not available.
2 = Part-time help not available.
3 = Equipment down.

59

Fig. 4-4

MEDIA DISTRIBUTION

Name _____ Dept. _____ Phone _____ Stud. Served _____
Del./P.U. Pt. _____ Use Date _____ Time _____ Bldg. _____ Room _____
Course _____ Sec. _____ Return Date _____ Time _____

N.F. Code

Quan.	Equipment	Dist. Code	Quan.	Equipment	Dist. Code	Quan.	Equipment	Dist. Code
	16mm			Filmstrip			Dual 8m	
	OH			CART			Screen, Prt	
	S 8 So			Rec Play MS			Tpe Rcr MS	
	CRSL			Cass S Sync			TV I/2 RR	
	CASS			VCR 3/4			R 8 LOOP	
	Monitor MC			TV RR Ens			OTHER	
	Fm strp cass			Fm strp R/P			OTHER	
	S8 LOOP			3 I/2 x 4			OTHER	
	TV VCR Ens			Opaque			OTHER	

Materials

Shelf No.

Notes

Booked by _____
Operator _____

staff member takes down only the information necessary to confirm the order which includes the equipment requested, dates for use, students served, and client's name. Availabilities are quickly checked and if the order cannot be filled on the date requested, alternate dates are suggested. Offering alternate dates can reduce the disappointment of not receiving the equipment while exhibiting a helpful attitude on the part of the staff. If alternate dates are not a viable solution, the appropriate code is placed in the "N.F. Code" slot. Instead of throwing away the form, which is typically the case, all "not filled" orders are kept. When utilization is tabulated the manager has a record of what was accomplished as well as what was not accomplished and even the reasons why certain requests were not filled. Although this example happens to deal with the distribution of audiovisual equipment, the same concept of documenting problem areas could be used for many media service areas.

SUMMARY

The main reason for collecting utilization data is to provide information which accurately shows the productivity and positive impact of a media center. First, the media manager must decide what to count which most accurately describes the mission of the media center. Secondly, service forms must obtain this key information. Third, a time frame must be established which most accurately illustrates work load fluctuations. Fourth, once collected, the data should be expressed by keeping the following qualities in mind for maximum benefit: (1) use terminology understood by upper management; (2) be concise; (3) provide options for decision flexibility; (4) stress how the media center contributes to the achievement of goals for the organization; and, (5) document negative along with positive media center utilization.

CHAPTER 5

Cost Accounting

C OST ACCOUNTING involves isolating costs, tabulating relevant costs, and determining relative cost effectiveness. The two major areas discussed with regards to cost accounting techniques are media productions and equipment.

The manager must be aware of operating costs for several reasons. A growing number of media centers use a charge-back system where a portion or all the operating budget is generated through charging for services. Those that charge for services require accurate cost data to ensure a continuing sound financial base. Properly applied, media technology can be less expensive than traditional lecture methods. Conversely, there are cases where the additional cost of mediated instruction is not justified. These situations justify the need for cost accounting methods capable of obtaining data the media manager can use to make intelligent decisions.

Although specific examples are used, cost accounting approaches discussed have general application and can be used in any media center. All procedures presented will build from simple to more complex examples so you can select the approach that best fits your own local conditions. Hopefully, the chapter will help the media manager to keep better cost data, manage current expenditures, and plan more accurately for future budgets. All figures used for labor, materials, and equipment costs are only for example purposes and should not be considered official quotations. Examples are kept simple to explain cost accounting concepts. Once understood, concepts can be altered to fit individual media center needs.

COST ACCOUNTING PRODUCTIONS

Television productions are used as examples in this section because television can involve a number of production elements, each with unique cost considerations. Once cost accounting techniques for television are mastered, other less complex media productions such as photography or audio recording should pose no problem.

Determining Costs

No matter whether a proposed audiovisual production is simple or complex, it is imperative to determine as closely as possible the exact production requirements. Any number of behavioral objective models can be used to determine the target audience, instructional goals, and media required. From a realistic viewpoint, this process need not be complicated for many of the simple production requests coming to a media center. With a clear idea of the production elements involved, the media director can more accurately determine possible costs. One note of warning for the manager initiating cost accounting techniques. Do not become too preoccupied with identifying every *source* of cost. This chapter will move from very simple to more sophisticated cost accounting models and the manager should do the same. A staff can quickly become overloaded with paper work and forget the primary mission of the media center which is instructional support. The costs discussed below start with the simple areas of labor and materials and then move to the more complex area of overhead.

Direct Costs. Labor and materials expended on a specific project are direct costs. There could be other expense classifications directly chargeable to a production but labor and materials are the two major categories covering most costs.

Indirect Costs. Costs that are not the direct result of doing a production are called overhead. These costs are not as specific, covering general operating expenses such as equipment depreciation, administrative and secretarial support, office supplies, utilities, and maintenance. Another way of looking at overhead is to group all expenditures required to maintain the basic operation of the media center which cannot be charged to any specific project. Overhead has also been called "the cost of doing business." Media managers in education seldom have to figure overhead costs. Conversely, media centers in industry and commercial production houses usually must cover overhead as a part of production charges. Methods for recouping overhead costs are probably as varied as media center organizations, with no two being exactly alike. Managers who do not have to figure overhead costs, by all means, rejoice! Overhead costs can be extremely complex. Although several methods for figuring overhead are discussed, the manager will no doubt have to create a system custom-suited to local conditions.

Tabulating Costs

Once all appropriate sources of cost have been identified, the next step in production cost accounting involves tabulating costs. Several methods will be discussed, moving from simple to more complex.

Fig. 5-1

TELEVISION PRODUCTION COST SUMMARY

	Student Hours	Professional Hours	Total Hours	
LABOR	($3/hr)	($8/hr)		
Planning		46	46	$
Graphics		3	3	
Studio	8	25	33	
		Sub Total	82	$

MATERIALS		Average Cost × No. of Items	
Graphics			
slides	.30	× 30 =	$ 9
overheads	1.50		
tv cards	.20	5	1
charts & graphs	1.00		
other			
Videotape			
½ hour cassette	20.00	4	80
1 hour cassette	35.00		
Photo			
16mm film & processing	8.00		
slides (on location)	.46		
prints	.85		
Other			
lumber & hardware			30
travel (40 miles @ 25¢)			10
		Sub Total	$
		Grand Total	$

Direct Costs. Keeping a record of all labor and materials expenses can be time consuming. Personnel costs can be complicated, especially if a number of different people, all at different pay scales and classifications, are involved in a production. Trying to record the exact cost for all materials can also become very involved. Using average costs can reduce record keeping problems. In a production department with different job classifications and pay ranges, an average per hour rate for the area can be established. Instead of trying to figure the exact cost for each slide produced, again an average cost for a finished slide is used. Averaging does not provide exact data but is easy to implement for the media center just starting cost accounting procedures.

Figure 5-1 shows a cost summary for a simple television production using the averaging technique for labor and materials. Often students are used as studio crew on a part-time basis in media centers. Professional hours represent full-time staff. The average rate for each labor classification is multiplied by the number of hours expended on the production for a total labor charge. Materials are figured the same way with the average costs already listed on the sheet. Production personnel fill in the number of items to figure materials cost. Adding labor and materials expenditures provides the total cost of the production. Notice labor represents the largest cost in this production and is typical of most media productions. Consequently, labor costs are a primary concern for media managers.

One additional note. Figure 5-1 represents a closed-end design in that all pricing information is printed on the sheet and space is only provided for final totals. A closed-end form can be restrictive and necessitates keeping rough figures on another sheet for transfer to a cost summary sheet. Some people like a log or open-end form. Figure 5-2 shows an open-end form with the same cost information shown in Figure 5-1, expressed in a different way. The form is open-end because plenty of spaces are provided to fill in information as the project develops. As was noted in Chapter 3, "Designing Service Forms," it is always best to leave yourself some flexible space. Figure 5-2 has more flexibility, especially in the materials area, by leaving space to write in the specific expenses instead of listing all possible item prices as is the case in Figure 5-1. With either Figure 5-1 or 5-2, some might still want to keep a separate log or running record of expenses. When the production is completed all relevant information can be transferred to the one-page cost summary sheet.

If the production is properly conceived, most time is spent in preproduction and post production activities. The actual production time in a studio or on location should be the smallest portion of the total time expenditure because this is where the cost per hour is the highest. Staying with television production as an example, usually a number of people are involved in the actual videotaping, including the producer, director, content specialist, engineers, and crew. Note in Figure 5-2 the actual production cost of $11 per hour is the sum of staff and student per-hour costs, whereas the preproduction and post production cost is only the professional staff cost of $8 per hour. Many people are carried away with the glamour of production, forgetting that most successful programs are developed on paper in laborious preproduction planning sessions. A comparison of the time spent in preproduction planning versus actual production is analogous to the iceberg illustration in Figure 5-3. All the unglamorous yet crucial planning steps involving determining target audience, defining instructional needs, preparing instructional objectives, defining strategy, selecting media, evaluating the pilot program and revising content based on evaluation,

Fig. 5-2

TELEVISION PRODUCTION DATA SHEET

Program Title __POINT OF PURCHASE STRATEGY__ Job No. __239__ Date __3/1__
Department __MARKETING__ Client Contact __SMITH__ Phone __8-3524__
Series/Project Title _____

LABOR[1]
Professional Hours

PRE					PRODUCTION		POST			
Client Conf.		Research Script		Set Const.		Pro Studio /Field	Graphics	Edit.		Eval.	
Date	Hrs.	Date	Hrs.	Date	Hrs.	Date	Hrs.	Date	Hrs.	Date	Hrs.	Date	Hrs.

Client Conf. Date	Hrs.	Research Script Date	Hrs.	Set Const. Date	Hrs.	Pro Studio/Field Date	Hrs.	Graphics Date	Hrs.	Edit. Date	Hrs.	Eval. Date	Hrs.
3/1	4	3/5	5	3/12	4	3/15	4	3/12	3	3/16	9	3/26	3
3/2	3	3/8	5			3/18	2			3/23	6	3/31	3
3/3	5	3/9	6										
3/11	4	3/10	8										
					44				9			21	

= [74] × Average Wage [$8] = [$592]

Student Hours

Date	Hrs.	Date	Hrs.	Date	Hrs.	Date	Hrs.	Date	Hrs.	Date	Hrs.	Date	Hrs.
1/15	4	1/18	4										

= [8] × [$3] = [$24]

MATERIALS

Videotape	Graphics	Sets/Props	Photography	Other
4 ½-hr tapes @ $20 = $80	5 cards @ $.20 = $1	lumber, hardware, etc. $30	30 slides @ $.30 = $9	Travel: 40 mi @ $.25 = $10

------------ = [$130]

NOTES

Fig. 5-3

PREPRODUCTION PLANNING ICEBERG ANALOGY

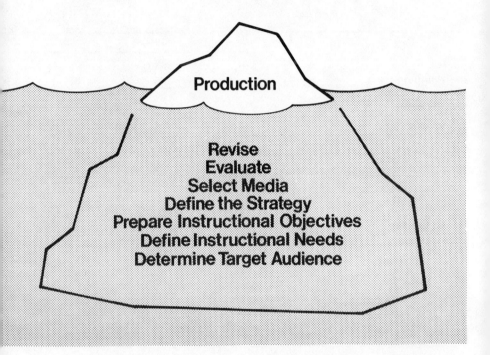

all should take place before production work begins. All important planning steps in Figure 5-3 are "below water," seldom seen, and yet form the very foundation for the visible production phase. The exciting production phase, resulting in a finished program, is what everyone sees. Yet without the foundation elements of preplanning, the finished production could not float! Indeed, the final production does represent only the tip of the iceberg! Certainly there are cases where extensive preproduction planning is not required. However, more often than not, the planning process is short changed, resulting in mediocre productions. Extensive changes should be kept to a minimum during actual production to keep costs down. Time for another media axiom: *eraser dust is less expensive than changing a finished program.* The studio or remote production site is the place for execution, not planning.

Indirect Costs. Overhead can quickly become a very complex source of cost. Several approaches for tabulating overhead are discussed. These are certainly not the only ways to incorporate overhead costs in a total production budget summary. It is hoped that this section will give the manager not familiar with overhead a point of departure and a better understanding of the sources of overhead costs.

One very simple method for figuring overhead is to add up the annual budget for all costs not related to a production and divide by the number of

Fig. 5-4

TELEVISION PRODUCTION COST SUMMARY

	Student Hours	Professional Hours	Total Hours	Tot Cos
LABOR	($3/hr)	($8/hr)		
Planning	_____	46	46	$36
Graphics	_____	3	3	2
Studio	8	25	33	22
		Sub Total	82	$61

MATERIALS Average Cost × No. of Items
Graphics

slides	.30 ×	30 =	$ 9
overheads	1.50	_____	_____
tv cards	.20	5	1
charts & graphics	1.00	_____	_____
other	_____	_____	_____

Videotape

½ hour cassette	20.00	4	80
1 hour cassette	35.00	_____	_____

Photo

16mm film & processing	8.00	_____	_____
slides (on location)	.46	_____	_____
prints	.85	_____	_____

Other

lumber & hardware	30
travel (40 miles @ 25¢)	10
Sub Total	$ 13

OVERHEAD Cost per hour × total hours
Sub Total

$14 × 82 = $114

Grand Total $189

Fig. 5-5

WORK HOURS PER YEAR

OVERHEAD & DIRECT CHARGEABLE HOURS
52 weeks × 40 hours/week   2,080

OVERHEAD HOURS
Vacation & Holidays: 20 days × 8 hours/day   = 160
Lunch & Unassigned Time: 240 days × 1 hour/day = 240
                                                400   −400

DIRECT CHARGEABLE HOURS   1,680

---

production hours available in a year. Only general operating expenses such as utilities and office supplies are considered overhead. There is no attempt to compute overhead labor costs. Based on this formula, Figure 5-4 includes a $14 per hour overhead charge. This means it is costing $14 per production hour just to keep the television facility open, above and beyond the direct cost of actual productions. Figures 5-1 and 5-4 are very similar except in Figure 5-4 the total of 82 hours directly charged to the production is multiplied by the $14 per hour overhead charge.

Refining the concepts presented in Figures 5-1 and 5-4 can result in a more accurate yet increasingly complex computation for overhead. Figure 5-4 does not consider personnel overhead. A production facility open 40 hours per week with a staff of six, represents 240 work hours per week. However, 240 hours of 100 percent staff productivity per week is unrealistic since some time is consumed in breaks and unassigned time. The portion of each staff member's time not spent on a production represents overhead. Labor that is not chargeable to a given project can represent a very large overhead cost. Figures 5-5 to 5-11 take a look at this whole problem of refining specific overhead charges.

Figure 5-5 provides a method for determining the annual number of overhead hours not assigned to any specific project. Three key figures should be noted in Figure 5-5: 2,080 total overhead and direct chargeable hours; 400 total overhead hours; and 1,680 total direct chargeable hours. These three totals form the basis for overhead costs developed in Figures 5-6 to 5-11. The 400 overhead hours include all vacation, holidays, and breaks, for which an employee is paid. All time technically available for work is represented by the 1,680 direct chargeable hours. Overhead and direct chargeable hours together represent a total of 2,080 hours that an employee is paid for per year.

Key totals from Figure 5-5 can then be incorporated into Figure 5-6 where the per hour overhead cost is determined. In this example, the supervisor works half time as a television director. The supervisor duties represent half of the 1,680 available hours or 840 hours. The 840 hours spent in supervision plus 160 hours spent on vacation, and 240 hours spent on breaks, total 1,240 hours of overhead. The 1,240 hours represent overhead because none is expended di-

Fig. 5-6

TELEVISION PRODUCTION PER HOUR OVERHEAD SURCHARGE[a]

Overhead Labor Cost	Overhead Hours/Year	×	Number of Employees	=	Total Overhead Hours	×	Cost/Hour	=	Total Overhead Cost
TV Director/Supervisor	1,240		1		1,240		$9		$11,160
TV Director	400		3		1,200		8		9,600
Engineer	2,080		1		2,080		7		14,560
Secretary	2,080		1		2,080		4		8,320
			6		6,600				$43,640

	Total Paid Hours		Number of Employees						
Total Chargeable Hours	2,080	×	6	=	12,480	−	6,600	=	5,880

Total Overhead Cost

Labor	$43,640
Office Supplies	600
Repair Parts	9,000
Telephone	1,600
Travel	200
Equipment Depreciation	15,000
	$70,040
Per Hour Overhead Surcharge	$70,040 ÷ 5,880 = $12

[a]Includes labor overhead and general overhead (i.e. office supplies, repair parts, telephone, etc.)

Fig. 5-7

TELEVISION PRODUCTION COST SUMMARY

MATERIALS

	Cost per Item	×	No. of Items	=	Total
Television					
½ hr. videotape	$20		2		$40
Audio					
7″ reel	3		1		3
Photo					
1 roll 16mm film	8		1		8
slides	.40		30		12
8 x 10 print	.50		10		5
					$68

LABOR

	Cost per Hour	×	No. of Hours	=	Total
Television	$8		65		$ 520

COST SUMMARY

Overhead	$12	×	65	=	$ 780
Materials					68
Labor					520
Total					$1,368

rectly on any production. Only 400 hours (160 hours of vacation plus 240 hours of breaks) is considered an overhead cost for each production employee since the rest of his/her time can be charged against a specific project. Since the engineer spends a great deal of time on general maintenance of the studio, the entire 2,080 paid hours is considered overhead. Secretarial support, like the engineer, is not charged to any specific production so the entire 2,080 paid hours is considered overhead. All overhead hours per year can be multiplied by the number of employees and their respective hourly rate to obtain total overhead labor costs per year. This total overhead labor cost can be added to the other overhead costs in Figure 5-6. A per hour overhead rate is determined by dividing total chargeable hours (total work hours less total overhead hours) into total annual overhead costs. This per hour overhead rate is then used to generate a proportion of the general operating budget by attaching a surcharge to the basic production hour and materials costs for a project.

Figure 5-7 shows how all direct and overhead costs are brought together to arrive at a total project cost summary for a typical television production. Mate-

Fig. 5-8

GRAPHIC PRODUCTION PER UNIT OVERHEAD SURCHARGE [a]

Annual Overhead Labor Cost	Overhead Hours/Year	×	Number of Employees	=	Total Over-head Hours	×	Cost/ Hour	=	Total Overhead Cost
Supervisor	2,080		1		2,080		$7		$14,560
Artist	400		5		2,000		6		12,000
Photographer	400		1		400		6		2,400
Secretary	2,080		1		2,080		3		6,240
			8		6,560				$35,200

Total Overhead Cost

Labor	$35,200
Office Supplies	50
Telephone	200
Printing	50
Equipment Depreciation	500
Per Unit Overhead Surcharge	$36,000 ÷ 24,000 = $1.50

Estimated Total Annual Units to be Produced

[a]Includes labor overhead and general overhead (i.e. office supplies, repair parts, telephone, etc.)

Fig. 5-9

GRAPHIC PRODUCTION COST SUMMARY

MATERIALS

	Cost per Item	×	No. of Items	=	Total
Storyboards	$.05		100		$ 5
Colored paper	.25		120		30
Strathmore	.15		60		9
Presstype	2.50		2		5
Zipatone	1.50		2		3
Slides	.40		80		32
					$84

LABOR

	Cost per Hour	×	No. of Hours	=	Total
Artist	$6		240		$1,440

COST SUMMARY

	Cost per Unit	×	No. of Units	=	Total
Overhead	$1.50		80		$ 120
Materials					84
Labor					1,440
Total					$1,644

rials and labor represent direct costs. By computing labor costs we also obtain total production hours which can be multiplied by the per hour overhead surcharge to obtain the total overhead cost. An inherent problem with this system is the assumption that all direct chargeable hours for production staff will be used. If all direct changeable hours are not used, the per hour overhead surcharge must be adjusted upward to cover overhead operating costs and downward if the reverse is true.

Another way of tabulating overhead is based on determining all overhead costs and dividing by the number of projected finished units to arrive at a per unit overhead surcharge. A unit is defined as a finished piece of media such as a slide, overhead transparency, videotape, or print. Figure 5-8 shows how a per unit overhead cost could be tabulated for a graphic production area. Notice that Figure 5-8 looks much like Figure 5-6 except the "Total Chargeable Hours" section has been eliminated. The total overhead cost for the year is divided by the number of estimated finished units to arrive at a per unit overhead sur-

Fig. 5-10

TELEVISION PRODUCTION PER HOUR LABOR CHARGE [a]

Overhead Labor & Direct Chargeable Labor Cost	Hours/Year	×	Number of Employees	=	Total Hours	×	Cost/Hour	=	Total Labor Cost
TV Director/Supervisor	2,080		1		2,080		$9		$18,720
TV Director	2,080		3		6,240		8		49,920
Engineer	2,080		1		2,080		7		14,560
Secretary	2,080		1		2,080		4		8,320
									$91,520

Total Labor and Overhead Cost [b]

Labor	$ 91,520
Office Supplies	600
Repair Parts	9,000
Telephone	1,600
Travel	200
Equipment Depreciation	15,000
Per Hour Labor Charge	$117,920 ÷ 5,880 = $20

Total Chargeable Hours [c] ←

[a]Includes direct chargeable labor, labor overhead, and general overhead (i.e. office supplies, repair parts, telephone, etc.).
[b]Does not include direct chargeable materials.
[c]Refer to Figure 5-6, p. 70.

74

charge. Each finished unit would receive the same charge when figuring the total cost for a production.

Figure 5-9 shows how the cost summary sheet might look for a graphic production using the per unit overhead surcharge technique. All direct mateirals and labor costs are figured. The 80 slides are multiplied by the per unit overhead cost of $1.50. This approach works better for some media departments than for others. For example, a television production department might have total operating overhead of $112,500. If the television department estimates doing 250 programs during the year this total would be divided into $112,500 to arrive at a per unit overhead surcharge of $450. However, this figure is somewhat misleading since one television program might be simple and another very complicated, yet the overhead cost is the same. The varying complexity of media jobs is the whole reason behind an overhead surcharge based on the number of hours expended on a production. When the overhead surcharge is multiplied by the number of hours spent on a project, the overhead cost is commensurate with the sophistication of the production. However, the per unit overhead surcharge technique can work, especially in areas where the unit volume is high and jobs do not vary much in complexity.

The same problem noted earlier in using as estimate of chargeable hours is evident here in estimating the number of finished production units. At the beginning of the fiscal year a production area must accurately estimate the number of media units to be produced. Estimates must be done at the beginning of the year since this is when operating budgets and working cash flow are established. During the course of the year, if an area is below the projected unit volume, the overhead surcharge will have to be adjusted upward to generate sufficient revenue to meet expenses and, conversely, if the number of units is over the projected volume there will be surplus funds. Adjustments may be necessary to come out even at the end of the year.

All overhead formulas presented list overhead as a separate charge. In many cases the overhead cost can be higher than other direct charges. In Figure 5-7 overhead is $780 while labor and materials are only $520 and $68 respectively. Clients could contend there must be mismanagement with such high overhead in comparison to other charges. For this reason some media centers do not show overhead but incorporate a certain amount of overhead in direct charges. True, the direct materials and labor charges are higher, but many clients are less disturbed by this than by a separate breakout of overhead costs.

Figure 5-10 shows how labor overhead and general overhead can be incorporated in the per hour labor charge. The top part of Figure 5-10 looks like Figure 5-6 except that 2,080 hours per year (includes overhead labor and direct chargeable labor) is used for each employee. Total labor costs are then added to general overhead and divided by total chargeable hours to determine the per hour labor charge. Note that chargeable materials are not incorporated in the per hour labor charge because many clients want to see the specific materials costs for their project. Figure 5-10 includes all labor (overhead labor and direct chargeable labor) and general overhead for a $20 per hour labor rate while Figure 5-6 includes only labor overhead (not chargeable labor) and general overhead for a $12 per hour overhead surcharge.

The project cost summary in Figure 5-11 looks much like Figure 5-7 except the per hour labor charge is $20 instead of $8. The $12 difference is included in the labor cost in Figure 5-11. Note, in both Figures 5-7 and 5-11, the total production cost is $1,368. In Figure 5-7, all direct labor and materials along with a surcharge for general overhead must be figured for each production while in Figure 5-11 only direct labor and materials must be computed. Summarizing, the approach used in Figure 5-11 has these advantages: (1) only labor and materials have to be figured: and (2) overhead is not visible as a separate cost because it is already included as a part of the labor charge.

Many approaches can be used to express and recoup overhead expenses. The several overhead formulas presented in this section should not be construed as the *only* approaches. These formulas are presented to help explain some major considerations when faced with figuring overhead. Once the sources of overhead are isolated, the method for recovering overhead costs is highly dependent on local financial and operational policies.

Making Comparisons

After costs have been identified and information tabulated, comparisons are possible. Cost comparisons can be used to determine if a production is cost effective and to keep projects within budget.

Estimate and Actual Cost. Estimating production expense is an extra cost accounting step not used in many media centers. The estimate *before* production has several advantages. Production people are forced to think more carefully about the implications of a production. Usually by providing an estimate the production staff is better prepared and has a clearer idea of the finished product. A thorough understanding of production requirements and objectives translates into more efficient use of production time, resulting in lower costs. Estimates also tend to keep production people on track by providing a target figure they must stay within. Once a production person has submitted an estimate he/she usually feels a commitment and will work hard to stay within his/her own budget figures.

Figure 5-12 shows how the estimate procedure can work. Based on the preproduction meeting with the client, the artist would complete the "est" or estimate columns for materials and labor. Estimates set the budget targets for the project. When the project is finished the "act" for actual cost columns are completed as shown in Figure 5-13. Ideally, the artists wants the estimate and actual figures to be the same. However, nothing in media production is ideal! Note that while the materials section is fairly close, the difference between estimated and actual labor charges is much larger. This is typical since most people, even experienced production personnel, often underestimate the amount of time necessary to complete a job. Certainly a media axiom is appropriate here: *everything always takes longer than you estimate.* This axiom leads to another, often the reason behind the first: *if something can go wrong, it will.* Although neither of these axioms is terribly original, both are germane to the world of media management. Although the final cost in Figure 5-13 is $70 over the estimate, it could have been much worse. Media personnel just starting to project costs will quickly learn to appreciate actual costs which are only $70

Fig. 5-11

TELEVISION PRODUCTION COST SUMMARY

MATERIALS

	Cost per Item	×	No. of Items	=	Total
Television					
½ hr. videotape	$20		2		$40
Audio					
7" reel	3		1		3
Photo					
1 roll 16mm film	8		1		8
slides	.40		30		12
8 x 10 print	.50		10		5
					$68

LABOR

	Cost per Hour	×	No. of Hours	=	Total
Television	$20		65		$1,300

COST SUMMARY

Materials	$ 68
Labor	1,300
Total	$1,368

over the estimate. Usually when initiating estimating procedures, actual costs will far exceed estimates. With practice, however, a staff can quickly become very proficient at developing accurate estimates.

Cost Effectiveness. A concept receiving increased attention in media management is cost effectiveness. Whenever possible, cost effectiveness should be expressed in terms of cost per student or trainee served, since the learner is the final recipient of materials and services provided by a media center. The production of programs without a constant concern for student development negates the whole purpose of instructional technology and the media center manager's role in delivering that technology.

Determining what is or is not cost effective is totally dependent on local conditions. There is no national average indicating that everything below a certain cost per student or trainee served is automatically cost effective. For example, American Airlines has a $40 million training complex close to the Dallas/Fort Worth Airport. About 10,000 training cycles are completed each

Fig. 5-12

GRAPHIC PRODUCTION COST SUMMARY

MATERIALS

	Cost per Item ×	No. of Items		Total	
		est	act	est	act
Storyboards	$.05	80		$4	
Colored paper	.25	80		20	
Strathmore	.15	40		6	
Presstype	2.50	2		5	
Zipatone	1.50	2		3	
Slides	.40	80		32	
				70	

LABOR

	Cost per Hour ×	No. of Hours		Total	
		est	act	est	act
Artist	$6	230		$1,380	

COST SUMMARY

	Cost per Hour ×	No. of Hours		Total	
		est	act	est	act
Overhead	$1.50	80		$ 120	
Materials				70	
Labor				1,380	
Total				$1,570	

year at a cost of $15–20 million.[1]* Pilots use the latest audiovisual programs and equipment along with expensive simulators that accurately duplicate the movement of a plane during take-off, flight, and landing. A simulator can cost $3 million and $450 per hour to operate.[2] Yet use of simulators can save over 28 million gallons of fuel representing an annual cost savings of at least $8 million.[3] The annual training expense for a pilot can range from $13,800–27,200.[4] But, a new commercial aircraft, depending on size and type, can run $20–50 million.[5] A $15–20 million annual training expense that can reduce fuel consumption and increase the safety of passengers, crew, and a

* Notes are referenced at the end of this chapter.

Fig. 5-13

GRAPHIC PRODUCTION COST SUMMARY

MATERIALS

	Cost per Item	×	No. of Items		=	Total	
			est	act		est	act
Storyboards	$.05		80	120		$ 4	6
Colored paper	.25		80	100		20	25
Strathmore	.15		40	60		6	9
Presstype	2.50		2	2		5	5
Zipatone	1.50		2	2		3	3
Slides	.40		80	80		32	32
						$70	$80

LABOR

	Cost per Hour	×	No. of Hours		=	Total	
			est	act		est	act
Artist	$6		230	240		$1,380	$1,440

COST SUMMARY

	Cost per Hour	×	No. of Hours		=	Total	
			est	act		est	act
Overhead	$1.50		80	80		$ 120	$ 120
Materials						70	80
Labor						1,380	1,440
Total						$1,570	$1,640

fleet of expensive airplanes is indeed cost effective! However, if a media director in a small school district suggested developing instructional programs for a mere $15–20 million, there would be grounds for dismissal by reason of insanity! Simply stated: cost effectiveness is a relative measurement, dependent on local conditions.

About the only constant regarding cost effectiveness is that it is a relative measurement. Any instructional media approach that is cost effective represents the least expensive method of satisfying all stipulated objectives and judged by local authorities to be worth the expenditure. This definition applies to mediated instructional packages, media equipment, and operational processes.

Comparing Costs of Instructional Approaches. Some definitions are necessary to differentiate between traditional and mediated instruction. Traditional instruction is course content provided by the teacher, primarily in a lecture format. Mediated instruction is an instructional product made up of material, devices, and techniques in combination designed to achieve specified objectives. Most or all of the essential content is provided through media programs and materials rather than the teacher.[6] Traditional and mediated instruction each have advantages and disadvantages. Any comparison in this section will be between traditional and mediated forms of instruction. Since most instruction is still delivered by using the traditional approach, emphasis is placed on advantages of the mediated approach when properly applied. Please note that in order for mediated instruction to be effective, the teacher must be in a position of control, managing the instructional experience.

A major advantage of mediated instruction is that it can be more cost effective than traditional instruction. Sometimes cost effectiveness can completely overshadow another major advantage, increased instructional effectiveness. Mediated instruction may, in many cases, cost more, but increased learning may be worth it. However, improved learning requires sophisticated documentation which is usually the reason media center managers, out of convenience or survival, stress cost effectiveness rather than instructional effectiveness. Cost effectiveness is more easily proven and understood by administrators. Since this chapter is restricted to cost accounting, there will be no indepth discussion of instructional effectiveness, but this should not be construed as an attempt to minimize its obvious importance. Several publications with material on instructional design and methods for measuring instructional effectiveness are listed in Resource Section 2: A Selected Bibliography.

There are numerous methods for comparing instructional programs costs but only two basic concepts will be discussed here. One method is a comparison of in-house production costs versus outside commercial production costs. This approach is especially useful in metropolitan areas having professional production agencies. A media center within an organization established to break even, will usually be less expensive than the outside production agency which must make a profit. The significant savings realized by doing the production in house can make a big impression on upper management. Figure 5-14 shows the estimated comparative cost figures for a production done in house versus using the services of an outside production agency. The media manager could argue that doing the production in house will result in a savings of $374. Managers could run such comparisons as a regular part of any production estimate. At the end of the year total net savings realized by doing productions in house can be impressive. The manager could state in the annual report to upper management that in-house productions saved the "XYZ Company" or "ABC School District" $150,000 in outside production costs. Such figures can be a very understandable expression of cost savings having a positive impact on administrators. Conversely, using such a comparison can also indicate when certain productions, such as television programs with elaborate special effects, are best done by an outside production agency. Again please note, such cost comparisons are easly implemented and only practical in metropolitan areas having numerous outside production agencies.

Fig. 5-14

GRAPHIC PRODUCTION COST COMPARISON:
IN-HOUSE VERSUS OUTSIDE PRODUCTION AGENCY

		In-House Production		Outside Production Agency	
	Units	Cost per Unit	Total	Cost per Unit	Total
LABOR					
Illustrator	3	$3.00	$ 9	$5	$ 15
Graphic Artist	20	5.00	100	15	300
MATERIALS					
Transparencies	3	1.00	3	2	6
Slides	10	2.00	20	15	150
Posters	1	5.00	5	25	25
Prints	6	.50	3	3	18
Total			$140		$514

Outside Production Agency	$514
In-House Production	140
Net Savings	$374

Another more sophisticated technique is to compare the costs of traditional and mediated instruction. In Figure 5-15, taking for granted that the traditional and mediated versions of the course both satisfy instructional objectives, the mediated approach costing $10 per student served is more cost effective than the traditional approach costing $50. This cost comparison is based only on instructional cost per course offering and does not include development cost. Isolating all relevant cost areas for traditional instruction may be difficult. An instructor may be assigned half-time to a course. Three instructors may work as an instructional team on a course, only to be replaced the following year by three more instructors all at different pay scales. Where accurate cost information can be obtained for traditional instruction, the media center manager may be able to make a convincing argument in favor of mediated instruction.

The impressive cost difference between $10 per student served for mediated instruction versus $50 per student served for traditional instruction does not include development cost. Typically, the startup or development cost for mediated instruction is more than for traditional instruction. Figure 5-15 shows this difference in development cost with $4,000 for traditional versus $16,000 for mediated instruction. The increased cost is for media production since research cost is the same with either approach. However, over the long run, the cost of providing instruction is usually much less with a mediated approach.

Figure 5-15, under "Instructional Cost Per Course Offering," indicates a net savings of $2,000 per course offering by using mediated instruction:

$$\begin{array}{ll} \text{Traditional Instruction} & \$2,500 \\ \text{Mediated Instruction} & \underline{-\ 500} \\ \text{Net Savings} & \$2,000 \end{array}$$

The $2,000 savings can be used to recoup the $16,000 development cost for the mediated instruction if the course is offered eight times:

$$\frac{\text{Development Cost for Mediated Instruction}}{\text{Savings Per Course Offering}} \quad \frac{\$16,000}{\$2,000} = 8 \text{ Course Offerings}$$

Fig. 5-15

TRADITIONAL VERSUS MEDIATED INSTRUCTION COSTS[a]

	Traditional		Mediated
DEVELOPMENT COST			
Research			
Instructor Time	4,000		4,000
		4,000	4
Production			
Instructor Time			1,000
Media Labor Cost			10,000
Media Materials			1,000
			12,
Total Development Cost		$4,000	$16,
INSTRUCTIONAL COST PER COURSE OFFERING			
Instructor cost[b]	2,500		
Instructor cost[c]			400
Videotape playback cost[d]			100
Total Instructional Cost		$2,500	$
COST PER STUDENT			
50 students per course offering	$\frac{2,500}{50} = \$50$		$\frac{500}{50} = \$10$

[a]Traditional instruction refers to teaching course content through the lecture approach. Mediated instruction is an instructional product made up of material, devices, and techniques in combination designe achieve specified objectives. Most or all essential content is provided through mediated instruction ra than the teacher. Definition for mediated instruction based on *Educational Technology: Definition and C sary of Terms, Volume I*, by the AECT Task Force on Definition and Terminology (Washington, D.C.: Asso tion for Educational Communications and Technology, 1977) p. 174.
[b]Represents the instructor's salary allocated to teach the entire course using the traditional mode of inst tion.
[c]Represents portion of instructor's salary allocated for managing the course which includes scheduling videotapes, assisting students with problem areas, and administering tests. The portion is less than for t tional instruction because the instructor does not spend as much time on the course as a result of b content being covered on videotape.
[d]Represents costs associated with playing back videotapes covering basic course content.

Fig. 5-16

SAVINGS BASED ON PROJECTED COURSE LIFE

PROJECTED COURSE LIFE

Sections Offered Each Semester	3
Semesters Course Will be Offered	×8
Number of Times Course Will be Offered	24

PROJECTED INSTRUCTIONAL COST

Traditional Instruction[a]

Cost per Offering	$ 2,500
Number of Times Course Will be Offered	× 24
	$60,000
Development Cost	4,000
Total Instructional Cost	$64,000

Mediated Instruction[b]

Cost per Offering	500
Number of Times Course Will be Offered	× 24
	$12,000
Development Cost	16,000
Total Instructional Cost	$28,000

PROJECTED SAVINGS

Total Traditional Instructional Cost	$64,000
Total Mediated Instructional Cost	− 28,000
	$36,000

[a]Traditional instruction refers to teaching course content through the lecture approach.
[b]Mediated instruction is an instructional product made up of material, devices, and techniques in combination designed to achieve specified objectives. Most or all essential content is provided through mediated instruction rather than the teacher. Definition for mediated instruction based on *Educational Technology: Definition and Glossary of Terms, Volume I,* by the AECT Task Force on Definition and Terminology (Washington, D.C.: Association for Educational Communications and Technology, 1977) p. 174.

Cost effectiveness can also be determined by using the projected life of a course as the basis for estimating savings. Course life is the length of time before major content revisions are necessary. Figure 5-16 shows that if the course is offered 24 times before major content revisions, the mediated approach will represent a $36,000 savings in instructional costs.

Another cost advantage resulting from the proper application of media is an increase in the amount of time the instructor has available for other activities. Mediated instruction can free a certain portion of the instructor's time usually spent just covering basic course content. The instructor can use the additional time in activities that may have a higher cost benefit such as more contact with students on an individual basis or development of new courses. Reallocation of a portion of an instructor's salary for more beneficial activities is another way of determining cost effectiveness.

COST ACCOUNTING EQUIPMENT

The two major considerations in cost accounting equipment are depreciation and cost effectiveness. Both points will be discussed by isolating costs, presenting various depreciation methods, and making cost comparisons to determine the most economical approach.

Determining Costs

In any area of cost accounting, isolating costs can quickly move from specific direct costs to more complex indirect costs. The media manager must decide what is relevant. There is no need to tabulate fascinating data that serves no purpose. Most emphasis in this section will be placed on purchase price and maintenance costs.

Purchase Price. No matter whether the manager buys direct from the dealer or must advertise for competitive bids, the initial purchase price is the basic foundation for any equipment cost accounting procedure. The amount of depreciation, cost effectiveness, and even maintenance expense are all related to purchase price.

Maintenance Costs. Over the life of the equipment, maintenance costs can have a more direct impact on cost accounting procedures than the purchase price. A piece of inexpensive equipment may seem like a wise purchase. In retrospect, when totaling maintenance costs, one may find that the original purchase price was paid many times over in repair bills. Conversely, a very expensive piece of equipment may seem extravagant but increased reliability and minimal maintenance may make the more expensive unit less costly in the long run. Taking for granted that essential requirements are satisfied by two pieces of equipment, one relatively cheap and one expensive, the old adage, "You get what you pay for," still holds true.

Depreciation

Once media equipment is purchased the manager is immediately faced with the fact that equipment will wear out. For some reason, this concept is seldom understood by upper management. When equipment wears out the reaction by upper management usually is, "But we just bought that 10 years ago!" Media managers must sometimes feel that management thinks media equipment will last forever! There are educational institutions that carry the original equipment purchase price on the inventory. Upper management looks at the total dollar figure and surmises the media center has a $100,000 equipment inventory when the actual depreciated valve is more like $25,000. Not being to depreciate equipment is misleading and should be avoided whenever possible. Depreciation, as with other aspects of cost accounting, is a numbers game and there are different ways to write off equipment costs. An indepth discussion of depreciation is beyond the scope of this book. However, the manager can look at the following basic depreciation methods and select those features that would

Fig. 5-17

TOTAL INVENTORY DEPRECIATION
SCHEDULE BY DECLINING BALANCE

Total Inventory Value (purchase price) $500,000

Annual Depreciation Rate: $50,000

Years	Annual Depreciation
1	$500,000
2	450,000
3	400,000
4	350,000
5	300,000
6	250,000
7	200,000
8	150,000
9	100,000
10	50,000

work best. Depreciation methods will be presented moving from simple to more complex.

Total Inventory. The easiest way to depreciate equipment is to develop a write-off schedule for the entire inventory. A set amount or percentage is subtracted from the remaining inventory value each year. There are numerous methods for establishing the set amount or percentage. The major advantage is that each equipment item is not written off separately, which would be a clerical nightmare and only practical if done by computer. The cumulative value of the total inventory, consisting of numerous equipment items, is depreciated as a whole. A total inventory depreciation or write-off schedule is especially convenient for the manager who has an established inventory but has never started a system for depreciation. Since the manager must start somewhere, the total inventory write-off can be an easy first step. Figure 5-17 shows how a total inventory write-off procedure might look using a ten-year depreciation period. Note this is a ten-year depreciation schedule for all equipment purchased within a given fiscal year. Equipment purchased in the next fiscal year would fall under a new ten-year depreciation schedule. Over a period of time there will be sections of the inventory being totally written off each year. The length of time used to depreciate equipment can depend on tax laws, estimated equipment life, and local financial considerations. The total inventory in Figure 5-17 is divided by 10 and that result is subtracted each year. Please note, when playing the numbers game there are many different ways to express the same information. In some organizations the reduced balance shown in Figure 5-17 is not accept-

Fig. 5-18

TOTAL INVENTORY DEPRECIATION
SCHEDULE BY DEPRECIATION RATE

Total Inventory Value (purchase price) $500,000

Annual Depreciation Rate: $50,000

Years	Annual Depreciation
1	$ 50,000
2	50,000
3	50,000
4	50,000
5	50,000
6	50,000
7	50,000
8	50,000
9	50,000
10	50,000
Total	$500,000

able so Figure 5-18 demonstrates another approach where the amount of write-off is shown each year, totaling the original cost of the inventory. Yet another example is shown in Figure 5-19 using a double declining percentage write-off. The first year 40 percent, or $200,000 of the total inventory is depreciated, leaving a remaining value of $300,000. Each year 40 percent of the remaining value is subtracted. At the conclusion of the tenth year the remaining balance is written off. Many corporations might use the double-declining method to write off equipment faster for tax purposes. Some organizations might feel the double-declining method better reflects the high initial use of new equipment. Notice in Figure 5-19 the amount of depreciation is large and then becomes smaller as compared to Figures 17 and 18 where $50,000 is written off each year. The important principle to remember is that Figures 5-17, 5-18, and 5-19 are showing exactly the same information expressed in different ways. All three examples also show partial depreciation of the total equipment inventory value in a given year regardless of equipment type or category. For example, overhead projectors, record players, slide projectors, and television receivers are depreciated as an aggregate, not as separate categories.

A more refined write-off schedule is shown in Figure 5-20 where each major equipment category is written off at a separate rate over a five-year period. The separate rate is the total dollar value of equipment in a certain classification divided by the number of years allowed for depreciation. As with other depreciation methods shown, equipment purchased in the next fiscal year would be on a new write-off schedule.

Fig. 5-19

TOTAL INVENTORY DEPRECIATION SCHEDULE BY
DOUBLE DECLINING PERCENTAGE WRITE-OFF

Total Inventory Value (purchase price) $500,000

Annual Depreciation Rate: Double Declining
(40% of remaining balance)

Years	Write-Off Amount	Remaining Value
1	$200,000	$300,000
2	120,000	180,000
3	72,000	108,000
4	43,200	64,800
5	25,920	38,880
6	15,552	23,328
7	9,331	13,996
8	5,599	8,398
9	3,359	5,039
10	2,016	3,023

Average Life Depreciation. A major disadvantage with some depreciation schedules is that the time period selected for write-off does not necessarily correspond with the actual useful life of the equipment. Often the time period selected is the result of local financial practices rather than equipment life. Average life depreciation then represents a more sophisticated write-off since a separate depreciation schedule is set up corresponding to the expected life for each major media equipment category. The Educational Products Information Exchange (EPIE) published a report citing average life figures for audiovisual equipment.[7] Based on average life figures from this report, Figure 5-21 shows what the depreciation schedule might look like for two pieces of audiovisual equipment differing greatly in cost, sophistication, and expected life. The average years of life for an equipment category is divided into the purchase price to determine the annual depreciation rate.

Although depreciation based on average life of equipment can be more accurate than some other write-off methods, there are several disadvantages. First, treatment and maintenance of audiovisual equipment can result in average life figures very different from national trends. A school in a rough metropolitan neighborhood may record a much lower average life for equipment than what might be reported by a medical school for the same equipment. The most accurate average life figures will be developed by the media manager reflecting local equipment handling and maintenance conditions. Second, even if local

Fig. 5-20

TOTAL INVENTORY DEPRECIATION SCHEDULE BY EQUIPMENT CATEGORY

Years	16mm PROJECTORS Annual Depreciation Rate: $3,600	SLIDE PROJECTORS Annual Depreciation Rate: $20,000	OVERHEAD PROJECTORS Annual Depreciation Rate: $1,200	AUDIO RECORDERS Annual Depreciation Rate: $500	PROJECTION SCREENS Annual Depreciation Rate: $875
1	$18,000	$100,000	$6,000	$2,500	$4,375
2	14,400	80,000	4,800	2,000	3,500
3	10,800	60,000	3,600	1,500	2,625
4	7,200	40,000	2,400	1,000	1,750
5	3,600	20,000	1,200	500	875

Fig. 5-21

AVERAGE EQUIPMENT LIFE DEPRECIATION SCHEDULE[a]

Average Years of Use	10 TV Sets @ $500 = $5,000 Annual Depreciation Rate: $1,000	5 Overhead Projectors @ $200 = $1,000 Annual Depreciation Rate: $100
1	$5,000	$1,000
2	4,000	900
3	3,000	800
4	2,000	700
5	1,000	600
6		500
7		400
8		300
9		200
10		100

[a] Based on average life span figures from annual report of 900 schools tabulated by the Bureau of Audio-Visual Instruction of the New York Public Schools cited in "Life Expectancy for AV Equipment: A User Report," *EPIE Report,* VI, No. 53 (New York: Educational Products Information Exchange Institute, 1973), p. 3.

data are used, average life figures can be distorted. Average life does not take into account individual pieces of equipment but rather basic equipment categories. One overhead projector may be used once a week while another will be used six times a day, yet the average life is the same. Third, tabulating average life figures is time consuming and usually not practical unless done by a computer.

If the media manager is blessed with access to computer technology, equipment depreciation is much easier. A computer program can make possible depreciation by equipment item. Many centers receive an inventory printout each year listing all media equipment. Equipment inventory printouts usually include information such as an abbreviated verbal description, property control number, purchase price, and purchase date. A computer program can be written to include the depreciation schedule for each piece of equipment. When equipment is purchased a depreciation rate can be assigned. When the inventory card is key punched, the depreciation rate is entered with other data.[8] Each year when the inventory is printed the depreciation rate is applied to reduce the value of the equipment item. Once the number of years has elapsed to fully depreciate the item, a zero appears in the price or current value column. Although the manager may elect to carry fully depreciated equipment on subsequent inventory printouts, at least the zero indicates that certain items have no remaining market value. Another approach might show an adjusted salvage value if equipment were traded in. The media manager at any time can express the present value of the equipment inventory based on the depreciated rather than original purchase price.

Operating Hours. The number of hours a piece of audiovisual equipment operates in its lifetime provides a very sophisticated data bank for depreciation. EPIE conducted a survey resulting in responses from 40 college-level users and 102 elementary and secondary schools.[9] Average life was not only expressed in years of use but also in hours of use. Figure 5-22 uses some of the data reported in this EPIE survey to establish a cost per hour depreciation rate for basic pieces of audiovisual equipment. For example, a filmstrip projector purchased for $138 will depreciate .028¢ each hour it is used.

The advantage of a depreciation schedule based on operating hours is increased accuracy. Actual operating hours for a category of equipment is much more refined than years of use. Even with averages, use hours is more accurate, covering only the period of time the equipment is actually operating. Several disadvantages must also be considered. First, a decision must be made on what constitutes a use hour. The simplest method for scheduling purposes is the time between check-out and return of equipment. However, there could be a large portion of time when the equipment would be in transit. A more accurate yet expensive approach would be to install meters on all equipment. Meters should be connected to the operational functions, not the power switch. Equipment can be "on" for hours and yet only be in an operational mode for a few minutes. Utilization would only require logging the meter reading when the equipment is checked out and upon return, with the difference providing the actual use time. The installation and maintenance of meters is costly and the tabulation of readings can be time consuming. As always, the manager must decide whether the cost of increased accuracy provides tangible results that directly benefit the media center.

Cost Effectiveness

Determining the cost effectiveness of audiovisual equpment, just as with instruction, is relative and dependent on local circumstances. The definition for cost effectiveness used earlier in this chapter when discussing instructional productions still holds: *any instructional media approach that is cost effective represents the least expensive method which satisfies all stipulated objectives and is judged by local authorities to be worth the expenditure.* Equipment needed to produce and deliver instruction is only one part of the entire cost-effective picture. Determining the cost effectiveness of an instructional production includes a portion of the cost of professional production equipment in the form of overhead. Professional production equipment as a source of overhead will not be covered here since it was previously discussed in this chapter under "Cost Accounting Productions." This section will be restricted to equipment used in training rooms to support instruction.

Cost Per Use. Not only is cost effectiveness for audiovisual equipment relative to local conditions, but it is also influenced by the purchase price and number of uses. Figure 5-23 shows one method for measuring cost effectiveness based on average life depreciation and cost per use. Each time a piece of equipment is requested represents one use. The left hand section of Figure 5-23 is based on the average life depreciation schedule first discussed in Figure 5-21. However, in Figure 5-23, instead of showing the declining balance of the

Fig. 5-22

AVERAGE LIFE EQUIPMENT DEPRECIATION
EXPRESSED IN COST PER HOUR

Equipment	Cost	Average Life in Hours [a]	Cost Per Hour
Filmstrip projector	$138	4,896	.028
16mm sound movie projector	970	4,742	.205
Reel-to-reel videotape recorder	895	4,689	.190
Portable audio cassette tape recorder	76	4,665	.016
TV receiver/monitor	350	4,624	.076
Phonograph	253	3,188	.079
Slide projector	320	3,176	.101
Disc sound filmstrip projector	335	3,051	.110
TV camera	960	2,784	.345
Cassette sound-slide projector	400	2,396	.167
8mm silent movie projector	219	1,546	.142
Cassette sound filmstrip projector	365	1,312	.278

[a] Figures taken from EPIE survey of college, elementary and secondary users cited in "Equipment Lifetimes," *EPIEgram Newsletter,* IV, No. 5 (December, 1975), p. 1.

inventory, the depreciation rate for write-off is shown each year. The average years of life for a specific type of equipment is divided into the purchase price to determine the annual depreciation rate. In Figure 5-23 the annual depreciation rate is divided by the total number of uses in a given year to determine the cost per use. Note in Figure 5-23 the key variable is the number of uses. For purposes of illustration, the general acceptability and use of the equipment tends to increase over the depreciation period. As the uses increase the cost per use drops. Conversely, if the number of uses happen to decline the cost per use would increase. Once the equipment is totally depreciated, costs may reverse and start to climb because of increased maintenance as the equipment becomes old.

Although cost per use is easy to figure there is a major disadvantage. The cost per use approach does not consider the number of trainees or students served by each use. Cost per use figures can be somewhat misleading since one use might serve 50 students while another might serve only 10, yet the cost per use is the same.

Cost Per Student. Figure 5-24 also has the depreciation schedule on the left but is based on the cost per student served. The instructor can indicate the number of students who will be served when ordering the equipment. Figure 3-6 in Chapter 3 (p. 45) shows a typical booking form with a place for noting the number of students served as a normal part of the booking procedure. The annual depreciation rate for an equipment category is divided by the number of students served to determine the cost per student. The variable at work in Figure 5-24 is the number of students served. As the number of students served

Fig. 5-23

AVERAGE EQUIPMENT LIFE DEPRECIATION AND COST EFFECTIVENESS SCHEDULE BASED ON COST PER USE

| Average Years of Use | AVERAGE LIFE DEPRECIATION[a] | | COST EFFECTIVENESS | | | |
| | 10 TV Sets @ $500 = $5,000 | 5 Overhead Projectors @ $200 = $1,000 | Number of Uses | | Cost per Use | |
	Annual Depreciation Rate: $1,000	Annual Depreciation Rate: $100	TV Sets	Overhead Projectors	TV Sets	Overhead Projectors
1	$1,000	$100	50	100	$20.00	$1.00
2	1,000	$100	75	110	$13.33	.90
3	1,000	$100	150	125	6.66	.80
4	1,000	$100	325	200	3.08	.50
5	1,000	$100	400	350	2.50	.28
6		$100		400		.25
7		$100		525		.19
8		$100		600		.33
9		$100		650		.15
10		$100		700		.14

[a]Based on average life span figures from annual reports of 900 schools tabulated by the Bureau of Audio-Visual Instruction of the New York Public Schools cited in "Life Expectancy for AV Equipment: A User Report," *EPIE Report*, VI, No. 53 (New York: Educational Products Information Exchange Institute, 1973), p. 3.

Fig. 5-24

AVERAGE EQUIPMENT LIFE DEPRECIATION AND COST EFFECTIVENESS SCHEDULE BASED ON STUDENTS SERVED

Average Years of Use	AVERAGE LIFE DEPRECIATION[a]		COST EFFECTIVENESS			
	10 TV Sets @ $500 = $5,000 Annual Depreciation Rate: $1,000	5 Overhead Projectors @ $200 = $1,000 Annual Depreciation Rate: $100	Number of Students Served		Cost per Student	
			TV Sets	Overhead Projectors	TV Sets	Overhead Projectors
1	$1,000	$100	1,250	2,500	$.80	$.04
2	$1,000	$100	2,080	3,020	.48	.03
3	$1,000	$100	4,500	5,750	.22	.02
4	$1,000	$100	8,200	6,800	.12	.014
5	$1,000	$100	10,000	9,010	.10	.011
6		$100		10,650		.009
7		$100		14,900		.007
8		$100		15,250		.0065
9		$100		16,300		.0061
10		$100		17,500		.005

[a]Based on average life span figures from annual reports of 900 schools tabulated by the Bureau of Audio-Visual Instruction of the New York Public Schools cited in "Life Expectancy for AV Equipment: A User Report," *EPIE Report*, VI, No. 53 (New York: Educational Products Information Exchange Institute, 1973), p. 3.

93

increases, the cost per student drops. Conversely, if the number of students served decreases, the cost per student increases. The big advantage is that cost is expressed in terms of students served. Cost per student is a more accurate statement of the economics at work since the capital investment in equipment is divided by the number of people directly served by that investment. Cost per student eliminates the inconsistency problem discussed with cost per use. Just in terms of impact, the cost per student served carries more weight and will persuade more administrators. From a cost-effective standpoint, overhead projectors costing $.04 per student served in Figure 5-24 is more impressive and more accurate than a cost of $1.00 per use shown in Figure 5-23. Also, when comparing overhead projectors in Figures 5-24 and 5-23, the decided impact of 17,500 students served over 700 uses should be obvious. Always try to express costs and utilization in terms of the actual population receiving the direct benefit of the service.

Figures 5-23 and 5-24 purposely use two pieces of equipment with different costs, depreciation rates, and application to again demonstrate that cost effectiveness is a relative value. The lower cost per use and cost per student served for the overhead projector does not mean the overhead projector is more cost effective than the television set. Each piece of equipment has unique capabilities making a direct cost comparison impossible.

SUMMARY

Responsible management of any media center must include good cost accounting techniques to project, control, and expand limited budgets. Cost accounting techniques for any media production involve determining realistic sources of costs, tabulating those costs, and comparing various production approaches to determine the most cost-effective choice. The final production should accomplish stated objectives for the least amount of money. Cost per student or trainee served is the most accurate way to express cost effectiveness. Only figure costs that result in useable information. Tabulating endless reams of fascinating data having no practical application is a waste of time. Accurate preproduction estimates can help determine whether a project is worth the expense. Preproduction estimates can also help keep the project on schedule and within budget. Overhead costs covering general media center operating expenses must be custom designed for each media center. Cost effectiveness of media productions is also relative to local conditions. A production may be very cost effective for one media center and totally over budget for another center.

Cost accounting procedures for media equipment follow the same general format used for media productions. Major costs include purchase price and maintenance. The manager should depreciate equipment to show true inventory value and what equipment is cost effective under appropriate conditions. There are numerous write-off procedures with depreciation of the total inventory being the easiest while average life operating hours is more complex and accurate. Cost per student should be used whenever possible to help establish the cost effectiveness of audiovisual equipment.

The manager who can develop relevant cost accounting techniques will be better able to justify budget requests and prove that properly applied mediated instruction is cost effective.

NOTES: Chapter 5

[1] "Training Facilities," *Training and Development Journal,* XXXI, No. 12, (December, 1977), p. 18.

[2] "At American Airlines," *Application Report,* Report published by the Public Relations Department of Control Data Corporation in cooperation with American Airlines, (Minneapolis, Minnesota: Control Data Corporation, 1978).

[3] D. C. Killian, "The Impact of Flight Simulators on U.S. Airlines," Conference paper presented by D. C. Killian, Manager, Audio Visual Center, 1977.

[4] "Flight Training Fully Allocated Costs," Table supplied by D. C. Killian, Manager, American Airlines Audio Visual Center, 1978.

[5] Letter, D. C. Killian, Manager, Audio Visual Center, American Airlines, to William T. Schmid, Director of Media Services, Illinois State University, May 7, 1979.

[6] Association for Educational Communications and Technology, *Educational Techology: Definition and Glossary of Terms, Volume I* (Washington, D.C.: Association for Educational Communications and Technology, 1977), p. 174.

[7] Educational Products Information Exchange Institute, "Life Expectancy for AV Equipment: A User Report," *EPIE Report,* VI, No. 53 (New York: Educational Products Information Exchange Institute, 1973), p. 3.

[8] Chapter 7 (p. 145) has a full explanation on how the depreciation rate can be used as a part of a computerized inventory process.

[9] Educational Products Information Exchange Institute, "Equipment Lifetimes," *EPIE-gram Newsletter,* IV, No. 5, (December, 1975), p. 1. As of this writing EPIE data on equipment lifetimes is being updated.

CHAPTER 6

Instructional Materials Selection and Purchasing Procedures

THE PROPER DEVELOPMENT and selection of instructional materials directly affects the success of a media center. Poorly conceived programs played back on the best media equipment will not guarantee desired learning. Media equipment can only transmit information. The instructional quality of information will not be made any better or worse by media equipment. This chapter was written since the effective development and selection of instructional programs represents an important media center responsibility. Emphasis will be placed on providing some practical guidelines for the selection and purchase of instructional materials. References in this chapter, along with several sections in Resource Section 2: A Selected Bibliography, will provide further information beyond the scope of this book.

This chapter begins with a discussion of instructional development techniques. A simple instructional development procedure is presented so you can become familiar with the important steps that must take place *before* any selection of media materials. Accurate selection cannot be made in the absence of a thorough knowledge of the instructional objectives. Once the need for instructional media has been determined, based on an accurate analysis of student needs, additional guidance is provided on the selection and purchase of instructional materials.

INSTRUCTIONAL DEVELOPMENT CONSIDERATIONS

The instructional development process can be as simple or complex as you desire. The emphasis here is to provide a simple overview of the basic steps which most authorities feel should be included in the instructional development process. Kemp summarizes it nicely by stating that instructional development starts with answers to three questions: (1) What must students learn (objectives)?; (2) What procedures and resources are required to accomplish the learning (the teaching and learning strategies)?; and (3) How will you know when the required learning has taken place (the evaluation)?[1]* Once you understand the essential steps required in the development of instructional materials you can then choose to acquire more indepth information in Resource Section 2: A Selected Bibliography. Even in the most sophisticated application, instructional development principles do not represent an exact science. Practical considerations such as available development time, staff talent, production capability, and operating budget will necessitate compromises.

Instructional Development Model

A typical instructional development model shown in Figure 6-1 usually includes the following steps:

1. *Determine the target audience.* What is the educational level of the student population? What knowledge and skills do they already possess? What is their socioeconomic background? Are the students motivated by professional advancement or prestige if they master the instructional material? Instructional development cannot be done in a vacuum. A thorough knowledge of the student is essential.

2. *Define the instructional needs.* What skills or knowledge are required to solve the training problem? Certainly a tangential concern when defining instructional needs is whether training will solve the problem. The old adage, "when in doubt, create another training program," may be ill-advised. Training and the use of instructional media will not solve every problem. If someone is experiencing difficulty operating equipment because parts are mislabeled, that is not a training problem. Training is not a solution for every problem which emphasizes the necessity to accurately define instructional needs.

Another important reason for accurately determining instructional needs is to make sure that if training is required it is designed to correct the real problem. Said another way, you cannot hit the target unless you know where it is! Development of an instructional program that does not solve the problem represents a tremendous waste of personnel and money.

3. *Prepare instructional objectives.* What measurable behavior must be observed to demonstrate the student has mastered the instructional material? Writing instructional objectives is not easy, especially for the uninitiated. Instructional or behavioral objectives must be specific and measurable. "The student will understand the company position on community service," is a vague, poorly written instructional objective. A more specific instructional ob-

* Notes are referenced at the end of this chapter.

Fig. 6-1

INSTRUCTIONAL DEVELOPMENT MODEL IN THEORY

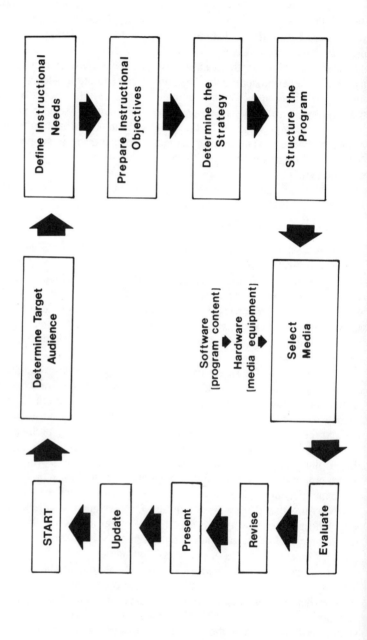

jective would require the student to list the five most important points of the company community service policy. If the objectives are not measurable there will be no method of determining when the student has mastered the instructional material.

4. ***Determine the strategy.*** What kind of learning must take place? Many authorities agree there are three basic kinds of learning: (1) cognitive domain relates to knowledge, information and other intellectual skills; (2) affective domain covers personal attitudes and values; and (3) psychomotor domain refers to skeletal-muscle use and coordination.[2] Depending on the instructional needs and resulting objectives, one or more kinds of learning will need to take place. Another strategy consideration is selecting the most appropriate teaching-learning pattern: (1) presentation; (2) individualized learning; or (3) small group interaction.[3] There are also choices regarding the category of learning experience that is most suitable: (1) direct experience; (2) verbal or printed word abstractions; and (3) vicarious, sensory experience.[4] The strategy step helps to formulate ideas and eliminate options regarding media selection.

5. ***Structure the program.*** What information should be included? In what sequence should the program develop? One of the toughest choices in instructional development, especially for the content expert or teacher, is deciding what content must be included so the student will attain the required instructional objectives. Selecting content essential for mastering instructional objectives requires making some hard choices. Teachers often want to include content that is entertaining or of personal interest. However, well structured programs can be entertaining, without drifting off on tangents that do not relate to instructional objectives. The primary question must always be: Is this content essential for the student to master the instructional objective? If the answer is "no," in most cases the content should be excluded. Determining the sequence of information is usually not as difficult as deciding on essential content. Sequence should be governed by moving from previous knowledge and skills to new information. Instructional development should move from simple to more complex. Sequence should always be governed by the learning pace of the student.

6. ***Select media.*** What medium or media will help the student master instructional objectives? Notice the selection of media only takes place after fundamental decisions have been made regarding target audience, instructional needs, instructional objectives, strategy and program structure. Once the learning activity has been thoroughly defined you will find it much easier to select media. Kemp has developed a very helpful selection chart with advantages, disadvantages, and relative cost for the following media: photographs, slides, filmstrips, recordings, overhead transparencies, motion pictures, television, and multi-image/multi-media.[5] A somewhat simplified version of Kemp's chart of media characteristics is located in Chapter 7, Media Equipment Selection and Purchasing Procedures. Anderson takes a slightly different approach with his media classifications: audio, printed material, audio-print, projected still-visual, audio-projected still-visual, motion-visual, audio-motion visual, physical objects, human and situational resources, and computers.[6] Although classification systems vary, decisions on selection must be made by deter-

mining how media characteristics such as audio, video, color, and motion will help the student master instructional objectives. Media selection will require making some compromises. A color videotape might be justified based on instructional objectives and media characteristics, but limited budget and production support might necessitate a less sophisticated approach. Media selection can also be influenced by available equipment, the need to quickly update information, and student control of program pace. With proper analysis of instructional requirements, media selection can be less complicated and more accurate. Also notice in the media selection step in Figure 6-1, software or program content will determine the choice of hardware or media equipment. The appropriate decision is whether the characteristics of overhead transparencies will help students master instructional objectives, rather than whether an overhead projector should be used. Program objectives should determine media selection which will, in turn, specify equipment needs. An indepth treatment of equipment selection is presented in Chapter 7, Equipment Selection and Purchasing Procedures.

7. *Evaluate.* Test the program on a sample of the target audience. Even if the steps in the instructional development process have been followed, some deficiencies will probably show up during evaluation. It is much better to catch problems during development rather than after the program is implemented. Some authorities recommend lean programming whereby student knowledge is intentionally overestimated and content is undertaught.[7] During evaluation students reveal where and to what extent teaching must be increased. Production can also be lean by using the least expensive approach to determine what is satisfactory and what learning will require more elaborate production techniques. Lean programming can reduce development and production cost because, based on evaluation, you need only upgrade those program sections where students are not mastering instructional objectives.

8. *Revise.* Make program adjustments based on the evaluation results. Only revise those sections of the program where students are not accomplishing the instructional objectives. Do not revise just for the sake of revision. If something works, leave it alone!

9. *Present.* Implement the finished program. If all the previous steps are followed in Figure 6-1, the finished program should represent the least expensive instruction that makes it possible for students to master the instructional objectives.

10. *Update.* Continual learner verification should be a part of any instructional development model to determine when changes in the program are necessary. Changes in the student's entry level skills could require program updates. New developments in a discipline will necessitate program changes. The instructional development cycle in Figure 6-1 is continually activated by the expansion of knowledge.

Instructional Development—Theory and Practice

The procedure outlined in Figure 6-1 is representative of the steps that should be included in an instructional development procedure. Figure 6-1 does not represent the most sophisticated approach but rather a realistic way to begin

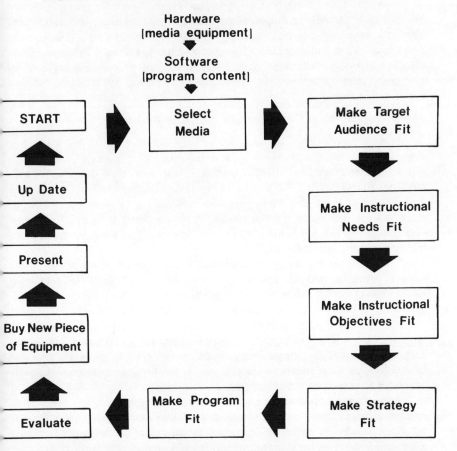

Fig. 6-2

INSTRUCTIONAL DEVELOPMENT MODEL IN PRACTICE

instructional development. Yet many teachers are not using instructional development procedures, hence the reason Figure 6-1 is entitled Instructional Development Model *in Theory*. People in education and training will publicly extol the virtues for developing instructional objectives. Privately, however, some educators feel instructional development procedures are too complex and time consuming. Many teachers feel much more comfortable following Figure 6-2, Instructional Development Model *in Practice*. Figure 6-2 probably looks more realistic to experienced media professionals. The client or teacher comes to the media center stating: "I want to do a slide program," or "I would like to make a videotape." Media selection, which should be one of the last steps in the instructional development process, is placed at the beginning. The rest of the instructional development process in Figure 6-2 must fit the initial hardware decision. People are more excited about technology and start with the inappropriate question, "How can I use videocassette recorders in my courses?" Using media equipment is fun and exciting, while developing instructional objectives is demanding, frustrating hard work. Yet a media manager who requires teachers to use a rigid instructional development process will probably not have any business. There must be a compromise where the media manager slowly initiates instructional development procedures without being too restrictive. Certain simple requests may not require elaborate instructional development procedures. More sophisticated learning requirements can start with some basic objectives. As clients become more familiar with the process and logic of instructional development we can continue to move away from Figure 6-2 and closer to Figure 6-1.

Learn Instructional Development Through Practice

Part of the resistance to using instructional development is that it imposes some structure and discipline on the learning process. It is much easier for the instructor to teach general information than it is to be held accountable for specific measurable results. Some media practitioners would much rather produce attractive programs than have to guarantee students will achieve a certain competency level after using their programs. A system that requires and measures very specific levels of behavioral change certainly can take the fun out of teaching and media production!

The secret to becoming proficient with instructional development procedures is getting started. By using a simple approach, such as the model shown in Figure 6-1, the instructor and media practitioner can slowly become comfortable with the basic techniques. Just like any new skill, at first there will be frustration, some setbacks, and even some failure! But we learn by failure just as we learn by success. With practice, improvement will overshadow failure because instructional development techniques are designed to guarantee success! Indeed, teaching and media production can be fun *because* instructional development helps create effective programs.

Instructional development procedures really represent a series of choices. In life we make choices everyday with few problems because we get plenty of practice. Usually the more we do something the better we become. The more we practice using instructional development procedures, the easier it becomes and the greater our proficiency. We can even move from a simple instructional development model shown in Figure 6-1 to more sophisticated models. Anderson has created a very elaborate series of development and media selection procedures.[8] At first glance, Anderson's tables, charts, and flowgrams might seem complicated. A typical first reaction might be, "I don't have time to work my instructional problem through a maze of diagrams!" Yet, if you use Anderson's instructional development and media selection procedures you quickly can work through various choices and have a clear understanding of how to accomplish the instructional task. The same can be said for Kemp's selection procedures.[9]

When we look at a road map, with infinitely more choices than sophisticated instructional development models, we do not immediately give up thinking the task is too formidable. We have had much practice using road maps. The road map lists many choices but, because we have defined our destination, we quickly can eliminate most options in favor of the most direct route. Good instructional development models like Anderson's and Kemp's should be viewed as road maps, listing many options from which you can choose the most appropriate media based on your learning objectives.

THE SELECTION PROCESS

Once student needs and instructional objectives have been established, the selection of educational media is much easier. Instructional development helps refine our thinking, eliminate unnecessary considerations, and focus more clearly on educational media possibilities that facilitate instructional objectives. With the learning requirements defined we are well prepared for the selection process.

Media Selection Considerations

Selection of commercially available educational materials is discussed first because, as a general rule, it is best to consider purchase before going to the expense of producing programs. A well worn cliche is "Do not recreate the wheel!" Do not go to the time and expense of production when the same basic program might already exist that would meet the learning objectives. Commercial program content tends to be broad in scope to appeal to a large segment of the market. A commercially produced instructional package might be appropriate if development procedures indicate the instructional needs and objectives have general application.

Resistance to Commercial Programs. Although the logic of purchasing rather than producing makes sense, some people resist commercial programs for several reasons:

1. ***Every organization likes to think it is unique.*** No two organizations are exactly alike yet there is some common sphere of problems that might be solved using the same instructional program.
2. ***Some people have a built-in prejudice against "canned" or "packaged" programs.*** It is not intellectually respectable to "pick something off the shelf" to solve an instructional problem. Not all commercial programs are well conceived which could also be said for locally produced programs. If the commercial program facilitates the instructional objectives, whether it is "canned" is a moot point.
3. ***There are teachers, trainers, and media specialists who feel if the commercially produced program does not meet all expectations it should not be used.*** The creative teacher or media practitioner might use part of a film or learning package that does satisfy student needs rather than discard the whole program. People can become very concerned over minor points in presentation or style that have nothing to do with course objectives. You must be able to stand back from the details to see if the overall impact of the program facilitates desired learning.

Advantages of Commercial Programs. Resistance to commercial programs can be countered with important advantages:

1. ***Commercial productions can be better than locally produced instructional programs.*** A large production budget can more easily be justified for a program that will be sold nationally, than for a program that will only be used locally. There are many commercial programs that could

never be justified as local productions. A well developed, produced and validated commercial production can make possible certain learning experiences not otherwise possible at the local level.

2. *Commercial productions can save time and money.* Some commercial programs can cost $400–5,000. Yet, when you consider the staff time and money required to develop the same program, the commercial package could be considered a bargain! When considering commercial programs always ask yourself, "Can I produce the same or a better program for less cost?" In many cases the answer will be "no!" The large initial expense and failure to produce effective programs are two major reasons why much expensive production equipment falls into disuse at the local level.

3. *Purchase of commercial programs will allow for better use of the local training and production staff.* The time and money saved by obtaining a commercial program can be more appropriately expended on instructional problems that cannot be solved through commercial purchase.

4. *Commercial programs are ready for immediate use.* A commercial program can be the answer when a training program must be implemented quickly.

Tips for Selecting Commercial Materials. There are some techniques that can be used to simplify the selection process and increase the likelihood of obtaining materials that will satisfy instructional goals:

1. *Let instructional objectives be your guide.* This chapter started with a discussion of instructional development procedures because a clear statement of instructional objectives can make the selection of commercial materials or local production much easier. With the wide variety of both good and bad commercial programming available, it is essential that instructional objectives be used to focus your consideration on a relatively small number of choices. Unless the scope of consideration is limited, the selection process will be time consuming and frustrating.

2. *Develop a file of resource material.* There are many sources of information on commercial instructional materials: promotional brochures and flyers; catalogs from commercial producers and distributors; reviews in trade journals and magazines; displays at professional conventions; trade books; colleagues; and professionally compiled resource directories and bibliographies. Several publications with good reference lists are located in Resource Section 2: A Selected Bibliography. Always remember the major types of learning activity that take place in your organization so you can keep your resource file current and limited to your specific needs.

3. *Establish a review panel.* A panel of people directly responsible for teaching activities should be established to review available materials and make purchasing recommendations. The media center manager should not select instructional materials in a vacuum. Realistically, there are political as well as pedagogical reasons for establishing a review panel. If certain individual interests within your organization are not represented, hurt feelings can block utilization of the best instructional material. Typical candidates

for the review panel should include teachers, content specialists, administrators, and media professionals. The list can be expanded or restricted, depending on local needs. A review panel large enough to satisfy political considerations might be too large to reach any purchase recommendations. The panel must function efficiently. At least one of the teachers or trainers who will actually use the material in the classroom *must* be on the panel. Teachers and content experts should have the ultimate responsibility for evaluation. The media center staff should facilitate the evaluative process rather than assume the role of evaluator.

4. *Look for commercially produced materials that have been validated.* Many commercial materials are produced to appeal to a training need but cannot guarantee a desired level of student performance. Well designed programs often describe evaluation procedures, the target audience tested, and the amount of demonstrated learning that took place.

5. *Always request a preview.* Educational materials should not be selected on the basis of attractive brochures. *Always* request to preview before purchase. If a preview is not possible, ask to rent the material in order to preview. Most reputable producers and distributors allow for free previews or previews at a reduced rental rate. There can be a tremendous difference between the description in a promotional brochure and a review of the actual program by teachers and media specialists.

6. *Do not make a large purchase before classroom use.* Even if a review panel is favorably impressed, a large purchase should not be made until the instructional materials have been tried out in training situations. Actual use in a learning situation is always the best test. Some producers and distributors will not want free preview copies used in a class, especially if the material is available for rental or purchase. Sometimes it is best to pay the rental fee so the material can be used in an instructional sequence for final evaluation. The rental rate can be much less costly than a large expenditure on materials that are never used.

7. *Develop practical effective evaluation forms.* The large and very important job of evaluation can be made easier and more reliable through well developed forms. With review panels or committees some standard method for rating materials for purchase is essential. A suggested evaluation form that is short and easy to complete is shown in Figure 6-3. When developing your own evaluation forms consider the following:

(a) Develop evaluation forms that are short and easy to use. A complex evaluation form is guaranteed to stifle teacher participation. There must be some compromises between a form that covers all aspects of evaluation and a form that is quick and easy to use.

(b) Develop evaluation forms that fit local needs. Do not require people to evaluate aspects of the program that have no relevance to local learning requirements.

(c) Evaluate material in terms of stated instructional objectives. The evaluation step must determine whether the material will facilitate desired learning.

Fig. 6-3

INSTRUCTIONAL MATERIALS EVALUATION FORM

1. Title: _____
2. Source: _____
3. Producer: _____
4. Copyright Date: _____ Cost _____
5. Format (videotape, slides, textbook, etc.): _____
6. Format description: sound ____ color ____ B&W ____ length ____
7. Subject area covered: _____
8. Courses or training this material might be used in: ____
   _____
9. Instructional objectives that must be accomplished:_____
   _____
   _____
   _____
   _____
10. Student target audience: _____
11. Number of students served annually: _____
12. Circle the number on the scale that most closely reflects your judgment:

	poor				excellent
Suitability of this material to meet instructional objectives stated above	1	2	3	4	5
Vocabulary	1	2	3	4	5
Content organization	1	2	3	4	5
Accuracy of content	1	2	3	4	5
Likelihood of content remaining current for five years	1	2	3	4	5
Presentation rate	1	2	3	4	5
Adaptability to various students	1	2	3	4	5
Quality of producer validation	1	2	3	4	5
Quality of teacher's manual	1	2	3	4	5
Sound quality	1	2	3	4	5
Picture quality	1	2	3	4	5

13. Overall rating   1 2 3 4 5
14. Would other teachers use this material?   yes _____ no _____
15. Would you use this material?   yes _____ no _____
16. Will additional equipment or facilities
    be needed to use this material?   yes _____ no _____
17. Purchase recommendation: _____ purchase immediately
                                _____ consider for future purchase
                                _____ do not purchase

Comments: _____
_____
_____
_____

Evaluator_____ Date _____

Fig. 6-4

STUDENT EVALUATION FORM

1. Title: _____
2. Format (videotape, slides, textbook, etc.): _____
3. Instructor: _____
4. Course: _____
5. What did you learn from this material? _____
   _____
   _____
   _____
   _____

6. What content was most effective? _____
   _____
   _____
   _____

7. What content was least effective? _____
   _____
   _____
   _____

8. What did you like most? _____
   _____
   _____
   _____

		poor				excellent
9. How was the sound quality?		1	2	3	4	5
10. How was the picture quality?		1	2	3	4	5
11. What is your overall rating of this material?		1	2	3	4	5

12. Comments: _____
    _____
    _____
    _____

Student _____ Date _____

(d) Evaluate content. Is the vocabulary appropriate? Are the examples realistic? Is the information accurate? Is the program pace too fast or slow for the intended students? Teachers and content specialists have a primary responsibility for answering these questions on the evaluation form.

(e) Evaluate the technical quality. Is the color realistic? Is the audio easy to hear? Are the pictures in focus? Can the print be easily read?

8. *Develop student evaluation forms.* The ultimate reason for selecting any instructional material is to facilitate student learning. However, seldom are students involved in the initial evaluation stage. Try to incorporate a student evaluation before final selection. A suggested student evaluation form is shown in Figure 6-4.

9. *Develop a priority list of materials.* You will probably not have enough budget to obtain all the materials receiving a favorable evaluation by a review panel. Use evaluation forms to place materials in priority classifications: (1) purchase immediately; (2) consider for future purchase; (3) do not purchase.

Purchase Versus Local Production. A thorough review of commercial materials in light of stated instructional objectives should indicate whether purchase or original production is the best approach. Acquisition is the next step if the selection process has revealed commercial material that meets instructional objectives and budget guidelines. If program needs are unique and nothing is available commercially, local production could be the best option. Staff talent, production capability, time, expense, and resulting instructional quality must also be reviewed when contemplating local production. A further consideration is whether to have the media center or an outside agency do the production work. Chapter 5, Cost Accounting, discusses cost effectiveness regarding local production.

Acquisition Procedures

Once the evaluation phase has been completed there are several points to remember regarding instructional materials acquisition:

1. *Review purchase and rental arrangements.* Several questions should be asked when considering purchase or rental of instructional materials: (1) How often will the material be used? (2) How much advance notice is required to obtain the material when needed? (3) How many students will be served? (4) How long will the content remain current? and (5) What is the difference between purchase price and rental rate? Although answers to these questions are all relative to local conditions, a general recommendation might be to purchase those materials that are used often, requested on short notice, will serve a large number of students, will not quickly become outdated, and where continued rental would quickly surpass the purchase price. A combination of purchase and rental will often represent the most flexible and advantageous acquisition program.

2. *Consider a three-level acquisition budget.* Suggested priorities are: (1) high use purchase and replacement; (2) infrequent rental; and (3) reserve funds for unexpected requests. Funds must be available for purchasing new titles and replacing worn out materials. Rental funds can assist when purchase is not prudent. There should be some reserve funds for unexpected requests that will always occur.

3. *Consider lease or rent-to-own contracts as an acquisition option.* A major advantage of lease and rent-to-own is that both contracts allow you immediate use of a number of programs for less than it would initially cost to purchase the same programs. Lease and rent-to-own contracts are often used for videotape and 16mm film programs. When the lease expires the programs must be returned to the distributor. Such a lease arrangement can be very beneficial, especially if the programs might quickly become out-

dated. For example, leasing programs on computer technology might be more advantageous than purchase, since computers represent a rapidly changing field. There are various lease arrangements such as the option to purchase at the expiration of the lease by paying the difference between what has been paid and the original purchase price. Rent-to-own is a time payment plan used to purchase programs. With a rent-to-own contract you receive an agreed upon list of titles and make payments until the programs have been purchased. A big advantage of rent-to-own over a lease contract is that, when the rent-to-own contract is paid off, you own the films. Consequently, rent-to-own can be a wise acquisition plan for programs that will not quickly become outdated.

4. *Consider cooperative acquisition plans.* Several organizations can jointly enter a purchase, lease, or rent-to-own contract. If sharing arrangements for the acquired programs are well defined, cooperative acquisitions can make a variety of media materials available that no single organization would be able to afford. The cooperative purchase arrangement can also be used by a media center on a smaller scale within an organization. When purchase requests exceed budget, a cooperative plan could be used where the media center would pay a percentage of the acquisition cost provided the requesting department would fund the balance. A limited acquisition budget can then be used as matching or seed money to stimulate the release of additional funds for cooperative purchasing.

5. *Inspect instructional materials before releasing payment.* On rare occasions 16mm films can come from distributors without a sound track! Always make sure instructional materials are technically satisfactory before releasing payment.

6. *Plan for a materials maintenance budget.* Instructional materials can become damaged during use. Films might require replacement footage, especially in the first 50 feet. Learning kits might require replacing parts such as slides or audiocassettes.

CATALOGING

Once materials have been purchased, a cataloging system should be used for easy accession. Methods for cataloging print and nonprint instructional materials have been the subject of numerous volumes. Since this book concentrates on media center management rather than library skills, a discussion of cataloging techniques will not be presented here. However, cataloging is an important skill and, therefore, some key sources have been listed in Resource Section 2: A Selected Bibliography under "Library Skills."

SUMMARY

The selection process must start with some basic instructional development steps to determine: (1) target audience; (2) instructional needs; (3) instructional objectives; (4) program strategy; (5) program structure; (6) media; and (7) evaluation. A thorough knowledge of student needs and resulting instructional objectives can make the decision to purchase or produce instructional materials much easier. Many commercial programs are excellent and often less expensive than trying to produce the same material locally. However, unique instructional objectives might require local production. Selection procedures for commercial materials should include: (1) a review based on instructional needs; (2) a resource file of information on commercially available materials; (3) a review panel consisting of content experts, media personnel and teachers who will actually use the material; (4) a review of validation procedures used for materials; (5) a preview of all materials considered for purchase; and (6) evaluation forms for the review panel and students using the material. Acquisition considerations include: (1) a priority acquisition list; (2) a review of purchase, rental and lease arrangements; (3) a flexible acquisitions budget based on a combination of planned purchase, rental and reserve funds for unexpected needs; (4) inspection of materials before payment; and (5) a maintenance budget. Once materials have been purchased a cataloging step is necessary to insure easy accession. Teachers, content experts, and students should be the primary source for the evaluation and selection of media materials. Media center personnel should coordinate the selection process rather than assume the role of evaluator.

NOTES: Chapter 6

[1] Jerrold E. Kemp, *Planning and Producing Audiovisual Materials* (3rd ed.; New York: Thomas Y. Crowell, 1975), p. 6.

[2] *Ibid.*, p. 17.

[3] *Ibid.*, pp. 4–5.

[4] *Ibid.*, p. 48.

[5] *Ibid.*, pp. 46–47.

[6] Ron H. Anderson, *Selecting and Developing Media for Instruction* (New York: American Society for Training and Development and Van Nostrand Reinhold Co., 1976), p. 29.

[7] *Ibid.*, p. 31.

[8] *Ibid.*, pp. 16–29.

[9] Kemp, *ibid.*, pp. 46–47 and p. 49.

CHAPTER 7

Equipment Selection and Purchasing Procedures

THIS CHAPTER provides a rationale for the proper selection and purchase of media equipment. Techniques discussed can be used to purchase anything from a simple audiocassette tape recorder to a sophisticated color television studio. By using the selection and purchase procedures outlined in this chapter, the media manager should be able to buy appropriate equipment for the lowest possible price. Although equipment will be emphasized, much of the information presented could also be used for selection and purchase of media programs and materials. Additional information on the evaluation and selection of media equipment is in Resource Section 2: A Selected Bibliography.

CAUTIONS REGARDING EQUIPMENT SELECTION

The media center manager should be cautioned regarding several points in the equipment selection process.

Plea for Media Center Equipment Review

Selection and purchase of media equipment should be a media center responsibility. The evaluation process should not be restricted to equipment for the center but should include any media equipment requested by other departments within the organization. Media practitioners work with equipment on a daily basis and are best qualified to select reliable models having the necessary capability to accomplish stipulated instructional objectives. Where media professionals are not given final authority for equipment selection, the result is usually a conglomeration of mismatched equipment, purchased as a result of personal whim, cosmetic appeal, or sales pressure. Most people who do not circulate, operate and maintain media equipment do not understand the costly ramifications of selecting the wrong equipment. Inappropriate purchases can result in equipment that: (1) does not operate well; (2) is difficult to repair; (3) is too expensive to operate; (4) does not meet minimum safety standards; (5) does not interface with other equipment or accessories; (6) may not be accepted by those who will use it; and (7) may not facilitate instructional objectives. Media directors should always push for the authority to make all final decisions on media equipment purchases.

Creeping Complexity

The growth of media equipment technology has always been way ahead of program development. Rapid development of media equipment has also created a disease affectionately referred to as creeping complexity. This disease can quickly be diagnosed when someone gradually becomes preoccupied with additional equipment options. Such individuals usually are mesmerized by the glitter of chrome-plated knobs, dials, switches, hand-rubbed imitation mahogany finishes, and a host of little windows housing all sorts of impressive meters. Euphoria soon sets in and we find wild-eyed individuals purchasing attractively packaged boxes of technology!

Television can cause extreme cases of creeping complexity. A person starts off with a harmless videotape recorder, camera, and television receiver. Soon the advantages of a second camera are evident. Once you have two cameras, a switcher is required. But, what is a switcher without special effects? By this time, creeping complexity is well established. Soon editing becomes necessary, so an additional videotape recorder is purchased. Usually a character generator and more sophisticated audio and lighting equipment are then added. Typically, time base correctors are waiting in the wings to be followed almost immediately by a bevy of image enhancers. Depending on production requirements, all these steps in creeping complexity might be needed, but there are numerous instances where additional sophistication is not required.

The term, creeping complexity, is very appropriate because even experienced media professionals may not realize they are slowly moving into more sophistication than is required to meet stated objectives. Without objectives, there is almost certainly going to be creeping complexity. The whole point is to beware of creeping complexity and use the following rule in any equipment purchase: *the simplest piece of equipment for the lowest price that accomplishes the required tasks, is the best purchase.*

Instructional Development—Theory and Practice

Instructional development is a systematic process used to create a learning experience that will yield a guaranteed level of measurable results. Two instructional development models first used in Chapter 6, "Instructional Materials Selection and Purchasing Procedures," Figures 6-1 and 6-2 (pp. 100–101) have equal application in this chapter. Figure 7-1 shows, ideally, where the equipment selection process should occur in the systematic development of instruc-

Fig. 7-1

INSTRUCTIONAL DEVELOPMENT MODEL IN THEORY

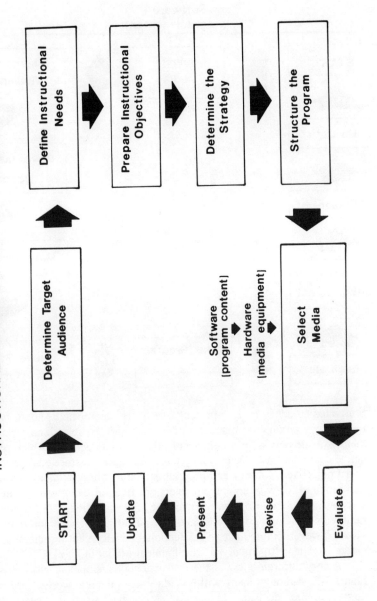

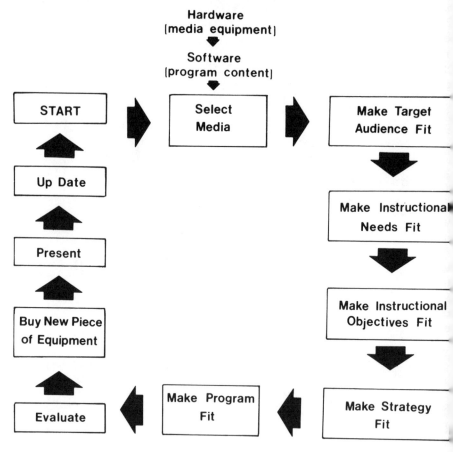

Fig. 7-2

INSTRUCTIONAL DEVELOPMENT MODEL IN PRACTICE

tion. This model is fairly representative of the steps which should be incorporated in any rational development of instruction. The selection of media equipment is made only after a number of other crucial decisions which, ultimately, define equipment use. Determining target audience, instructional needs, instructional objectives, strategy and program structure will provide essential information required for wise equipment selection. Even in the "select media" phase, software, or program content dictates the hardware utilized. Since few can find fault with the logic of instructional development, they give it appropriate lip service. However, limited use of instructional development principles is why this model is called "Instructional Development Model in *Theory*."

A very different view of the instructional development process is given in Figure 7-2. Although many will not admit it, in the real world, hardware selection is the *first* decision. In the "select media" stage, hardware determines software and all other steps are made to fit. In this illogical sequence, the equipment is blamed if the instructional program does not work. The only conclusion must be to "buy a new piece of equipment" and start the whole process over again. How many times have we heard that instructional television is boring and therefore television is not a good teaching tool? The blame is inappropriately placed on television technology rather than on the programming. Poorly conceived television programming may be boring but not television technology. Media equipment only *transmits* information, it does not *create* information. Whatever we put into media equipment is what comes out and the choice is ours: poor programs in, poor programs out; or, good programs in, good programs out.

There are several factors that contribute to the real-world situation diagrammed in Figure 7-2. Most clients coming to a media center have no experience in instructional development. Using instructional development procedures, even under the guidance of a person trained in educational technology, is hard work and often viewed by clients as an unnecessary bother. Some clients have already made up their minds on the media format before coming to the center. They come in saying, "I want to make a videotape," instead of "Here's my problem, how would you suggest solving it?" Hopefully, the second approach will become more prevalent as clients develop more trust and respect in the judgment of media practitioners.

Media personnel must make the best possible equipment selections realizing the limitations of the real world outlined in Figure 7-2, while constantly trying to achieve the logical analysis outlined in Figure 7-1. This chapter should provide assistance by, first, describing steps for selecting appropriate equipment and, secondly, outlining some procedures for purchasing the best equipment at the lowest possible price.

EQUIPMENT SELECTION

The approach used in this section is based on clients requesting the purchase of media equipment by a media center.

Determine Equipment Function

The first step in the equipment selection process is to determine what must be accomplished by the equipment. Any selection process should elicit instructional *function* rather than type of equipment. The first step should concentrate on content or software requirements rather than hardware. Once program content and objectives have been well defined, equipment selection becomes a much easier, more rational process.

The biggest problem with defining function is that most clients do not think in terms of instructional objectives. Clients come to a media center with a predetermined idea of what equipment will be required along with a basic description of content. There are cases where the client has a firm idea of equipment needs but is vague regarding program content. Requiring a needs assessment, complete with instructional objectives, before purchasing equipment will probably be considered as a frustrating waste of time by the client.

Screening Questions. There are ways of uncovering required information without becoming involved in a lengthy instructional design session. Most clients requesting equipment are more comfortable talking about equipment rather than instructional objectives. The suggested questions below are oriented towards equipment while really uncovering the instructional function of the program. Such questions could be used in an interview or incorporated

into a printed form that clients would complete. The media manager can select
those questions that best fit local screening needs.

1. *What is the instructional problem and how does the equipment solve that
problem?*

   This question allows the client to talk in terms of equipment while really expressing program concerns. By asking what the instructional problem is the client can talk in general terms without being intimidated by the
threat of having to state behavioral objectives. Ideally the client *should* be
able and willing to list behavioral objectives. But, this book deals with reality, not ideal situations. In the real world of media center management
few clients will be prepared to justify equipment requests on the basis of
behavioral objectives. This question is very important because it generates
information about instructional programs and how the equipment relates to
these programs.

2. *How does the equipment make better use of class, instructor, and/or
student time?*

   One of the major advantages of properly utilized media technology is
increased cost effectiveness and instructional effectiveness. Cost effectiveness represents situations where money is saved through use of media
equipment. Instructional effectiveness refers to situations where, through
appropriate use of media equipment, increased learning takes place. Although clients may not be requesting equipment to be more cost effective,
this question could start them thinking in the right direction. In most legitimate requests the equipment does make better use of time. However, time
savings resulting in increased cost effectiveness should not be the only
measure of whether or not to purchase a piece of media equipment. An
equally important factor is instructional effectiveness. There may be cases
where the use of media equipment will increase costs yet students will
benefit by learning more. Cost effectiveness and instructional effectiveness
must always be considered together.

3. *What is the rate of use and number of students served by the equipment?*

   By asking how often the equipment will be used and the number of
students served, the media director can make some judgments about cost
effectiveness. If a decision must be made between a request where a piece
of equipment will be used once a week to serve six students and another
where the equipment is used 12 times a week to serve 2,400 students, cost
effectiveness will heavily favor the latter.

4. *What is the projected demand for this equipment?*

   This question can circumvent the problem of purchasing equipment to
satisfy a short-term demand. If equipment is only needed for a limited
period of time, loan or rental might be a much better use of limited funds.
There is nothing worse than making a sizeable equipment investment only
to find a year later that the equipment the client "had to have" is gathering dust. Proper documentation of projected demand is a hedge against
disuse.

5. *How did you figure the number of units needed?*

This question tries to determine use volume in relation to the amount of equipment requested. Many times clients will not order enough equipment, especially sufficient back-up equipment, to satisfy projected use. When answering this question clients should be thinking about: (1) sufficient back-up equipment to cover maintenance periods; (2) instructional programs that may trigger high demand where a large volume of students need to use a program during a short time period; or (3) instructional programs that are totally self-paced, making it hard to estimate a particular pattern of use. Posing a question about the number of equipment units needed will at least start clients thinking about the volume implications.

6. *What software packages are planned for this equipment?*

This is one of the most important questions because it requires an explanation of program content. Such a question forces the client to describe the programs that will be produced or played back with the requested equipment. In most cases if the client has no software plans there is no need to purchase the equipment. Program content is the important part of mediated instruction. The equipment which receives all the attention and excitement is simply a conduit for information. Media equipment will not realize *full* potential without well designed programs.

7. *How much money has been set aside for equipment incidentals?*

A typical problem occurs when clients become so engrossed with the desire to purchase equipment that they forget or are totally unaware of hidden costs. Very seldom can equipment be purchased without some continuing costs for such items as maintenance, accessories and supplies. Television represents the classic example where the initial purchase of a videocassette recorder, camera, and television receiver is only the beginning. Next comes the need for videocassettes, cables, connectors, adapters, and, most of all, good technical support. This question should prompt consideration of equipment incidentals so that necessary budget preparation can be made *before* purchase. Such an approach can alleviate the classic problem of equipment left idle because of insufficient funds for supplies or maintenance.

8. *Is this equipment replacing old equipment? If yes, why?*

This question may be useful since some dealers will take trade-in equipment and provide an additional discount for new equipment. There is a good chance that new equipment will not stand idle if the client has a history of wearing out equipment through heavy use rather than abuse. Media equipment must be used to be cost effective.

9. *What security provisions have you made for this equipment?*

Media equipment is heavily susceptible to theft and damage. Security should be a major concern for those wanting media equipment. This question forces the client to develop proper security measures before purchasing the equipment.

Well designed screening questions allow the client to talk in terms of equipment while really providing valuable information about program content. This process is not as threatening to the client as a requirement to state specific behavioral objectives. The above list forms a good basic screening instrument but should not be considered comprehensive since other questions could include:

1. What instructional function does the requested equipment replace?
2. What has the demand been in the past for this equipment, specifically in terms of students not served?
3. Why is the equipment needed in lieu of some other less expensive equipment?
4. Can the equipment be used periodically on loan from the media center?
5. Can the equipment be rented?
6. What utilization records are planned to document use of the equipment?
7. How would you rank equipment in priority order?

A manager might consider additional questions that more closely fit local concerns. The goal is to select the shortest possible list of questions that define the instructional function of the desired equipment.

Case Study. The best way to show how the screening questions work is by example. In this case study the client wants a videocassette recorder, camera and television receiver, to record basic financial accounting techniques. Once on videocassette, the accounting techniques will be used in several business courses. Justification for the television equipment is presented through answers to the nine basic screening questions discussed above. This case study will be used as the basic example for the rest of this chapter.

1. *What is the instructional problem and how does the equipment solve that problem?*

   Instructors presently spend too much time drawing accounting forms and charts on the chalkboard. A videocassette recorder, camera and television receiver are requested so we can produce a series of short programs showing basic accounting techniques. These short instructional programs would be used by instructors in several business courses. We need a videocassette recorder and television receiver so the instructor can control the presentation rate in class. We will be able to show students how to complete simple to complex accounting forms and have students interact with the instructor in a discussion format. Forms and charts will be presented in a systematic developmental format so students can recognize basic differences in accounting procedures. The instructor being videotaped needs to interact with visuals by showing students how to complete various accounting forms. Instructors require equipment that is simple to operate and, therefore, a videocassette recorder has been requested.

2. *How does the equipment make better use of class, instructor, and/or student time?*

   Class time isn't spent drawing time-consuming accounting forms and charts on chalkboard. Once videotaped, the instructor's preparation time is cut. There is more efficient use of class time by having students deal with actual content instead of watching the instructor draw detailed forms and charts on the chalkboard.

3. **What is the rate of use and number of students served by the equipment?**

Classroom	Course	Time	Days	× Students	= Students Served
201	Accounting I	9 am	MWF	50	150
405	Auditing	1 pm	MWF	75	225
320	Accounting II	10 am	TR	50	100
405	Finance	11 am	TR	30	60
325	Bookkeeping	2 pm	TR	50	100
510	Accounting III	3 pm	TR	30	60
				Grand total:	695

4. **What is the projected demand for this equipment?**
    We expect an increase of approximately 15 students per semester based on admission office figures.

5. **How did you figure the number of units needed?**
    One unit is sufficient, since all classes meet at different times in the following rooms: 201, 405, 320, 325, and 510.

6. **What software packages are planned for this equipment?**
    All forms, charts, and graphs put on chalkboard will be made into TV cards for videotapes. An instructor will explain on the tape how to complete and work with this material.

7. **How much money has been set aside for equipment incidentals?**
    $4,500   videotape
     4,050   art supplies for TV cards
    $8,550   total for 150 finished videotapes

8. **Is this equipment replacing old equipment? If yes, why?**
    No.

9. **What security provisions have you made for this equipment?**
    Equipment will be locked in storage cabinet and moved to classrooms for each use.

Select Equipment to Fit Function

Once the justification for the equipment has been developed, the next crucial phase is to select media formats that will satisfy the required program functions. Please note this is *not* the phase where equipment brand names are considered. This phase only concerns matching the appropriate media characteristics with the instructional functions outlined in the previous screening questions. Decisions must be based on format such as whether to use slides, overhead transparencies, audiotapes or videotapes, not whether to use slide projectors, overhead projectors, audiotape recorders or videotape recorders. The emphasis must be on program content, not on media hardware. Key questions such as the following can help zero in on the media format required:

1. Is the instruction for individual or group study?
2. Will simple or complex equipment be required?
3. Will instructors and students know how to operate the equipment?
4. Can the instructional sequence order be changed and updated easily?
5. Should the instructional sequence order remain the same? Are there times when the instructional sequence should not be changed?
6. What is the cost of production and duplication?
7. What is the cost of presentation and production equipment?
8. Is motion required?
9. Is audio required?
10. Are still pictures required?
11. Does the student need printed material such as a manual or diagrams?
12. Does the instructional information require color or black-and-white visuals?
13. Must programs be saved or can they be erased?
14. Must programs be widely distributed and is sufficient presentation equipment available in the field?

There are numerous guides available outlining characteristics of different media. Figure 7-3 is based on a media characteristics chart developed by Kemp.[1]* For purposes of this case study, Figure 7-3 represents a much simplified version of Kemp's chart. Key advantages and disadvantages for six basic media formats are described. Figure 7-3 also compares the relative cost and complexity of production and presentation equipment along with the cost of software or program material. A scale of 1-5 is used, with 1 representing the least complex or least costly approach and 5 the most complex or expensive. For example, in Figure 7-3, the cost and sophistication of production and presentation equipment for a motion picture is much higher than for an overhead transparency. The resulting cost of a motion picture is also much higher than for an overhead transparency. In some cases the whole 1-5 scale is used because of a wide range of complexity and cost for a particular medium. The 1-5 scale is used only to provide a general idea since there are exceptions in all cases.

Advantages and disadvantages of media are defined by application. An advantage of the filmstrip is that it is always in the proper sequence, yet a disadvantage is that you cannot easily rearrange the sequence. If you do not want the sequence rearranged the disadvantage is not a disadvantage but, rather, an important advantage. The following are some definitions of media characteristics:

1. *individual study:* the rate of learning can be controlled by the student (i.e. a student can control the presentation rate of slides in a slide projector whereas a student cannot control the presentation rate of a program broadcast by a television station);
2. *large group study:* the media material can easily be presented to large groups (i.e. overhead transparencies are designed for large group projec-

---

* See notes at end of this chapter.

tion whereas photographic prints cannot be shown to a large group unless presented in another format such as slides);

3. *presentation equipment easy to use:* with little or no training the instructor can operate media equipment used to present information to students (i.e. the overhead projector can be operated by most teachers with no instruction whereas the setup and playback of a videotape usually requires some training);

4. *can update segments:* the media format allows for easy updating of particular segments (i.e. slide programs can be easily updated by simply pulling specific slides and inserting new ones whereas a filmstrip is one continuous piece of film, making quick selective updating difficult);

5. *standard format:* one agreed upon design and set of dimensions for a media format that will ensure its use with a specific type of media equipment (i.e. a 16mm film can be projected through any 16mm projector whereas videotape comes in various widths of open reel and videocassette requiring different types of equipment for playback);

6. *can control presentation rate:* the instructor can easily control the presentation rate (i.e. the instructor can control the rate of a slide presentation with the forward and reverse buttons on a slide projector whereas a 16mm film advances at a precise rate of speed not controlled by the instructor);

7. *always in proper sequence:* the information will always appear in the proper sequence as designed (i.e. since a filmstrip is a continuous piece of film all individual frames are always in the correct sequence whereas if the instructor is not careful, slides can fall out of a tray or mysteriously get out of sequence, usually about one minute before a major presentation!);

8. *systematic developmental format:* being able to move from already acquired knowledge to new information in a logical sequence controlled by the instructor (i.e. information can be added to an overhead transparency in a logical progression through use of overlays, or revealing information in steps, whereas the same systematic development of material on a filmstrip would be a more complex and possibly expensive approach);

9. *easily interact with visual:* the instructor can easily point to, write on or manipulate the material for more effective instruction (i.e. the instructor can draw on an overhead transparency or use overlays to highlight certain points whereas with a videotape the instructor has little opportunity for direct physical interaction with the program);

10. *easy to prepare:* the media material can be easily prepared by someone with no training or access to sophisticated production equipment (i.e. the instructor can draw charts or graphs on a piece of clear acetate for projection on an overhead projector whereas making a 16mm film requires training and sophisticated production equipment);

11. *can show actual motion:* the media material can easily show natural sequential continuous motion (i.e. a videotape can accurately and realistically show the continuous natural motion of a subject whereas slides can only show segments of continuous motion);

12. *automatic presentation rate:* when started the program will automatically advance at a predetermined rate of speed (i.e. when started, a 16mm film

Fig. 7-3

MEDIA CHARACTERISTICS

	Advantages	Disadvantages	Production Complexity 1–5	Equipment Cost 1–5	Presentation Complexity 1–5	Equipment Cost 1–5	Software Per Unit Cost 1–5
SLIDES	Individual or large group study Presentation equipment easy to use Can update segments Standard format Can control presentation rate	Require some photo equipment and skill Can get out of sequence Cannot show actual motion	1–5	1–5	2	2	1
FILMSTRIPS	Individual or large group study Always in proper sequence Standard format Presentation equipment easy to use Can control presentation rate	Can rearrange sequence Can update segments Requires some photo equipment and skills Production equipment can be very expensive Cannot show actual motion	2–5	2–5	2	2	2
AUDIOTAPES	Individual or large group study Always in proper sequence Presentation equipment easy to use Can control presentation rate	Not visual Overuse as oral textbook Multiple formats Production equipment can be very expensive Cannot arrange sequence Cannot update segments Cannot show actual motion	1–5	1–5	2	2–3	2

	Advantages	Disadvantages					
OVERHEAD TRANSPAR-ENCIES	Large group study Can present information in systematic, developmental sequence Can easily interact with visual Standard format Easy to prepare Presentation equipment easy to use Can control presentation rate	Not for individual study Can require special production equipment and skills Cannot show actual motion	1–5	1–5	1	2–3	1
MOTION PICTURES	Individual or large group study Can show actual motion Always in proper sequence Automatic presentation rate Standard format	Requires fairly sophisticated production equipment and skills Cannot rearrange sequence Special design required to control presentation rate	4–5	3–5	3	5	5
VIDEOTAPES	Individual or large group study Can show actual motion Always in proper sequence Can reuse videotape Automatic presentation rate	Requires fairly sophisticated production equipment and skills Cannot rearrange sequence Multiple formats Cannot update segments Special design required to control presentation rate	4–5	5	3–5	5	3–4

will advance at a specific rate of speed whereas the presentation rate for a series of overhead transparencies is determined by the instructor).

By using answers to the screening questions in the case study and the media characteristics in Figure 7-3, certain statements start to provide a profile of what is actually needed:

1. *"Instructors require equipment that is simple to operate. . . ."*
    A videocassette recorder is relatively easy to operate in comparison with other types of television equipment. However, there is certainly less complicated media equipment available. Slide, overhead, and filmstrip projectors are much easier to operate than a videocassette recorder. Of these three items, the overhead projector is the simplest piece of equipment to operate.

2. *". . . show students how to complete simple to complex accounting forms and have students interact with instructor in a discussion format." "The instructor . . . needs to interact with visuals. . . ." ". . . instructor can control the presentation rate in class."*
    Students cannot interact directly with the instructor on a videocassette. Slides or overhead transparencies allow for better instructor eye contact with the class and more chance for live instructor-controlled interaction. Through the use of overlays and reveals overhead transparencies can build from simple to more complex information. Overhead transparencies also allow the most potential for direct instructor interaction with the visuals and the class. The instructor could have overhead transparencies of ledger sheets prepared ahead of time. In class the instructor could work with the class completing these ledger sheets by writing the information on the overhead transparency. Through good eye contact the instructor could also know when to slow down or speed up the instructional sequence.

3. *"Forms and charts . . . presented in systematic developmental format. . . ."*
    By "systematic developmental format" the client wants to move from already acquired knowledge to new information in a logical sequence controlled by the instructor. Presenting accounting ledger sheets and forms in a systematic logical sequence can be done on videocassette. But the same goals can also be accomplished with slides, filmstrips, or overhead transparencies, all usually less expensive than producing a videocassette. The overhead transparency has additional advantages by allowing the instructor to write on prepared transparencies of ledger sheets and use various overlays to highlight important points.

4. *"Class size 30–75."*
    Class size is an important consideration when making decisions based on media characteristics. Certain media formats are designed for large group while others are better suited for small group or individualized instruction. There are several estimating procedures used for television re-

ceivers in relation to class size. Equating the diagonal measurement of the television screen to the number of students viewing is one popular estimating technique. A television receiver measuring 25″ diagonally usually should serve no more than 25 students. Using this estimating procedure there certainly are some problems with one television receiver, as requested by the client, serving classes ranging from 30 to 75 students. If television is going to be used the client will need at least two and, ideally, three television receivers to adequately accommodate the class sizes indicated. Other visual media formats such as slides, overhead transparencies and filmstrips can easily accommodate a class size of 30–75 students for less production and equipment expense. Of these three format options, the overhead transparency is specifically designed for large group presentations.

5. *"Class time isn't spent drawing time-consuming accounting forms and charts on chalkboard." ". . . instructor's preparation time is cut." ". . . more efficient use of class time. . . ."*

Well designed videocassette programs can accomplish the objectives of more efficient use of class and instructor time. But other media formats such as slides, filmstrips, and overhead transparencies can accomplish the same objectives for less money. If material is prepared ahead of time in any media format usually less class and instructor time will be required. Overhead transparencies might represent an ideal solution since there is a stated need to complete accounting forms and charts with class interaction. All necessary ledger sheets, charts, forms and graphs could be produced in advance as overhead transparencies. The instructor could use a water soluble pen on acetate sheets placed over the transparencies for completion in class. With a master set of overhead transparencies the instructor's preparation time has been cut and certainly class time is used more efficiently.

6. *"Equipment will be . . . moved to classrooms for each use." ". . . all classes meet at different times in the following rooms: 201, 405, 320, 325, and 510."*

The standard ¾″ U-matic videocassette record/playback machine was a giant step forward in ease of operation but a step backward in size, weight and portability. Most U-matic videocassette machines have no handles, weigh more and are larger than reel-to-reel and videocassette ½″ videotape recorders. The response to this screening question uncovers some interesting problems. How will the equipment be moved from class to class? No cart was requested which is a necessity with U-matic videocassette equipment. Hopefully, the building has an elevator since even a cart will not help if the requested videocassette recorder must be moved up and down stairs. Based on physical and logistics problems other media formats should be considered, resulting in the use of smaller, lighter weight, more portable equipment. Such formats include overhead transparencies, slides, and filmstrips. Also, for the money spent on one videocassette recorder and television receiver, an overhead projector could be placed in each classroom eliminating the need to move any equipment.

It is important to note at this time that crucial information needed in the screening process often comes out indirectly through a combination of responses. The client's desire to move the videocassette recorder and television receiver to each class is uncovered through answers to questions 5 and 9. There is no direct question about moving the equipment. But, question 5 regarding the number of units needed also determined the classes are on different floors. Question 9 regarding security uncovered that the videocassette recorder and television receiver would be "moved to classrooms for each use." Look at questions separately and in total to develop a better understanding of intended use.

7. *"$8,550 total for 150 finished videotapes."*

Possibly $8,550 need not be expended to satisfy the stated functions. The original art work necessary for camera cards could be used for slides, filmstrips or overhead transparencies, all of which can be less expensive to produce than videocassette programs. Overhead transparencies again seem to be the best choice since the art work is simple yet with the added benefits mentioned above regarding instructional application.

There are additional media formats available such as print, photo, or computer-assisted instruction. But, for purposes of this case study only some of the basic popular media formats are discussed.

After reviewing the client's justification using the screening questions and the media materials characteristics in Figure 7-3, overhead transparencies seem to be a better choice than videocassettes to satisfy the described function. In Figure 7-4 the advantages and disadvantages of media formats that relate to this case study have been highlighted in bold type. Overhead transparencies have the largest number of advantages and fewest disadvantages of the basic media formats presented. Notice that the entire review concentrated on instructional function rather than specific brand and model of equipment.

Evaluate Equipment

Once the instructional function has been determined, more intelligent decisions can be made regarding specific models and brands of equipment. Since overhead transparencies will help accomplish the instructional tasks the overhead projector is the equipment choice. One question remains. Which model overhead projector is best suited for this function? There are several sources that can help answer this question.

Essential Needs. Anyone who has shopped for a house or car starts off with one set of requirements and usually adjusts to another set with the very effective altering force being money. The same process is also true when purchasing media equipment.

Dugan Laird, in the *A-V Buyer's Guide: A User's Look at the Audio-Visual World,* talks about selecting the proper medium by putting requirements in one of three categories: (1) "must haves;" (2) "should haves;" and, (3) "nice to haves."[2] The original intent was to use the progressive stages of

Fig. 7-4

MEDIA CHARACTERISTICS

	Advantages	Disadvantages	Production Complexity 1–5	Equipment Cost 1–5	Presentation Complexity 1–5	Equipment Cost 1–5	Software Per Unit Cost 1–5
SLIDES	**Individual or large group study** **Presentation equipment easy to use** Can update segments Standard format **Can control presentation rate**	**Require some photo equipment and skill** Can get out of sequence Cannot show actual motion	1–5	1–5	2	2	1
FILMSTRIPS	**Individual or large group study** Always in proper sequence Standard format **Presentation equipment easy to use** **Can control presentation rate**	Cannot rearrange sequence Can update segments **Requires some photo equipment and skill** **Production equipment can be very expensive** Cannot show actual motion	2–5	2–5	2	2	2
AUDIOTAPES	**Individual or large group study** Always in proper sequence **Presentation equipment easy to use** **Can control presentation rate**	**Not visual** Overuse as oral textbook Multiple formats Production equipment can be very expensive Cannot rearrange sequence Cannot update segments Cannot show actual motion	1–5	1–5	2	2–3	2

Fig. 7-4 (*Continued*)
MEDIA CHARACTERISTICS

	Advantages	Disadvantages	Production Complexity 1–5	Equipment Cost 1–5	Presentation Complexity 1–5	Equipment Cost 1–5	Software Per Unit Cost 1–5
OVERHEAD TRANSPARENCIES	**Large group study** **Can present information in systematic, developmental sequence** **Can easily interact with visual** **Standard format** **Easy to prepare** **Presentation equipment easy to use** **Can control presentation rate**	Not for individual study **Can require special production equipment and skill** Cannot show actual motion	1–5	1–5	1	2–3	1
MOTION PICTURES	Individual or **large group study** Can show actual motion Always in proper sequence Automatic presentation rate Standard format	**Requires fairly sophisticated production equipment and skills** Cannot rearrange sequence **Special design required to control presentation rate**	4–5	3–5	3	5	5
VIDEOTAPES	Individual or **large group study** Can show actual motion Always in proper sequence Can reuse videotape Automatic presentation rate	**Requires fairly sophisticated production equipment and skill** Cannot rearrange sequence Multiple formats Cannot update segments **Special design required to control presentation rate**	4–5	5	3–5	5	3–4

Fig. 7-5

OVERHEAD PROJECTOR FEATURES

Requirement Stages	Features
1. Must haves	1. 10 x 10″ aperature 2. adjustable objective lens 3. fan cooled 600 watt lamp 4. 14″ f 3.5 lens 5. 10-foot grounded AC cord
2. Should haves	1. low noise fan 2. thermal couple fan 3. safety interlock switch 4. non-glare fresnel lens 5. spare bulb compartment 6. removable fresnel lens for cleaning
3. Nice to haves	1. objective lens convertible to wide angle lens 2. high-low switch for lamp 3. spare bulb automatic changeover lever 4. retractable registration pins 5. transparency roll attachment

"must haves," "should haves," and "nice to haves," when selecting a medium to accomplish instructional objectives. Laird's concept can also be applied when evaluating models of equipment. "Must haves" should cover only absolutely essential equipment requirements necessary for the program to meet objectives. The "should haves" provide added convenience but are not absolutely essential. "Nice to haves" usually provide added features which, although not used in every instructional situation, do provide greater flexibility and convenience. Figure 7-5 has examples of features for each of these three requirement stages for an overhead projector. The whole idea is to select the piece of equipment providing all the "must haves," most of the "should haves," and the largest number of "nice to haves" possible within budget.

Operating Environment. One area of evaluation many people forget about is the operating environment for media equipment. Dirt, temperature and humidity are chief concerns. Basic types of audiovisual equipment have a reasonable latitude for acceptable operating conditions. Usually the same temperature and humidity requirements for human comfort also work well for media equipment. The more sophisticated the equipment usually the more stringent the operating environment requirements. Typical environmental considerations to keep in mind are the following:

1. Will the equipment be housed in areas with proper heating, ventilating, and air conditioning requirements? These climatic factors, along with humidity control, are important for the proper operation of media equipment and storage of certain media programs such as audiotapes and videotapes.

2. Is the dust or dirt level high in the area where the equipment will be used?
3. Are there sufficient electrical outlets in proper locations where media equipment will be used? Are the electrical circuits large enough to accommodate the media equipment power requirements?
4. Is there proper security to discourage theft, vandalism, and unauthorized movement of equipment? Theft is sometimes not as much of a problem as the instructor who sees a projector in a classroom, and takes it to another classroom. Meanwhile, another instructor goes to the classroom where the projector was located, finds it missing, blames the media center for not delivering it, and pulls a projector from another room. The confusion can be reduced by using chain and padlocks to secure equipment in rooms. Resorting to chain and padlocks may be bizarre and unsightly, but it works! After several bouts of equipment security problems, aesthetics soon give way to practicality.
5. Where are windows located in the classroom? Will drapes or blinds adequately control light?
6. Are interior lights controllable through dimmers or banks of lights which can be turned off independently? Being able to control overhead lights near the projection screen is very important.
7. Is seating arranged so everyone has a good view of the screen?
8. Is the operating noise level of the equipment loud and distracting?
9. Is external noise easily transmitted into the room where the audiovisual equipment is being used?

Safety. Media equipment being considered for purchase should be evaluated for safety, using the following suggested questions:

1. Does the equipment use a three-prong grounded plug and a permanently attached power cord?
2. Is the equipment Underwriters Laboratories (UL) approved?
3. Are all corners and edges rounded to avoid cuts, pinches, or punctures?
4. Is heat emission properly ventilated?
5. Is access to electrical components only possible through a safety interlock that cuts all power to the equipment?
6. Is the equipment well constructed with welded joints, proper reinforcement struts, and rubber guards around any wiring going through metal panels?
7. Does the equipment have a thermocouple to activate a ventilation fan?
8. Does the equipment have a fuse or resettable breaker to prevent electrical overload damage?
9. Does the equipment have well constructed, comfortable handles? The handle that feels comfortable for 30 seconds may not after five minutes. How long will the equipment typically have to be carried?
10. How heavy is the equipment? Will it have to be lifted? Will a cart be necessary for transporting?

Personal Experience. For some reason people tend to discount their own experience when evaluating equipment. Often a consultant is hired to review equipment needs and make recommendations. The expert advice often represents the same conclusions local media center personnel would have developed if they had done the review. Do not discount personal experience as a valuable evaluation source. Personal experience can be especially valuable if you have used a particular brand of equipment for a number of years. You know best how well that equipment will function in your operation. Personal experience is much less expensive and possibly more accurate than outside consultants. When considering a new line of unfamiliar equipment a consultant can be a wise investment.

Evaluation Forms. When unfamiliar with new equipment try to see and operate the models under consideration. Most reputable dealers will provide an equipment demonstration either on site or in their showroom. Test operating a new piece of equipment is desirable since promotional brochures and specification sheets cannot tell the whole story. When not familiar with a new line of equipment, request a demonstrator unit for evaluation.

Design evaluation forms for basic types of equipment to make sure all testing is objective. A good source for evaluation forms is in *Mediaware: Selection, Operation and Maintenance* by Raymond Wyman.[3] Figure 7-6 shows a typical evaluation form for an overhead projector. Basic technical information should be covered in the evaluation along with any special considerations unique to a media center. The evaluation process should include a technical review by media personnel and an operator review by people who will actually use the equipment. Notice in Figure 7-6 certain areas dealing primarily with operating the equipment are footnoted, calling for user review. Consulting users before purchase can be a helpful public relations tool by making them feel a part of the purchase procedure. Users often look at equipment from a different perspective than media professionals. Often media people have a high technical aptitude and can quickly, by instinct, learn to operate a new piece of equipment. Instructors do not always share this same technical aptitude yet have to use equipment selected for them by media personnel. What may seem very easy for the media practitioner may be extremely difficult for the classroom instructor. A piece of media equipment will not be used if the instructor thinks it is difficult to operate. Obtain evaluations from typical users before purchase and, for your own salvation, listen to what they have to say!

Published Material. There are numerous equipment evaluations available in books, magazines, and special reports. Several equipment evaluation sources are listed in Resource Section 2: A Selected Bibliography. An important distinction must be made between reviews and evaluations. Reviews usually describe equipment features whereas evaluations usually rate equipment against some type of standard or comparable piece of equipment. The latter approach is the most valuable. Trade magazines such as *Broadcast Management and Engineering (BM/E), Videography, Training,* and *Educational and Industrial Television,* have staff writers or outside authorities who write articles comparing different types of equipment. Other magazines such as *Previews,* provide evaluations on instructional programs and materials. *ITN, International Television News,* published by the International Television Association, has run evaluations on television production equipment typically used in education and training. Educational Products Information Exchange Institute (EPIE) has a full

Fig. 7-6

EVALUATION FORM—OVERHEAD PROJECTOR

Manufacture_____ Model _____ Date _____
Evaluator _____ Department _____ Price_____

A. Physical Considerations
   1. Sturdy body construction __ yes __ no
  *2. Sharp edges causing cuts, punctures, or pinches __ yes __ no
  *3. Vibration __ yes __ no
  *4. Excessive noise from fan __ yes __ no
  *5. Dimensions __ too large __ too small __ ok
  *6. Weight __ too heavy __ too light __ ok
  *7. Acetate roll easy to change __ yes __ no
  *8. Register pins __ yes __ no
  *9. Easy to operate __ yes __ no

B. Optics
   1. Projection lens: __ inch f. __
   2. Aperature: __ x __
   3. Distance of __feet between projector and screen to obtain required image
    of __ x__
   4. Focusing: rack and pinion __ or helical __
   5. Resolution: __ good __ bad
   6. Brightness: __ lumens; acceptable: __ yes __ no
   7. Focus location: objective lens assembly __ stage __ acceptable __ yes
    __ no
  *8. Focus knob easy to operate __ yes __ no
   9. Maximum screen elevation by objective lens assembly from horizontal axis
    __degrees; acceptable: __yes __no
  10. Space between post supporting objective lens assembly and stage
    __ inches; acceptable: __ yes __ no
  11. Objective lens designed to discourage theft __ yes __ no
  12. Projection lamp: quartz-iodide __, tungsten __, other __
  13. Projection lamp: __ watts; __ volts; __ rated hours life
  14. Spare lamp change over built in __ yes __ no
  15. Adequate spare lamp storage if changeover not available __ yes __ no
 *16. Lamp easy to change __ yes __ no
 *17. Glare from stage: __ excessive __ ok

C. Electronics
   1. Meets federal, state, and OSHA codes __ yes __ no
   2. Thermostatically operated fan __ yes __ no
   3. Electrical safety interlock __ yes __ no
   4. Power cord 3-wire grounded, permanently attached __ yes __ no
   5. Power cord length __ feet; acceptable: __ yes __ no
   6. Overload protection with fuse or resettable circuit __ yes __ no
   7. Adequate electrical cord storage __ yes __ no
   8. Accessory outlet __ yes __ no

D. Service
   1. Operating instructions supplied with each unit __ yes __ no
   2. Parts availability: __ excellent __ good __ fair __ poor
   3. Projector easy to maintain __ yes __ no
   4. Service manual available for each model __ yes __ no
   5. Standard warranty: __ one year __ 90 days __ 30 days __other

E. Comments (provide specific information on back of sheet for above areas receiving poor rating)

*Should be reviewed by people who will use equipment.

time staff evaluating audiovisual equipment and programs. EPIE publishes bi-monthly newsletters and releases several special reports each year. The EPIE newsletters cover late-breaking news items regarding problems and applications for media equipment and material. Special reports published by EPIE provide indepth evaluations of media equipment and programs. Additional sources can also be found in *Consumer's Index to Product Evaluations and Information Sources* which indexes approximately 120 journals and services. With the amount of printed material available the problem is not finding information, but deciding what sources are best for your particular needs.[4]

Buyer's List. One of the best methods of evaluation is to contact people who have purchased the same equipment you are considering. Usually the dealer or manufacturer will supply a list of buyers who have purchased specific equipment models. These people are using equipment in the real world of application, not the idealized world pictured in equipment promotional brochures. Most media professionals are very candid and willing to admit when they have been disappointed with an equipment purchase. Remember to talk with people who are using the equipment in situations similar to your own. If you are considering purchase of a 16mm projector for heavy use every day, do not talk with someone who only uses the same model projector twice a month. Good dealers will supply a buyer's list because a satisfied customer will sell the equipment much faster than the best salesperson. The consumer has no vested interest, whereas the salesperson is motivated by profit. A dealer unwilling to supply a buyer's list may indicate the equipment in question has not performed well or the dealer does not have a good reputation with customers. Always try to find a dealer willing to supply a buyer's list. A dealer willing to supply a buyer's list is also probably interested in providing good customer service.

EQUIPMENT PURCHASE

After determining equipment function in relation to achievement of in-structional objectives, selecting equipment to fit the function and evaluating equipment brands, you are prepared to make an intelligent equipment purchase. There are a number of steps to follow in the purchasing process to obtain the best equipment at the lowest possible price. Figure 7-7 provides an overview of typical steps involved in the equipment purchasing process. Refer back to Figure 7-7 if necessary as the various steps are discussed.

Bid Procedures

A short explanation of the bidding process is required before discussing purchasing techniques. In the bid process dealers will independently submit quotes on specified merchandise in hopes of having the lowest price. A purchase order is usually awarded to the dealer with the lowest price for merchandise that meets stated specifications. The bid process works since usually the cost for goods and services tends to be higher where only one dealer or manufacturer is available. Many media centers are required to advertise for bids on equipment orders above a certain dollar amount. Other centers, by choice, use a competitive bid system to try and obtain the best price. Often the lowest price does not necessarily represent the best purchase. Other important considerations

Fig. 7-7

TYPICAL EQUIPMENT PURCHASING PROCESS

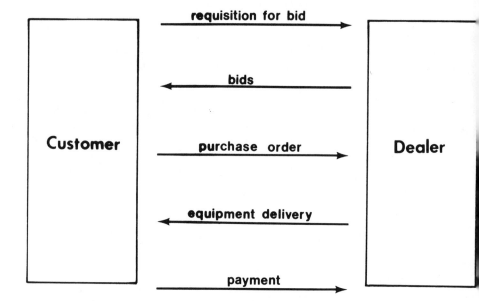

include equipment reliability and availability, replacement parts, service, and the dealer's general reputation. These considerations should be spelled out in the bid request for your protection so dealers fully understand the criteria for bid selection.

The bid process will be used in this section for several reasons. While not as convenient as direct purchasing, bidding can usually deliver the lowest possible price. Bidding can also create the largest number of problems. Dealers in a bid situation may submit an alternate, a less expensive piece of equipment, often with specifications different from what was originally requested. Vague bid specifications can result in a less expensive alternate you never heard of and do not want from a dealer working out of the trunk of a '57 Chevy! "Here Today—Gone Tomorrow AV Inc." is not who you want to do business with. Knowing how to write good precise specifications can make bidding work for you, instead of against you. Developing good specification writing skills is important since most media centers probably have to use competitive bidding for at least some equipment purchases. Please note that bidding and purchasing regulations vary greatly from state to state and from one organization to another. Concentrate on how the basic principles presented can be applied in your purchasing situation.

Two Types of Requisitions

A requisition is a formal request for dealers or vendors to submit bids on specified merchandise. Knowing how to write good requisitions for purchasing equipment is important whether or not a bidding procedure is used. An accurate description of the requested equipment must be developed in the form of a requisition.

Short Form Requisition. Many people write a short form requisition by listing only the brand name and model number of the equipment requested. Others may include basic specifications they feel are important. The requisition usually requires dealers to submit quotes on a specific brand of equipment or an alternate with similar specifications. Figure 7-8 is an example of a short form requisition. In situations where there are restrictions against using the brand name, only the type of equipment and important specifications can be listed. Model numbers and basic specifications can be obtained from product information supplied by the dealer or manufacturer. Probably the most comprehensive and convenient information source for audiovisual equipment is *The Audio-Visual Equipment Directory*, published by the National Audio-Visual Associa-

Fig. 7-8

REQUISITION

Complete name and address of suggested dealers

P.O. No. _____

P.O. Date _____

To Be Shipped on or before _____

F.O.B. Point _____

Voucher No. _____

Voucher Date _____

Invoice No. _____

Invoice Date _____

	Qty.	Units	Unit Price	Amount

CLEAR VIEW OVERHEAD PROJECTOR

Model:	3651	
Aperature:	10 × 10″	
Lamp:	FFJ, 600 watt; fan cooled	
Lens:	14″, f/3.5	
Weight:	16 lbs.	
Power:	120V, 60 Hz	
Dimensions:	22–3/4 × 12–3/8 × 13–3/4″	19 ea

Quoted price shall include complete maintenance manual and parts list. Equipment shall be warranted against defective parts, including fresnel lens, for one (1) year.

Any suggested alternate must satisfy above specifications. Dealer must supply complete technical data and, if requested, send suggested alternate for ten (10) day evaluation.

BY SIGNING BELOW, I CERTIFY I AM A FRANCHISED DEALER FOR THE EQUIPMENT BEING BID.

_____
Signature

Distribution:
  Sociology Department   4
  History Department   10
  Accounting Department   5

Fig. 7-9

REQUISITION

Complete name and address of suggested dealers

P.O. No. _____

P.O. Date _____

To Be Shipped on or before

_____

F.O.B. Point _____

Voucher No. _____

Voucher Date _____

Invoice No. _____

Invoice Date _____

Qty.	Units	Unit Price	Amount

OVERHEAD PROJECTOR, AS SPECIFIED BELOW:

Option #1
1. Shall provide a 10 x 10" aperture
2. Objective lens shall be 14", f/3.5, designed to discourage theft, mounted to focus at an image size of 50 x 50" and larger
3. Elevation to screen image must be accomplished by tilting the objective lens assembly rather than the projection stage of machine
   a. must permit at least 36° elevation from horizontal axis
   b. post supporting objective lens assembly must be mounted at the corner of machine, or at least 2" space must be provided between platen and post
4. Lamp shall be FFJ type 600—watts in intensity, and shall be of the quartz-halogen type
   a. quiet fan cooling shall be provided which is adequate to prevent curling or other damage to acetate materials, and to plastic fresnel lens
   b. fan shall be thermostatically activated
5. Shall be warranted against defective parts, including fresnel lens, for a period of one (1) year
6. Weight shall not exceed twenty (20) pounds
7. Shall have accessory outlet
8. Shall have safety interlock so when stage or door is opened bulb and fan are defeated
9. Shall have 1½" flange on body to accept 1" hole without drilling through interior of body for 3/4" security chain
10. Shall have 10' power cord permanently attached with 3—prong plug grounded to inside of machine
11. Shall have maintenance manual and parts list
12. Shall have all welded seam construction
13. Shall have all rounded corners with no sharp edges resulting in cuts, punctures, or pinches

Option #2, includes all of above plus
1. Shall have changeover device for spare projector bulb
2. Shall have durable plastic dustcover
3. Shall have acetate roll attachment

Equipment bid by dealer must satisfy above specifications. Dealer must supply complete technical data and, if requested, send equipment for ten (10) day evaluation.

BY SIGNING BELOW, I CERTIFY I AM A FRANCHISED DEALER FOR EQUIPMENT BEING BID.

Signature _____

Distribution:
Sociology Department   4
History Department   10
Accounting Department   5

tion.[5] Many media managers use this directory for basic information needed when writing requisitions. Media directors who are not legally required to take bids like the simplicity and convenience of short form requisitions. The disadvantage of the short form, especially in a bid situation, is that important specifications may be left out. When important specifications are not included, the dealer can easily submit an alternate which is the same general type of equipment but usually at a lower price. Alternate bids may involve less expensive equipment, lacking necessary features and having a poor service record. The short form invites the use of alternates by dealers because the specifications are not detailed. All alternates are not necessarily bad since there are times when a substitution may be perfectly acceptable. However, often, an alternate is less desirable than the original equipment requested and there may be no way of disqualifying the dealer because the short form requisition was not specific enough.

 Long Form Requisition. The long form requisition, especially in a bid situation, is probably the best approach because the equipment specifications are more complete. The exact equipment requirements are written in detail. If properly written, there is little chance for a dealer to submit an undesirable alternate. The dealer also likes a detailed exact requisition with complete specifications so time is not wasted quoting prices on equipment you have no interest in purchasing. If the requisition is well written, stating exact requirements, an undesirable alternate can usually be disqualified because it fails to satisfy specifications. Figure 7-9 is an example of a long form requisition with specific equipment information. While many of the specifications are standard items, such as bulb size and aperature, unique needs can also be included such as "shall have a 1½" flange on body to accept 1" hole without drilling through interior of body for ¾" security chain." This specialized requirement would not be included in a typical short from which lists just brand, model, and basic specifications. If you have unique needs the long form requisition is always the best choice.

Requisition Writing Tips

 There are a number of techniques which can be helpful when preparing any equipment requisition:

1. Be concise. The best specifications should contain only the minimum amount of information required to describe exactly what you want to purchase. Lengthy, elaborate descriptions are a waste of everyone's time if the information does not relate exactly to a purchase decision.
2. Try to use standardized measurements such as lumen, watt and decibel when stating specifications. Saying a projector should have a "clear, bright image" is too vague to screen out unwanted alternate brands.
3. State specifically what you do not want as well as what you do want. Often media managers emphasize what they want in a piece of equipment with little attention to what is unacceptable. You can stipulate what you do not want in a requisition and you do not have to give reasons. If you do

not want equipment with a plastic body, state in the requisition "will not accept plastic equipment body."

4. You can state "the purchaser must be able to test all equipment specifications before purchase." A media center with proper test equipment and skilled technicians can disqualify any equipment that does not meet stated specifications.

5. Include a statement "If dealer suggests alternate, all technical data must be sent and, if requested, a unit for evaluation." There is nothing worse than a dealer who supplies an alternate and gives you no specification sheet for comparison. With the above suggested phrase, failure to supply the information or a demonstration unit for evaluation would be grounds for eliminating the dealer's bid from further consideration.

6. If you are accepting bids on a sophisticated system involving interconnection of numerous components and you do not have people with sufficient technical background, you should request that dealers bid on a "turn key" system. The bid should include the cost of all components, installation and a proof of performance test. With a turn key approach the dealer must supply, install, and demonstrate that the equipment works satisfactorily before payment.

7. You might want to include the cost of installation for certain types of equipment such as a 16mm auditorium projector. This is not the same as a turn key operation where there are a number of equipment components which must be interconnected.

8. Remember to make arrangements for any necessary remodeling of facilities to accommodate new media equipment. Typical remodeling might include additional electrical service, increased air conditioning or more sound insulation. By mentioning remodeling requirements early, facilities can be made ready so when equipment arrives installation can be completed immediately. There is nothing more embarrassing than having $20,000 of new television equipment sit idle because someone forgot to consider the amount of electrical service needed. Local building engineers and maintenance personnel who do much of the remodeling work greatly appreciate advance notice when areas must be renovated for new equipment. Always try to plan ahead for the ramifications a new equipment purchase might have on facilities, people, and budgets.

9. You can request that a service manual and parts list be included in the bid price. Usually only an operator's manual is included with purchase. But, the operator's manual tells only how to operate the equipment and usually offers little information on maintenance. A service manual and parts list can be fairly expensive, especially for sophisticated equipment. Certain television equipment can require a service manual and parts list costing about $50. If requested as a part of the purchase, sometimes maintenance manuals and parts lists are included at no additional cost.

10. A "service what you sell" phrase might be needed in the requisition if you do not have local repair talent. This phrase means you do not want dealers to bid on anything they cannot service. You can further stipulate that dealers must have a guaranteed turnaround time for repair and replacement

equipment available during the time of repair. Replacement equipment is especially important for areas such as television where one videotape recorder out of commission can stop all studio production work. Some dealers may provide "loaner equipment" free or at a reduced rental rate as long as they are doing the maintenance on the customer's equipment.

11. Consider a service contract as a part of the bid price with a guaranteed turnaround time and option to renew. The service contract would be like an extended warranty to cover major repairs. A service contract can also cover routine preventive maintenance. The actual requirements of the contract depend on stipulations you outline when writing the requisition. Naturally, the more inclusive the service contract, the higher the cost.

12. Include a stipulation that the dealer must sign the following statement: "By signing below I certify I am a *franchised dealer* for the equipment being bid." A franchised dealer usually must honor equipment warranties and maintain desirable standards of customer service. A dealer who is not franchised may sell the equipment but is under no legal obligation to honor a warranty or service standards. Most manufacturers will supply a list of their franchised dealers and may even tell you, off the record, who has been the most reliable. Manufacturers want responsible dealers representing their products and will often cancel franchises if they receive numerous complaints. Franchise cancellations and other changes in the marketplace can cause some turnover in dealers. Contact manufacturers at least once a year for an updated list of franchised dealers.

13. Strive for high volume buying. This is one of the biggest advantages of centralized purchasing. The more units purchased, the lower the price per unit. Large volume purchasing also reduces paper work. Notice in Figure 7-8 and 7-9 that the number of overhead projectors needed in each department is stipulated, totalling 19 projectors. All 19 projectors can be ordered together to obtain a better price.

Selecting a Good Dealer

There are a number of criteria that help determine a good dealer. One important fact management finds hard to understand is that the best dealer is not necessarily the least expensive. A full service dealer will probably: (1) maintain a good equipment and parts inventory; (2) have a service department; (3) provide loan equipment; and (4) conduct on-site demonstrations of new equipment. Cut-rate dealers seldom have many services and pass the savings on to the customer. Full service dealers are more expensive because of the increased overhead. There may be nothing wrong with selecting the cut-rate dealer if the additional amenities of the full service dealer are not needed. The real question is whether the additional service is worth the increased price. Many media managers would answer a resounding "yes!" You must stipulate in the requisition the kind of services you want so you end up only comparing price quotes from similar dealers.

In the previous section on writing good requisitions, several desirable dealer qualities were mentioned: (1) being a franchised dealer for products represented; (2) having demonstration equipment available for evaluation; (3)

providing loan equipment; and (4) having a good parts inventory and service department. Other considerations when selecting a dealer should include:

1. What kind of relationship does the dealer have with the manufacturer? By calling the manufacturer you can usually find out how well the dealer represents the product. If a manufacturer is not happy with a dealer the dissatisfaction usually is not kept a secret. Some manufacturers may even suggest other dealers that do a better job representing their product. The reverse is also true where a dealer may not recommend a particular line of equipment because of supply and quality control problems with the manufacturer.

2. How long has the dealer been in business? A dealer who has been in business for a while has had an equal opportunity to establish a good or bad reputation. A well-established dealer with a good reputation of customer satisfaction is certainly a good choice. However, do not discount the new dealer who may be striving very hard to establish a good clientele.

3. Does the dealer keep a current inventory of new equipment? Some dealers are very slow in obtaining new equipment for their inventory. Others do not order equipment until they receive a purchase order, so as to eliminate carrying much inventory. Many dealers borrow the money to establish an inventory which results in two overhead expenses: (1) storage space; and (2) loan payments. Not having an inventory does extend the delivery time.

4. Does the dealer have a history of customer satisfaction? Opinions regarding customer satisfaction can be obtained from equipment manufacturers or by calling other organizations using media equipment supplied by the dealer.

5. Does the dealer have up-to-date product information? If the dealer cannot supply current product information this may be the first sign of other problems, such as not being able to supply the equipment.

6. Does the dealer stand behind factory warranties and any dealer guarantees?

7. Does the dealer have fair prices? The bid procedure can be very helpful by being able to compare independently submitted prices.

8. Is the dealer a member of the National Audio-Visual Association (NAVA)? A dealer who is a member of NAVA is supposed to conduct business according to a desirable code of ethics. NAVA also runs a training institute and annual convention each year to keep dealers current on new equipment trends and utilization techniques.

Evaluating Sales

Equipment sales can be a double-edged sword. On the positive side the dealer may be discounting equipment to reduce inventory and to make room for new models. On the negative side the dealer may be trying to move discontinued or undesirable equipment, and any such sale should be researched before purchasing.

Equipment Check-in Procedure

When equipment arrives a rather festive atmosphere can envelop the media center. In the excitement of unpacking new equipment some crucial mistakes can be made. A logical standardized check-in procedure for new equipment can eliminate much of the possible confusion. Here are some helpful tips:

1. Set up a form such as the one shown in Figure 7-10 to standardize the check-in procedure. All information is recorded on one form, such as the purchase order number, dealer, requisition number, equipment description, serial number, missing parts, and other data regarding the status of the order. The "back ordered" column is very important since many times a dealer will ship what is available and partially fill an order. Some dealers require a percentage of the full payment with partial deliveries. However, customers may state in the requisition that payment in full will be made only when the order is complete. Withholding payment until the order is complete or damaged merchandise has been replaced, gives the customer some financial leverage. Partial payment of incomplete orders is usually practical only among customers and dealers that have had a long, cordial business relationship.

   All parts of the form in Figure 7-10 must be complete, up to the double line, before any physical identification can be placed on the equipment. Sometimes in the excitement of unpacking, identification numbers will be placed on equipment before any operational or parts check has been completed. Identification numbers may be applied, using such irreversible techniques as permanently glued tags, etching pens, or stencils and spray paint. This usually happens as a shortcut for equipment seldom failing to operate upon delivery, such as overhead projectors. If, perchance, an overhead projector is found defective after the identification stage, no dealer in the world will be able to take it back if graced with your "flamingo pink" identification letters. The unit has been defaced and the dealer and manufacturer have every right to refuse to provide a replacement. Most defective units are examined at the factory and usually can be fixed and sold as "factory rebuilts," depending on local trade laws. However, a unit with "flamingo pink" identification letters is yours forever!

   There is also a place on the form in Figure 7-10 for a signature to confirm who checked in the equipment. When someone has to sign for something he/she tends to be more conscientious, which increases quality control. Another signature is used when equipment is delivered to another department for permanent assignment. The person receiving the equipment from the media center must sign, affirming the order is complete. This second signature puts the responsibility on the recipient, not the media center, and can eliminate later charges that the order was not complete.

2. Figure 7-11 shows an equipment history form that can be started when each piece of equipment is checked in. All pertinent purchasing information is listed across the top with maintenance information below. This form can be as simple or elaborate as local conditions require.

3. With some slight modification to eliminate duplication, all records for a piece of equipment can be kept together. The purchase and check-in information can be on one side of a card as shown in Figure 7-10, and the equipment history on the other side as shown in Figure 7-11.

4. Designate a specific area for checking in equipment. New equipment can

Fig. 7-10

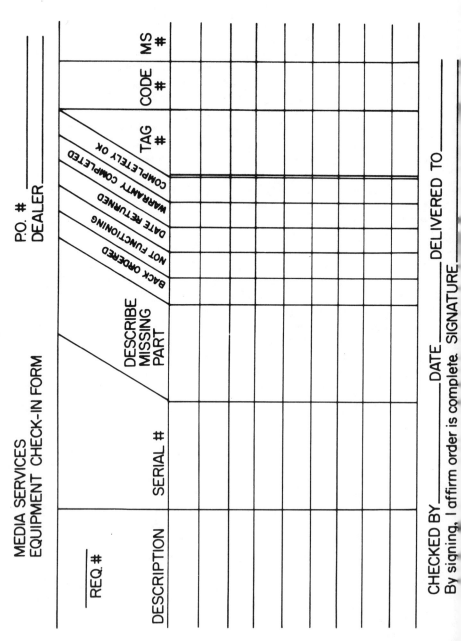

MEDIA SERVICES
EQUIPMENT CHECK-IN FORM

P.O. # _____
DEALER _____

REQ. # _____

DESCRIPTION	SERIAL #	DESCRIBE MISSING PART	BACK ORDERED	NOT FUNCTIONING	DATE RETURNED	WARRANTY COMPLETED	COMPLETELY OK	TAG #	CODE #	MS #

CHECKED BY _____ DATE _____ DELIVERED TO _____
By signing, I affirm order is complete. SIGNATURE _____

EQUIPMENT HISTORY

Acct.# _____ Req.# _____ P.O.# _____ Dealer _____ Purchase Price _____

DESCRIPTION	SERIAL #	LOCATION CODE	INVENTORY #	EQUIPMENT CODE	M S #

MAINTENANCE RECORD

DATE		Repairs	Parts	Labor	Total
OUT	IN				

143

be lost or mixed with the existing equipment inventory if not kept in a separate area until the check-in procedure is complete.

5. Do not throw away all the shipping cartons in case some equipment must be returned. Usually if a piece of equipment is defective, it is much easier to send the unit back to the dealer in the original shipping carton. If all the shipping cartons are gone and you send the unit back in a makeshift carton, there is a good chance for additional damage. The dealer or manufacturer may not be able to tell if the defect happened on the assembly line or in shipping. The dealer and manufacturer have every right to refuse replacement of equipment returned in substandard packaging.

6. As long as the defective merchandise is returned in the original shipping carton, a new replacement unit should be sent by the dealer. Requesting a replacement unit often can be faster than waiting for a part. You have every right to expect that equipment will work when unpacked. Do not become involved in trying to fix the equipment with replacement parts unless there is no other solution. If the dealer does not send a new unit but instead does major repairs on your initial purchase, you could try negotiating an additional discount for a factory rebuilt model.

7. When unpacking equipment make sure everything is complete. Most manufacturers include a packing slip with the equipment, listing all items which should be included in the shipping carton.

8. Complete all warranty information and sent it in immediately. This is a crucial step yet often forgotten because warranty cards can be easily lost.

9. Make sure the equipment operates properly under environmental conditions where it will be used. Television equipment may operate well in the clean air-conditioned check-in area with low humidity. Yet, when moved to a classroom, heat, humidity, and dirt may cause the television equipment to not operate properly. Either the environment must be changed or television equipment must be purchased with broader climatic tolerances.

10. If the order is complete and the equipment operates properly, release payment immediately. Prompt payment is a good business practice and common courtesy. Few people realize dealers often borrow money to purchase equipment from the manufacturer. The dealer needs your prompt payment to help pay off the loan. Conversely, if the equipment is defective, holding up payment is advisable since you have the bargaining advantage. The dealer needs your money to make payments on the loan and will usually do everything possible to correct an unsatisfactory situation.

Inventory Procedure

The inventory or property control identification is usually a rather long number, etched or glued to the body of the equipment in some unobtrusive place. Each inventory number is used to identify a specific piece of equipment on the inventory. Once checked in and operating properly, an inventory number should be put on the equipment immediately. There are insurance companies that will not pay a theft or damage claim unless there is inventory identification. The inventory number is usually entered on an inventory card along with other required information about the equipment item. Inventory cards are often key-punched for a computer printout. Many people find the printout pages easier to work with because many equipment items appear on each page rather than each item on a separate inventory card. When the inventory is conducted, the number on each piece of equipment should be checked against the number on the inventory sheet. After making corrections and depreciation adjustments, a new set of inventory cards or a printout can be processed. Usually an inventory is updated at least once a year. Typical information on inventory cards or a printout could include:

1. *Institution:* Organization owning the equipment.
2. *Department:* Where the equipment is assigned.
3. *Department Code:* A number designating the department where the equipment is assigned.
4. *Property Control Number:* A number assigned to the specific equipment item for identification purposes.
5. *Purchase Price:* The original price paid for the equipment.
6. *Purchase Date:* Date when final payment was made on the equipment.
7. *Description:* A very short description of the equipment item starting with a broad equipment classification and then becoming more specific such as "projector, overhead."
8. *Equipment Code:* A number assigned to identify the broad classification and specific type. For example, "008" could stand for "projector, overhead." The numerical equipment code is especially useful if the inventory is on a computer program.
9. *Depreciation Rate:* Designates the method for writing off the equipment cost. For example, the overhead projectors in the case study for this chapter could each cost $165. If the depreciation rate is 10 percent per year, then $16.50 will be subtracted each year. The total cost of each overhead projector will be written off in ten years. As was discussed in Chapter 5 "Cost Accounting," whether or not equipment is depreciated and if so, the type of depreciation, is dependent on local financial conditions.
10. *Depreciation Balance:* Represents the remaining balance yet to be depreciated. If an overhead projector is purchased for $165 with a 10 percent annual depreciation rate, each year that a new inventory is printed, $16.50 will automatically be subtracted from the depreciated balance. After two years of depreciation, a total of $33 will have been subtracted from the original purchase price, leaving a balance of $132. This depreciation balance of $132 shows the amount yet to be depreciated. Item by item depreciation on an annual basis is only practical if the inventory is on a computer program.
11. *Inventory Date:* The date of the most recent inventory.

Distribution or Circulation Coding

Much of the equipment purchased by a media center is circulated for client use. The inventory number can be too long for circulation purposes. Visual identification can also be difficult since the inventory number is usually located in an inconspicuous place on the equipment. A short number or letter abbreviation system is desirable for circulation purposes. The physical size of numbers and letters should be large to be easily read from a distance. A numbering system can be a two-part system such as 008-1, with 008 standing for overhead projector and 1 indicating the number of that overhead projector. Number designations can be used as input for various computer applications. A numbering system for circulation purposes would allow for computer scheduling of equipment and various special reports on equipment utilization.

Another coding system uses letter abbreviations such as OH-1 for overhead projector; OP-1 for opaque projector; and, SP-1 for slide projector. In each case, the 1 stands for the number of that particular piece of equipment. If the equipment is circulated by part-time personnel where there is high turnover, the abbreviated letter system might be easier to learn than a system based on numerical codes.

Make the circulation code as ugly as possible! Ugly does not mean sloppy but rather, by using stencils and bright paint, a circulation number or letter abbreviation can be applied that is unattractive yet big, bright, and functional. The physical size of the code number should be as large as possible so it can be easily read from a distance on the equipment shelf or in a room. Large circulation identification numbers also discourage theft because few people want media equipment with bright yellow numbers painted on the side!

SUMMARY

Media managers should be responsible for the proper selection and purchase of media equipment. Creeping complexity or the ever-increasing sophistication of equipment can be enticing yet misleading, in terms of what is really needed to do the job. The simplest piece of equipment satisfying the instructional function is always the best choice.

The first step in selecting equipment is determining what instructional functions will be facilitated by the equipment. Considerations could include whether the instructional functions call for large or small group learning or direct interaction between students and the instructor. Once the instructional functions are defined it is easier to select equipment that best fits these functions. Evaluation of equipment brands is the next step. The equipment evaluation process determines the "must haves" (absolute necessities); "should haves" (added conviences); and "nice to haves", (not essential but can provide added flexibility and convenience). An evaluation of equipment brands and models should consider the following: (1) operating environment; (2) equipment safety features; (3) personal experience with the equipment; (4) evaluation forms covering operational and technical features; (5) published equipment reviews; and, (6) interviews with people using the same equipment under consideration for purchase. Evaluation techniques should lead to selection of a brand and model of equipment that has the required characteristics to satisfy the specified instructional functions.

The purchasing process involves: (1) writing a requisition that states concisely what is needed; (2) selecting reputable dealers; (3) evaluating equipment sales; (4) checking in equipment properly; (5) providing the necessary information for inventory; and, (6) coding equipment for circulation. This chapter should provide the media manager with the necessary information to purchase dependable equipment that will satisfy instructional functions at the lowest possible price.

NOTES: Chapter 7

[1] Jerrold E. Kemp, *Planning and Producing Audiovisual Materials* (3rd ed.; New York: Thomas Y. Crowell, 1975), p. 46–47.

[2] Dugan Laird, *AV-Buyer's Guide: A User's Look at the Audio-Visual World* (2nd ed.; Washington D.C.: National Audio-Visual Association, 1974), p. 10.

[3] Raymond Wyman, *Mediaware: Selection, Operation and Maintenance* (Dubuque, Iowa: William C. Brown Company, 1975). At the end of each chapter covering a type of audiovisual equipment there is a form which could be used as a basis for evaluation.

[4] Complete citations for all publications noted in this section are available in Resource Section 2: A Selected Bibliography.

[5] National Audio-Visual Association. *The Audio-Visual Equipment Directory*. (Washington, D.C.: National Audio-Visual Association, published annually.)

CHAPTER 8

Promoting Media Center Services

MEDIA MANAGERS may have an excellent background in media production and utilization but lack ability to promote such services. Often managers in education and industry do nothing to advertise their programs. Others assume sufficient promotion is a printed brochure circulated to potential clients. They may feel that promotional activities take too much time from producing programs and providing instructional support services. Certainly an equitable balance must be established between time spent on services and promotion. Yet the media center is highly susceptible to cutbacks and excellent services should have the first priority, quickly followed by promotional activities that generate client interest and maintain a positive public image.

Within budget and service limitations, promote your media center as much as possible. You can never promote a media center too much. No matter how much you publicize services there will be people who are not totally familiar with your services. At worst, there may be a person who says, "I've worked here 25 years and I didn't know we had a media center!" In short, promote—promote—and then promote some more!

PUBLIC RELATIONS

There are several reasons why a media center should have a strong public relations program. Whether the center is in a profit or nonprofit setting, there are many influential people who feel the products and services provided are an unnecessary luxury. Consequently, when budget reductions are required the media center is usually reviewed critically. In difficult periods, many media centers have received major budget cuts or have been closed. A continual and aggressive public relations program that gives the media center positive visibility and justification for existence can help offset any tendency to eliminate programs without careful deliberation. There are a wide variety of publications and activities that can be used for promotion.

Brochures

Brochures, an effective promotion device, must be directed to the proper audience. Often brochures are designed from the point of view of the media staff, not the clients of the center. Terminology used and services stressed may hold a particular fascination only for staff while not being understood or appreciated by clients. Brochures must be designed for the target audience. What you think is an important service may not be of interest to others, especially first-time clients. You may be impressed by the capabilities of your full-color television production facility whereas a majority of your clients are ready for and need slides or an overhead projector. Let your brochure promote your basic services. Give your sophisticated services that have limited appeal only limited space.

A brochure must be attractive, concise, and designed to generate interest. Learn from prospective clients exactly what they would find useful and stress those services. Design the brochure to be simple and easy to use. Use short words, phrases, and sentences. Consider using magazine advertising layout techniques. A brochure must communicate a message immediately! If you have trouble in cutting content remember: if the brochure is short and to the point they *might* read it; if it is long and involved they *will not* read it. Do not waste time and expense printing a brochue that no one but the media center staff will read. A brochure should generate interest and motivate clients to use a service, or at least to call for additional information. If you do not compromise these objectives, a well designed brochure can be a valuable and productive promotional piece.

Exhibits

Exhibits can be effective if properly designed and located for the right target audience. Picture displays about the media center or sophisticated media demonstrations can be used for exhibits. If exhibits are kept simple and designed primarily for impact, most people will be impressed. Exhibits are also staff morale boosters as they provide media center personnel with an opportunity to tell others about their work. Locations for exhibits might include the lobby or cafeteria or a company or school which has a media center. If people have to wait in line to eat or wait in a lobby for an appointment, they could be reading about your media center. Well-planned exhibits in the right location can generate additional interested clients who will use your center. Remember in your exhibits to use language that the target audience will understand. Use promotional flair in displays that communicates quickly and clearly. Exhibits should present your services to the largest possible client audience, the objective being to tell your story, emphatically and memorably.

You might want to generate community support for your media center, in which case public areas such as a shopping center might be an appropriate location for an effective exhibit. Many shopping centers make their enclosed mall areas available for community exhibits—everything from antique car shows to art festivals have become weekend features. Media centers can also take advantage of free publicity space by presenting an exhibit of equipment and materials. Remember that many citizens have never seen a filmstrip projector or television camera. Once an exhibit is produced it can be taken to numerous locations such as schools, museums, fairs, and community gatherings.

Staff Speakers' Bureau

Staff members of a media center often forget the importance of their jobs. But, if given the opportunity to talk about their profession, they can become effective goodwill ambassadors and receive public recognition for their work at the same time. By establishing a speakers' bureau for the media center, staff members can be given the opportunity to tell others about their work.

A speakers' bureau will give the staff an opportunity to answer questions and clear up misunderstandings. Many administrators, teachers, or citizens base their impression of your service on one unfortunate incident or a distorted rumor, and the speaker's platform provides an opportunity to tell the other side of the story. Through questions and answers, the audience may obtain a better understanding of your service than is possible through any other approach.

Many community clubs and organizations are constantly looking for speakers to give presentations for their meetings. Develop an effective program, well supported with audiovisual materials, and train several staff members to deliver it effectively to help build support for the objectives of your media center.

Tours

Inviting groups to tour your media center is a very effective means of demonstrating your services. But, you must be thoroughly prepared since tours are often requested at an inconvenient time. Well planned tours and staff members thoroughly prepared as guides can simplify the process. Here are some ideas that can make visitors a pleasure rather than a problem:

1. Give visitors a brochure or handout that summarizes media center activities.
2. Show them activities that will convince them you are a service agency and have the resources available.
3. Use terms and figures that are easily understood and quickly make the point. Although annually you might fill 132,825 requests for service, to say that each client was served an average of 30 times this year has understandable impact and is easier to remember.
4. Use media in your tour. Sometimes a 6-minute sound-slide show can present an overview that makes the tour effective and saves time. A 3-minute videotape demonstrating a television special effects generator is much more interesting than a talk about it.

5. Keep the tour entertaining yet informative. Involve the guests in tour activities. Have people walk in front of a camera to see themselves on television.
6. As with any promotion, remember your audience. Stress the services most likely to be used by your visitors, as well as showing new possibilities. Use terminology people will understand. Simplify explanations.
7. Have several staff members trained to give tours
8. Have exhibits and displays in departments showing typical activities.

News Releases

A basic requirement of any public relations effort is to write news releases in a format that can easily be used by mass media. A story written in journalistic style, requiring little editing, has a much better chance of being used than if a reporter is requested to come and write the entire story. Unless it is a big story, the reporter will not have time for sufficient coverage. Media center managers must take the initiative and write their own news releases in order to receive the desired exposure.

Awards

In some organizations a program of awards for exceptional media development or use invites improvement in education and training for instructors or trainers. A printed certificate, trophy, or plaque that recognizes instructor time and effort may be an effective reward. In some situations, awards can be humorous and have great appeal, although taste and tact are required. Awards of any type can give clients a feeling of satisfaction about the hard work invested, and possibly might encourage them to return to the media center for another production.

Letters of Commendation and Appreciation

A well written letter to a client's supervisor regarding participation in an instructional production can be valuable. People sometimes are apprehensive about praising their own work, but the media manager can do it for them. A letter to a supervisor can bring attention to the fine work done by a subordinate in the production. Many times such letters are included as part of the performance review; positive recommendations are appreciated by both supervisors and subordinates.

Newsletters

The newsletter can be another good promotional piece, if properly designed for the right target audience. Newsletters should provide articles and information promoting media center services and programs. Such articles might include: new program acquisitions; new services, special workshops on effective uses of educational media; and notification of instructional programs available for preview. Just as with the brochures discussed above, the biggest mistake in most newsletters is that media people write for themselves instead of for potential clients. Articles tend to be too long, too involved, and written with a media vocabulary no one else can understand. Another problem is circulating the newsletter too frequently. After a while, two things happen: (1) novelty can wear off; and, (2) in order to fill space, long insignificant articles are used. In both cases, the result is the same: people stop reading the newsletter. There is only one worthwhile objective and that is to promote increased use of the media center. A newsletter that promotes a positive image for a center is nice, but increased production and service is much better.

Evaluation Forms

A media center that seriously seeks information on the results of its services and acts on that information will have a better image than a center that never elicits client reactions. Copies of production and service forms used by clients can have a place to rate quality of services received. Examples of this evaluation technique can be found on service forms provided in Resource Section 1: Service Forms. Facilitating client reactions has several advantages: (1) clients that normally would not be inclined to comment may complete the form because it is easier to do so than calling or sending a memo; (2) clients do not have the excuse that they could not reach the media center manager; and, (3) even if clients do not respond, an evaluation section promotes a positive image for the media center as a service interested in client reactions.

On some forms an invitation for an evaluation of services may not be reasonable. For instance, when equipment is borrowed, the client would be primarily interested in whether the equipment operates correctly and all necessary accessories are provided. Thus, each piece of equipment could have a "client's report form" on which may be reported equipment failure or other deficiencies. Not only does such a form provide the client with a quick way to report a problem but staff personnel can then take effective action. The evaluation section should only be used on service forms where it is appropriate.

A questionnaire to monitor client satisfaction and needs may also be an effective device. However, evaluation questionnaires sent too frequently will be considered a nuisance by clients. A questionnaire must be designed properly to monitor honest feelings and needs. Questionnaires must provide for both critical and positive comments. A well designed questionnaire should determine media center strengths as well as areas needing improvement. Through a rating system from "strongly agree" to "strongly disagree" or "highly important" to "highly unimportant" the client can react to present and proposed services. A questionnaire should be open ended and enourage the client to list needs or complaints the media center may not have considered. The same question often can be asked in different ways to be sure the respondent is consistent. A crucial part of the questionnaire design should be a forced ranking where clients have to make hard choices regarding desirable services. A question might be phrased: "From the list of 20 services below, list five in priority order, realizing these would be the *only* services available." This forces the client to seriously consider what is important, aware that some things may have to be cut to provide funds for new or expanded services. A forced ranking educates the client regarding the real world of educational media where every service has a price tag.

Client Feedback Sessions

Sometimes more indepth analysis is needed than can be articulated in a quick response form or a short questionnaire. A discussion situation may be more productive than a questionnaire reply and allows opportunity for a free exchange of ideas between media personnel and clients. More importantly, a discussion format facilitates clarification of any misunderstandings about services. If properly structured, a discussion can become a teamwork effort to resolve mutual areas of concern. A goal of better services through the cooperative efforts of clients and media center staff is far more productive than a "gripe session" where people may react from an emotiona', rather than a pragmatic level.

Extra Effort

Good public relations can be achieved in ways that have nothing to do with service capability. Often people call a media center wanting services provided by another department. Usually responses to these calls fall into a predictable pattern. Instead of just telling callers they have the wrong number, tell them who you are and give them the correct number for the area they are trying to reach. On a college campus, people may stop by the media center when needing directions to other buildings. Have maps available to help visitors with their quest. Another small point, yet one bound to leave a client or visitor with a good feeling about your media center. Keep an alphabetical file of client interests and when news of a new program or piece of equipment comes across your desk, give them a call or send a note or brochure. They may not be interested but they will remember you took the time to call or send a memo. When a client has done his/her first media production or has used a piece of audiovisual equipment for the first time, make a follow-up call to check on how things went. Even if there were problems, these difficulties can be quickly rectified before rumors are started about poor service. Develop positive habits. Planning and organization reduce the time required for little niceties that will set you apart from other service organizations.

POLITICAL RELATIONS

Being politically astute is an absolute requirement for growth, not to mention daily survival. The well-worn adage: "It's not *what* you know, it's *who* you know," certainly has application in the world of media management. You must learn to define your political environment and deal effectively with it.

Provide Reliable Service

New programs and services can be initiated and developed only on a foundation of satisfied clients. An appropriate service provides clients with what they want, not necessarily what they need. Note this important distinction. What clients want and what they need are not necessarily synonymous. Achieving clients' support is much easier when they are reasonably happy with existing services. Certainly this is not meant to endorse inappropriate use of media, but rather the realization that in a political environment growth is nurtured through a spirit of compromise. A media manager unwilling to accommodate ordinary client needs may win the battle but lose the war. Nothing can be achieved in the political environment until clients are first satisfied with basic media center services. Client satisfaction can be used as a solid foundation to add services clients really need and probably should use.

Learn the Real Organization Chart

Seldom does a formal organization chart accurately depict how things get done, or more specifically, reveal the emotions and drives that facilitate action. As a media center manager you must first find out who are the important, influential people in the organization. How much power do they have in the decision-making process? Whom do they like and dislike? Whom can they influence and who is beyond their influence? You can learn about the decision makers by: (1) tactfully talking with others in the organization; (2) noting who the decision makers socialize with; and, (3) closely observing how decision makers relate to other people in meetings. Once the people who really make decisions have been identified you can develop a strategy to obtain their support for your program.

Determine Motivation

With decision makers identified, the next challenge is to define their motivation. Everyone has some interest or desire that serves as motivation. Some school administrators may want a promotion. A plant manager may want to reduce overhead. A sales manager may want to improve the effectiveness of the sales force. There are numerous motivational drives. As media manager, your key concern is to determine those drives that can be advanced through media. If you can help people achieve their goals through media, you will likely have their attention and enthusiastic support.

Plan Initial Contact

People are receptive under different conditions. Some are best approached directly in their offices. Others are more receptive over lunch. Additional avenues include an indirect approach, through a golf match, social gathering, or meeting for another purpose. If the sales manager has a relaxed informal personality, a golf game might be the best time to describe ways educational media could be used to improve the training of sales personnel. A university dean of continuing education might be more receptive to a formal presentation showing how videocassette programs could be used to deliver instruction to branch campuses. Enthusiasm and receptivity of a decision maker are largely dependent on how new ideas are presented. The goal is to plan an initial meeting providing optimum receptivity to your ideas.

Solicit Client Participation

Clients will be more receptive to new services if they are part of the formulative process resulting in a new service, and encouraging participation in such development gives them a sense of part ownership. Clients no longer feel they are *subjected* to new services but rather that they helped to *develop* them. If the media center is considering the purchase of new 16mm projectors, clients should have an active role in the equipment evaluation process. Clients should be on committees reviewing the acquisition of educational materials and programs. The use of questionnaires and feedback forms mentioned earlier is a good way to obtain client reaction. But the media manager must always encourage clients to participate in the actual decision-making process that results in new services.

SUMMARY

Good promotional techniques must be stressed since media centers are often among the first to be considered for cutbacks. Public relations activities that might be helpful include brochures, exhibits, a speakers' bureau, tours, news releases, client awards, letters of commendation, newsletters, evaluation forms, client feedback sessions, and extra effort beyond regular services. Good political relations with the right people are also very important. Your political activities must be based on good service. Additional techniques that can enhance your political position include learning the real organization chart of the institution in which the media center operates, determining the motivation of decision makers, planning the right initial contacts, and soliciting client participation in the development of media services and program acquisitions. These public and political relations techniques can help publicize your services and build increased support for the media center.

CHAPTER 9

Developing Constructive Client Relationships

MEDIA CENTER MANAGERS are not in the media business, they are in the *people* business. The ability to work well with people permeates every aspect of instructional media center activity. Clients contact the center with instructional support needs. Personnel produce materials and deliver services. Students or trainees use programs and services. Add the administrators who must approve client programs and budgets and you have an idea of the number of people involved. Ability or inability of instructional media center personnel to work productively with people is a major factor in program success.

Whereas Chapter 8 concentrated on developing public and political relations which could favorably influence the right people, this chapter will concentrate more specifically on the client who requires production support from the instructional media center. No matter whether the project is a simple audiotape or a complex television production, there are many circumstances that can strain relationships between clients and media specialists. Establishing a harmonious production team consisting of the client and media professionals is a complex challenge because people are complex. However, a teamwork approach is crucial in production activities where much can be lost in terms of budget, time expenditure, and final results. Suggestions are offered on how the teaching professionals and media professionals can work together to develop effective uses of instructional technology.

Several definitions and generalizations are important at this point. Although primarily written for the media manager or director of a center, the concepts in this chapter have equal application for *all* media professionals who work with clients on production projects. The concepts used for client relations in *media* productions are also applicable for work with clients in *service* areas such as equipment and materials circulation. Throughout this book, "client" has been used as a general term for a wide variety of people who would request media center support. This chapter is more specific, concentrating on the instructor or teacher as the primary type of client involved in media productions. There is also no attempt to differentiate between the use of media[1] * or educational media[2] (i.e. slides or overhead transparencies) used to support the instructor's presentation or mediated instruction[3] (i.e. self-contained media programs such as videotapes or slide/audiotape packages) which need no direct involvement of the instructor. Media, educational media, and mediated instruction will be used interchangeably since the concepts presented have equal application for all three terms.

The best instructional program using media requires total cooperation between the instructor and media director. Cooperation can be achieved if the instructor and media director are aware of what each should be doing for the other. A productive working relationship requires complete honesty, objectivity, and a constant desire for improvement.

Requirements for the Media Center Director

Recognize the Instructor as the Content Specialist. A content specialist has final authority for the information in a program produced by a media center, and the instructor should be so recognized. The instructor has the important job of assembling information and ensuring the accuracy of content; without him/her there would be no program. A media production with poorly developed, inaccurate content is doomed from the start, hence a qualified instructor as the content specialist is a basic requirement for the program that satisfies stated instructional objectives.

Stress Instructor's Sources of Control. Many instructors who use media for the first time may feel humbled by the strange technology surrounding them. Suddenly the rather private world of instruction between teacher and student is thrust into the open, examined, and rearranged by media specialists. Instructors, quite naturally, may feel they are losing control over something which once was totally theirs. The media director must eliminate these concerns with technology by making the instructor aware that: (1) media equipment is only a means to an end; and (2) the instructor has several sources of direct control over media productions. The correct development of a program using instructional media depends heavily on guidance from the instructor. After production the program can have maximum effectiveness only if the instructor properly incorporates it into a learning sequence. As a manager of learning experiences the instructor *has* tremendous control and corresponding responsibility for the success or failure of mediated instructional programs. Media personnel must emphasize this crucial role.

Adjust to Different Personalities. Media professionals must work constantly with different personalities. This can be a challenge and often a source

* Reference notes are at the end of this chapter.

of frustration. There is no standard formula for producing every client program. Each project must be approached differently depending on the personality of the client and quickly, during the first meeting, the media director must analyze the instructor's personality and adjust to it. Some instructors might be apprehensive about the use of media while others show enthusiasm. The director should move carefully so as to sell the apprehensive client on the advantages inherent in media programs. With the enthusiastic client, the director may have to set some limits on what, realistically, can be accomplished within production and budget capabilities. Any type of media production is primarily a "people process" and the director who cannot adjust and work with many different personalities is ill-suited for the job.

Treat Ideas with Sensitivity. Ideas are personal and represent an extension of one's personality. During the production process the director will receive many ideas from the instructor which just will not work with media. Instructors often think in terms of printed material or lectures that can be deadly if transferred directly to slides or videotape. However, tact and sensitivity must be used in redirecting or rejecting the instructor's ideas. Since ideas are personal, being told such ideas are impractical or silly may often be misconstrued. Build from the positive by selecting and supporting those ideas offered by the instructor that do have effective media application.

In the first production meeting it is often effective to brainstorm. During this period the instructor and media director each offer ideas with the understanding that there is no such thing as a bad idea. A cardinal rule of brainstorming is that no idea is analyzed or questioned. To facilitate spontaneity have someone else write down the ideas on cards. The director must set the tone by encouraging participants to lose their inhibitions, and not be afraid to come up with ideas that may be wild or far-out; such ideas often trigger other ideas that are not so wild and, with some modifications, might work. After everyone has contributed without challenge, the instructor and media director can begin to refine the ideas. More important, in the brainstorming process a team spirit may begin to emerge.

Eliminate Technological Fears. During the initial stages of production, the media director, should keep technology in the background. Some instructors have a genuine fear of media. For example, the technical maze of lights, cameras, and engineering gadgetry associated with television may be particularly conducive to such apprehension. One way to ease this fear is to let the instructor actually touch the equipment, thus leading to the realization that there is no special secret to focusing a camera or pushing a button on a switcher bank. Media directors may be apprehensive about this technique since some instructors have been known to label media people as mere "button pushers"— unable to contribute to instructional planning. The crucial issue is not knowing *how* to push a button, but *when!* To be able to provide the right mix of production skills and resources represents a primary responsibility of the media director. A client's fears of technology can be put to rest by giving that client a sense of control over the equipment. The media director can also establish a leadership role as someone able to harness technological capability for the benefit of the instructor and students.

Fig. 9-1

LEARNER MOTIVATION RATIO

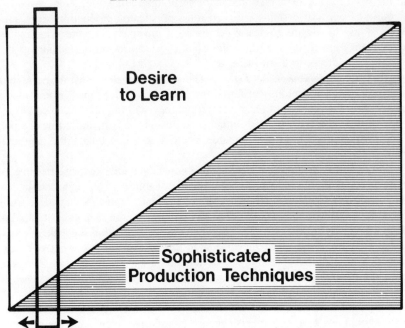

Keep Technology in its Place. A common fault with a media practitioner is to be so enamored with technological excellence that *content* is given inadequate attention. Media people primarily concerned with technology are easy to spot and often discourage an instructor's ideas for technical reasons. The media director must remember a basic rule to check uncontrolled zeal for technical quality: media productions must be of sufficient *quality* so as not to distract from content. That is *all* that is required. Any push for additional technical quality could represent overkill and a waste of time and money. If students remember technical imperfections or sophisticated technical effects instead of content, then the wrong balance between technology and content has been achieved. Media professionals must remember that technical quality should be the silent partner, not the dominant force, in a production.

A simple ratio is appropriate here: the higher the desire for students to learn, the less sophistication is required in the media production. Conversely: the lower the desire to learn, the more sophistication is required in the production. If you must inflate a life raft on a sinking ship your quest for knowledge will probably never be higher! As long as the instructions are clearly understandable, it does not matter whether the print is Helvetica or Futura Bold. You do not stop to weigh the relative merits of point size, color, contrast, and composition when you are trying to save your life! Conversely, the sophistication level must be high in a media production where the audience has little interest. Well done television commercials, especially for national viewing, are excellent examples of using sophisticated production techniques to entice an audience. Figure 9-1 graphically demonstrates the ratio between the desire to learn and the need for sophisticated production techniques. Imagine, as the window-bar moves from left to right, the need for sophisticated production techniques increases as the desire to learn decreases. Conversely, as the window-bar moves from right to left, the need for sophisticated production techniques decreases as the desire to learn increases.

Talk in Understandable Terms. The media director must learn to talk about production techniques in terms the instructor understands. Some media directors feel that the use of technical terminology will impress the client; experience shows, however, that resentment, confusion, and frustration on the part of the instructor are the most probable result. Use a vocabulary the instructor easily understands.

Be Tolerant of Limited Technical Knowledge. One favorite pastime of media directors is to trade stories regarding the inability of instructors to understand and work with instructional media. Typical comments include, "they wanted to know why they couldn't see any pictures on the videotape stock," or "they wanted us to take our 'television camera' and go 'film' a speaker," and, the old standby, "they said the television didn't work so we went over and plugged it in!" Although these can be humorous and even frustrating experiences, the media director must remember that the instructor is not supposed to be the media specialist. Much as in the patient-doctor relationship, the instructor comes to the media director to seek answers for instructional problems. The doctor should not scoff at patients because they do not understand the structure of the circulatory system. The patient is not paid to know such medical information any more than the instructor should be expected to understand media technology. Remember, the day when instructors know as much about media as your staff, will be the same day your services will no longer be needed. Be thankful clients make what appear to be silly mistakes and need your assistance!

Be Realistic About Instructional Design. Much has been written in recent years about instructional development and behavioral objectives. A typical instructional development model might include these steps: define target audience (i.e. educational level and motivation); define instructional need (i.e. what skills are needed); define instructional objectives (i.e. measurable behavior demonstrating that the target audience has mastered the skill); determine program structure (i.e. sequence of information and what to include); evaluate (i.e. evaluate program on a sample of target audience); revise (i.e. make program adjustments based on evaluation results); produce (i.e. produce finished program); and, implement (i.e. use program with appropriate target audience preparation and follow up). Many give lip service to the need for a systemized approach to planning instruction. In some quarters, being against instructional development principles is akin to not believing in the flag, motherhood, or Santa Claus! However, while many instructors pledge undaunted allegiance to educational objectives, few are probably using instructional development principles. Privately, teachers will admit they do not have time to systematically develop lessons; more important priorities are teaching overloads, large classes, and training deadlines. No one disagrees with the virtues of instructional development but few have put instructional development principles into full practice. Because of this reality, if you insist that instructors follow an elaborate instructional development process they probably will decide against using media. There may be value in not using a rigid, fully developed instructional development model, especially for the instructor considering media for the first time. Some media production requests may not even require indepth instructional development. The instructor who needs an overhead transparency to illustrate a point will probably not be enthusiastic about an indepth instructional analysis as a prerequisite for having the transparency produced. Be realistic and custom-fit instructional development techniques to the job and the client. On some simple projects, an abbreviated statement of objectives will work. As instructors gain experience in developing and producing media they will become more sophisticated in using thorough instructional development procedures. Do what you can to promote the use of instructional development principles, given the realities of the job, without ''turning off'' the instructor.

Develop a Sample Portfolio. Sometimes it is difficult for the instructor to imagine how a production technique will actually look. The media director should assemble a portfolio of samples showing techniques used in past productions. All types of media including slides, overhead transparencies, short videotape clips, and prints can be available. When you discuss using colored overlays to highlight an overhead transparency, show an example immediately to make your point and save time. Clients can quickly determine whether the technique will work for them. A portfolio of excellent examples gives evidence of competence and previous success which can be reassuring for clients. Sample scripts accompanying excerpts from programs can show instructors how print is transformed to finished media productions.

REQUIREMENTS FOR THE INSTRUCTOR

Be Prepared to Make Commitments

Instructors should realize that when they become involved in a media production they must make a commitment in personal energy and time. A television production can easily require 50 hours of planning for a half-hour program. The time spent in properly planning a production is directly proportional to instructional effectiveness. Deciding to do a media production usually represents a sacrifice for the instructor; unless additional time is provided, the instructor usually must take time from an already busy schedule.

The level of media involvement in an instructional sequence also can influence the teacher's commitment. Mediated instruction, in this section, can mean anything from developing a few overhead transparencies the teacher will use in a lecture, to producing a total program where the learner has little or no contact with the instructor. Producing a few overhead transparencies will probably require much less time and energy from the instructor and media center staff than a program that must be designed to teach essential content without assistance from the instructor. Numerous levels of media use are possible between these two extremes. Instructors must understand that their time and energy commitments are heavily influenced by the amount of educational media incorporated into a learning sequence.

Fig. 9-2

TIME COMMITMENT: LECTURE VERSUS MEDIA APPROACH

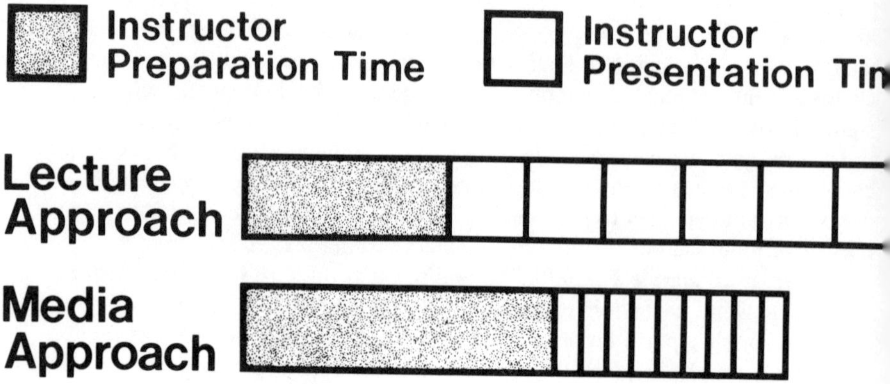

The instructor, understandably, may see no advantage in mediating a classroom presentation which has been acceptable. This is especially true when we realize that a mediated presentation will involve more planning than a conventional classroom lecture. A lecture recorded directly on videotape or film is usually a predictable disaster. To take full advantage of media capability, content usually must be substantially reworked. No wonder instructors are hesitant to consider using media when it will necessitate more development time than is required for a traditional lecture. However, in addition to the advantages of more effective instruction, often a mediated program can also save instructor time! These advantages of media may cause the instructor to invest more time initially to save time in the long run, and improve instruction. Figure 9-2 can help instructors see this point. Granted, the media approach will usually take more time to develop versus the lecture approach but, once implemented, the instructor will spend less direct time presenting information with the media approach. In Figure 9-2, the smaller increments of instructor presentation time illustrate that basic content can be taught primarily through use of media.

The logic of the above rationale is often followed by an argument that use of media will put instructors out of work. Nothing could be further from the truth. By mediating basic information that does not quickly change, the instructor is free to work with students on a more individualized basis or develop new courses. The instructor should be a manager of learning experiences, not a lecture robot repeating the same information each time the course is offered. Appropriate application of educational media allows for better utilization of the instructor's unique talents.

Time commitment also is influenced by media techniques employed. Usually the simpler the medium, the less time involved for instructors and media staff. In Figure 9-3, typical media characteristics are listed along the left-hand margin with selected basic media along the top. An ''x'' is placed across

Fig. 9-3

TIME COMMITMENT BASED ON MEDIA CHARACTERISTICS

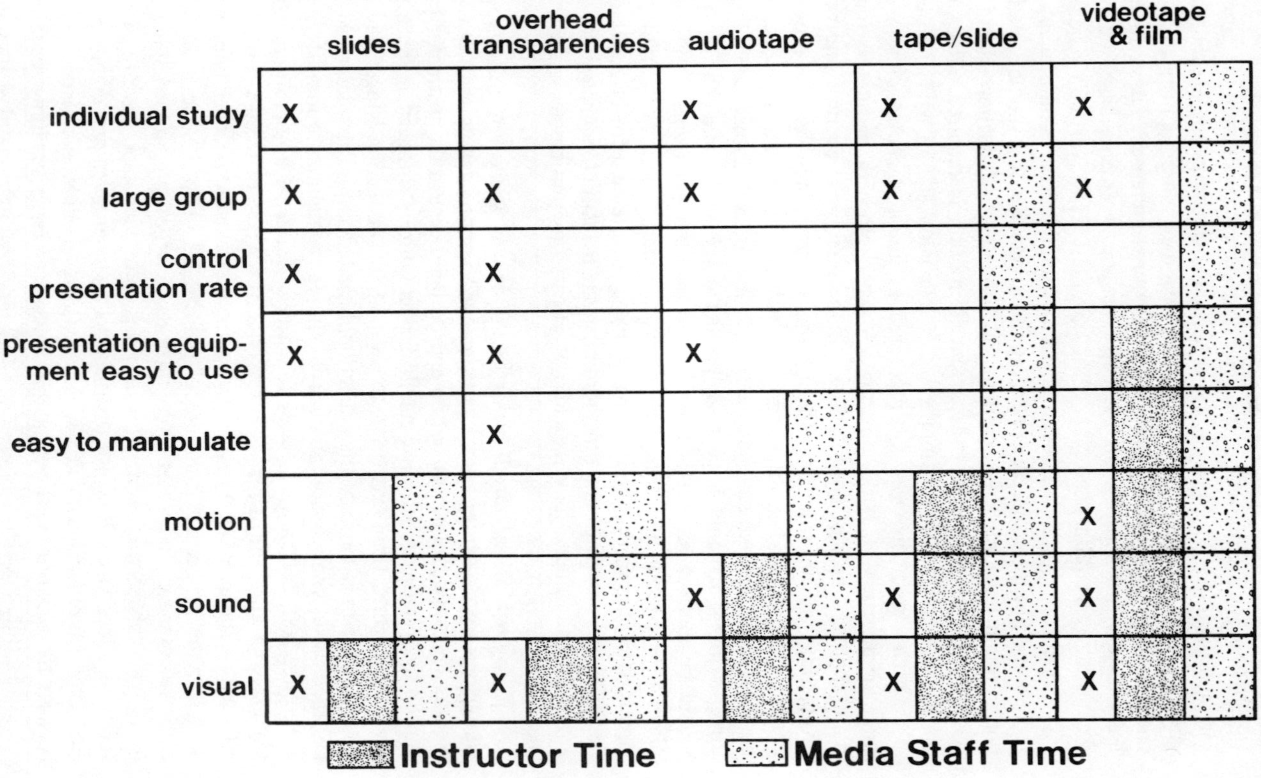

	slides	overhead transparencies	audiotape	tape/slide	videotape & film
individual study	X		X	X	X
large group	X	X	X	X	X
control presentation rate	X	X			
presentation equipment easy to use	X	X	X		
easy to manipulate		X			
motion					
sound			X	X	X
visual	X	X		X	X

▨ Instructor Time   ▫ Media Staff Time

163

from each characteristic that might apply to a particular medium. Both the characteristics and media cited are representative and not inclusive. But, this chart should help instructors see several relationships: (1) production time for instructors and media staff as it relates to a particular medium; and (2) the characteristics of each medium. As the medium becomes more sophisticated the time commitment for instructors and media personnel increases. These relationships are only general approximations, not exact measurements based on research. Actual ratios would depend on specific programs. However, in a general sense, Figure 9-3 can give the instructor an idea of relative time commitment. Instructors should not immediately decide on slides because of a smaller relative time commitment than might be required for a videotape. Selection should depend on instructional objectives and content. If motion is required, slides will not work and the larger time commitment of television or film will be required.[4]

Often media directors are pressured to do productions with insufficient time for preparation. If the director refuses to proceed, instructors may complain about a "lack of cooperation." If the director is coerced into doing the production with insufficient planning, the instructor may use the program and find it ineffective. Then the complaints may be that the media specialist is incompetent or that educational media are ineffective. Either way, the media director loses. It could have been predicted ahead of time that the program would be ineffective, not because of the medium but because of inadequate planning and production time. Generally, adequate time is not provided for instructors to plan media productions. A basic requirement for effective preparation of media materials is a time commitment. If instructors choose not to make a time commitment, they should not attempt to participate in instructional media production.

Recognize the Media Director as the Media Specialist. Instructors often come to a media center with a preconceived notion of how they want to use media. The application may not be appropriate because the instructor has seen and enjoyed someone else use media for an entirely different purpose. Sometimes ideas come from network television where production budgets are considerably larger than those of the educational media center. Instructors do not understand why you cannot produce a simple continuous zoom shot from a helicopter 200 feet above a forest to a freeze frame of a micro-organism on a leaf! "After all," they say, " 'The Wonderful World of Disney' used this very effective technique last week!" Professional conventions and conferences can also generate sincere yet misconstrued ideas. A client has seen an excellent color videotape on industrial safety hazards of large stamping machines and returns with this terrific idea: How about a color videotape covering industrial safety statistics since 1900 for distribution to underdeveloped countries? There are several problems with this idea. First, the client wants to do a videotape because the program on the industrial hazards of large stamping machines was effective. But, accidents regarding stamping machines required motion while statistics on industrial safety does not. A videotape covering safety statistics since 1900 should carry the following disclaimer: "Warning: This program may put you to sleep!" Distribution to underdeveloped countries is the finishing touch since most of these countries have limited videotape equipment.

Still, instructors can be adamant about doing the production "their way." Usually the results are not good, again with media technology being credited with the failure. The instructor tries to be both the media specialist and content specialist. Instructors must be encouraged to recognize the media director as the media specialist. The media director should never try to become the content specialist and the instructor should return the favor by not becoming a media specialist.

Establish Objectives. Instructors frequently come to the media center with no specific instructional objectives. They say instructional objectives are too hard to write or are not appropriate to their subject or teaching method. But, instructors should get something down on paper to tell what they want students to learn. As was discussed earlier, even if not perfectly written, the objectives represent a starting point for production planning. Broad goals or generalized objectives can always be made more specific. Much like a road map, objectives keep the instructor and media staff moving in the right direction. Spending some extra time writing specific, measurable objectives can save much time and money later in actual production and implementation of the final program.

Use Only Essential Content. One inherent advantage of the use of media is that it forces the instructor to organize and to be specific. Since the attention span of students is often limited, only essential content should be covered. Usually the longer a fully mediated program, the higher the risk that you will lose the student's attention. Conversely, the shorter the program, the lower the likelihood of losing student interest. A rule of thumb should be to keep mediated presentations as short as possible without sacrificing essential content. Figure 9-4 graphically shows this ratio. Imagine, as the window-bar moves from left to right, the likelihood of maintaining the student's attention span increases as the program length decreases. Conversely, as the window-bar moves from right to left, the likelihood of maintaining the student's attention span decreases as the program length increases. The instructor must be prepared to make some hard decisions on exactly what information is *essential* for the student to achieve the specified instructional objectives. Most of us find it very difficult to cut content. Instructors, fascinated by their subject, may think all information is important for students, and find it extremely difficult to cut content that is of personal interest but not necessary for student learning. Instructors must develop the objectivity necessary to make hard decisions on what is *essential* content.

Be Prepared for the Production. A media production usually involves a number of people. The instructor becomes part of a team that can involve graphic artists, television directors, audio production personnel, instructional designers, photographers, and equipment technicians. For example, in a television production, there is nothing worse than having the instructor take up studio time to select content. Certainly minor changes can be expected, but a major rewrite in the studio, while the entire crew stands around, is costly in terms of time, budget, and the final program. The instructor should arrive for the production on time and be totally familiar with the script.

Measure Effectiveness. A commitment of time does not stop with producing the program. There must also be a commitment to evaluate the program

Fig. 9-4

PROGRAM LENGTH RATIO

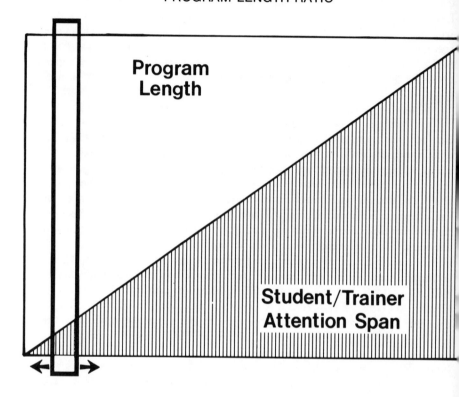

against the original statement of instructional objectives. When an instructor has finished a media production there is a sense of relief and a desire to get on with other pressing responsibilities. Evaluations often are subjective, with the instructor saying, "I really liked the program," or, "It works well in class." The instructor liking the program is inconsequential. A primary concern should be whether or not the students have achieved the instructional objectives as a result of program content. Saying, "The program worked well," is an obscure statement and could mean anything from achievement of instructional objectives to filling the last class period on Friday when the instructor was not prepared. Everything in a media production relates to good preproduction planning, including realistic objectives and tests designed to measure instructional effectiveness.

COMMON REQUIREMENTS FOR THE MEDIA DIRECTOR AND INSTRUCTOR

Keep an Open Mind

Both the instructor and media director must enter the instructional production process with an open attitude towards experimentation. Both individuals can adopt a routine automatic approach to solving certain instructional problems. People usually like to stay in an environment that is safe and predictable. But the instructor and media director must be willing to take some risks. The rapidly growing field of instructional technology requires experimentation for growth. The instructor and media director must each have an open and receptive mind and be willing to support each other in the pursuit of new instructional techniques.

Learn to Compromise

Probably after the successful evaluation and implementation of an instructional program, neither the instructor nor the media director is totally happy with the final product. However, under the best of circumstances, each has learned humility and the ability to compromise for the good of the program. The media director has probably sacrificed some technical quality standards and the instructor has had to cut some non-essential content. But, in the end, they have both won by developing a product that achieves the instructional objectives. Proper evaluation and testing of the program can also provide information to guide the instructor and media director in program revision and improvement.

SUMMARY

Media center managers are not in the media business, they are in the people business. These people are clients, instructors, administrators, staff, students, and the general public. An inability to work with and for these people will result in failure of any media program.

The production of instructional media materials represents a very special area where the media director must be able to develop an effective working relationship with an instructor. The media director should treat the instructor as a content specialist, stress the instructor's sources of control regarding media, adjust to personality differences, treat ideas with sensitivity, eliminate fears of technology, be tolerant of limited technical knowledge, be realistic about the use of instructional development techniques, and develop a protfolio of media samples. Instructors also have responsibilities in a media production. The instructor must make a time commitment, recognize the media director as the media specialist, establish objectives, use only essential content, be prepared, and be willing to measure the effectiveness of finished programs. Together, through cooperation and respect, the media director and instructor can form an effective production team.

NOTES: Chapter 9

[1] AECT defines media as all of the forms and channels used in the transmittal of information process. (AECT Task Force on Definition and Terminology, *Educational Technology: Definition and Glossary of Terms Volume I* [Washington, D.C.: Association for Educational Communications and Technology, 1977], p. 173).

[2] AECT defines educational media as the media born of the communications revolution

which can be used for instructional purposes alongside the teacher, textbook, and blackboard. (*Ibid.*, p. 171).

[3] AECT defines mediated instruction as an instructional product made up of a combination of materials, devices, or techniques designed to achieve specific objectives without additional input from other components such as live people. (*Ibid.*, p. 174).

[4] Dr. Jerrold E. Kemp has developed a summary of media characteristics and media selection diagrams. (Jerrold E. Kemp, *Planning and Producing Audiovisual Materials* [New York: Thomas Y. Crowell, 1975], pp. 46–50).

CHAPTER 10

Complaints:
Handling Them Effectively

E FFECTIVE CLIENT-MANAGEMENT relationships are basic for successful media center management. To achieve these relationships requires continual effort. As a manager you may spend a surprising amount of time initiating, maintaining, saving (and sometimes losing), productive working relationships with clients. You must develop an objective understanding of factors that lead to differences of opinion. Understanding causes of complaints will help you gain the necessary perspective needed to reach appropriate solutions. Ideally, the best insurance against service dissatisfaction is to identify possible problem areas and take corrective action *before* people have a chance to complain. But, it is impossible to predict every source of a problem. Therefore, it is essential for a successful media center program that you be able to handle complaints effectively because: (1) managers of instructional media centers will always have some complaints about service; and (2) effective solutions for complaints can yield large dividends in increased client satisfaction and patronage. Although the primary emphasis is on the manager, *all* media center staff members must become proficient at handling complaints effectively.

CLIENT-MANAGEMENT PERSPECTIVES

Clients and media managers have the same concerns, they just use different labels. Figure 10-1 shows typical client and management needs in a media equipment circulation department. Clients and managers express needs using different terms yet the lines connect those areas of mutual concern. A

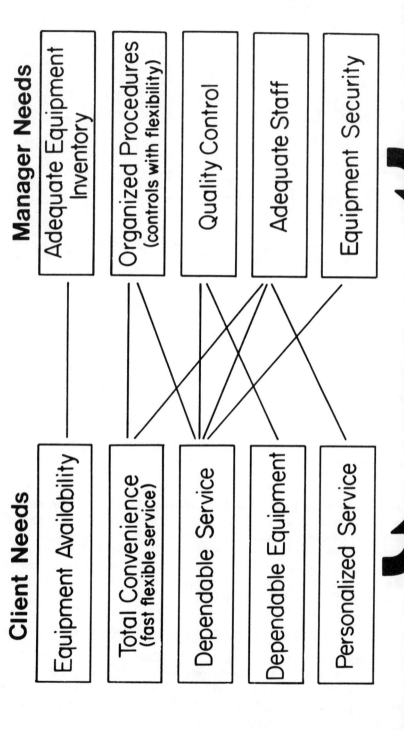

Fig. 10-1

CLIENT-MANAGEMENT NEEDS

Client Needs

Equipment Availability

Total Convenience
(fast flexible service)

Dependable Service

Dependable Equipment

Personalized Service

Manager Needs

Adequate Equipment Inventory

Organized Procedures
(controls with flexibility)

Quality Control

Adequate Staff

Equipment Security

desire for equipment availability by clients is the same concern management has for adequate equipment inventory. The client wants dependable media equipment while the manager wants quality control. Clients like personalized service while management wants adequate staff. The point is that clients and managers really want the same things. If clients and media managers realize they have the same goals, a base of cooperation can be established. Although service relationships may never be perfect, more program improvement is possible through cooperation than can be achieved in an adversary relationship.

HANDLING COMPLAINTS

If you have never had to handle a complaint you obviously are not managing a media center. Complaints are inevitable in media center management because, to some degree, the following conditions exist: (1) media centers usually try to do too much with too few resources; (2) there are numerous opportunities for communication errors, (3) media centers are staffed with people who cater to people, and people are not perfect; and (4) media equipment will fail. There are also some basic media management axioms regarding complaints: (1) *if you make a mistake with a client you will make another worse one quickly;* (2) *the size of the mistake will be directly proportional to the client's ability to complain;* and (3) *a client will remember only your mistakes when generalizing about the quality of your service.* These realities emphasize the need for devoting major attention to the effective management of complaints. When confronted with a complaint do take comfort in the realization that you are not alone.

We remember and cherish those who are visible in their praise of our media center. Conversely, we abhor those who are equally, if not more, visible in their displeasure with our services. There are certain complainers who become preoccupied with their ability to belittle you and your staff vocally and most creatively in letters or memos. They specialize in long letters that build with an increasing frenzy toward the ultimate conclusion that being born was your first big mistake! These letters seem to have a circulation rate equivalent to the *New York Times.* Everyone gets a copy. Those on the guest subscription list include all who can end your career in under five minutes. Catastrophic situations will expand the list to your staff, clients, future employees, friends, and, of course, your mother! The vindicative ability to make you squirm suddenly becomes more important than the original problem that prompted the anger. When irate clients say your service is two notches below worthless and that you have the native intelligence of a paperweight—stay calm!

When you and your staff are being severely criticized, it is difficult to stay composed. Even if your service is at fault there is a natural tendency to defend yourself, hope you can find someone else to blame, or select another career. Being confronted with complaints is never pleasant but there are some suggestions which can be helpful for you and your staff.

Be Courteous

Do not, under any circumstances, lose your composure. It is difficult to be courteous when a client is dismantling your office, stick by stick. Actually, even under such bizarre circumstances, you have no choice but to remain calm. You represent the only controlling factor in the situation. Obviously, the client running around the ceiling of your office is not in control. If you become upset, the whole situation is elevated to an emotional game of "Can You Top This Insult," instead of keeping the discussion on an objective problem-solving level. Also, if you become upset the client will say, "Not only was the service terrible, but the staff was discourteous." The bottom line in a complaint situation is: *do not give the client anything to complain about except the original problem*. If you find it difficult to stay calm, take comfort in the fact that some clients with a problem come in with the intent of making you upset. It is their way to get back at you for the problem they have experienced. When you stay calm and handle the problem in a courteous manner, they may feel frustrated because there is nothing left to complain about. It is a small victory but better than escalating what already is a problem into a more volatile situation.

Be Concerned

If you do not have a service orientation, a commitment to give more than 100 percent, and an interest in working with people, select another profession. Instructional media management is a people business, first and foremost. Exhibit a concern for the client's problem. Demonstrating a genuine interest in solving the problem will defuse many potential complaints quickly; even if it is a small problem and you find it difficult to become concerned, pretend. At least let the client think you are concerned. Exhibiting a concerned attitude will probably quell most complaints, or at least reduce them to a manageable level. After all, put yourself in the client's shoes. There is nothing more frustrating than expressing what you think is a legitimate problem only to have the service staff show little interest in suggesting a solution. Little or no staff response to your concern can be more upsetting than the original problem.

Put Yourself in Client's Shoes

People in service occupations must develop a refined ability to see the problem from the client's viewpoint. Looking at a problem from the client's perspective will help explain most of his/her frustration and help you to be genuinely concerned about the difficulty. Many media managers and staff people forget how they would react under the same conditions. Always ask yourself, "Based on the client's level of experience and background, how would I react under the same conditions?" Put yourself in a similar situation with a service such as an airline or phone company and ask yourself how you would react. If you are honest and objective, this little exercise can provide a perspective that will help you develop increased understanding and sensitivity for the client's concern.

Take Responsibility

If a person confronts you with a problem, act—even if the problem does not relate to the media center! Too many times in a complaint situation staff will look for another source to blame or the all too familiar response, "That's not my job!" If someone confronts you with a problem it is *your responsibility* and *your job* to assist in every way possible. Even if this assistance only means directing that person to the proper office where the problem should be handled. Always give the office to which the person was referred some advance warning so preparations can be made to solve the problem effectively.

Be in Control

In a complaint situation you must take control of the conversation quickly: (1) ask specific questions leading to the facts rather than exaggeration and misinformation; (2) be courteous yet firm; (3) do not become emotional; (4) do not make unnecessary concessions before you know all the details; and (5) do not become defensive regarding your services. Take charge immediately before the client has a chance to dominate the conversation. A professional, mature, courteous businesslike manner on your part tells clients quickly they are not going to benefit by threats and badgering and that you want to solve their problems.

Get the Facts

There is probably a direct correlation between how upset the client is and the accuracy of information regarding a problem. Exaggeration and generalization are major sources of distortion. Clients want impact when they are upset so, instead of simply saying, "The projection lamp burned out," they say, "The lamp blew during the most important part of my presentation and the class will give me a bad evaluation, hampering my chances for promotion." For additional impact, they may generalize from this experience saying, "The bulb *always* burns out when I use your equipment." Probably this is not the case, but if it has happened twice in ten uses, words like "always" and "every time" will slip into the description of the problem. Try to eliminate emotion and concentrate on the real facts. Working with facts is the only way to solve the problem. A solution based on emotional exaggeration and generalizations will probably be an incorrect remedy. Taking only the client's side of the problem and quickly acting can result in blaming the wrong people and making inappropriate adjustments in service. If someone said they "can never get a slide projector because your people are always unconcerned and too slow" you might replace the entire equipment circulation staff. When the problem still persists you might find it was due to not enough equipment and slow repair work from an outside dealer. This kind of over-reaction based on insufficient information does not build staff morale or provide a long-term solution to the original problem. Get all the facts, devoid of emotion, and then take action.

Always get all sides of the story. As a responsible manager you must be objective, gathering *all* the pertinent facts regarding the problem. Managers who jump automatically to the defense of their staff are paranoid and may find themselves in an embarrassing predicament if the staff is at fault. Never let anyone badger you into a snap decision without complete information. Clients may exaggerate, depending on how upset they are and staff may try to cover up if they feel their reputation or job is in danger. Your job is to ferret out the facts. Uncovering the facts can only be done by acting in an unemotional mature manner, asking direct forceful questions. When you act concerned but neutral in your approach, people will usually be honest with you. Once you have the facts, not emotional exaggeration, you can make rational decisions. When someone is trying to persuade you, the old non-committal standby, "I'll look into it," is very effective. Looking into the situation communicates your concern, does not take sides, and indicates your honest intentions to investigate quickly and resolve the problem in an equitable fashion. An objective search for the facts and a genuine concern with solving the problem will probably win you the respect of all concerned parties.

Act Quickly

The negative effects from a problem can be mitigated if you move quickly. Get all the facts needed and act. If someone is about to start a training sequence and a projector does not work, get another quickly. The only fact you need is that the projector does not work. You do not need to know why or who is at fault. Once the client has been taken care of, then solve the quality-control problem that created the situation. The quick resolution of a service problem is always your top priority.

Learn from Your Mistakes

Since people are not perfect and technology is not infallible, problems will occur. Nevertheless, perfection should always be your goal, any lower objective can cause more than a tolerable level of problems. Always learn from mistakes. A problem should be seen as a development tool to help you refine the present system. Learning from mistakes should be tempered by not overreacting; sometimes a simple problem is exaggerated by an extremely vocal, irate client. The action taken might solve the client's problem while creating some new ones by initiating service changes that are not well thought out. For example, if an equipment order is incorrect a client who is very upset may demand that confirmations be sent in the future. So you immediately implement confirmations on all equipment orders, which cuts down on the amount of available equipment because of increased processing time. Meanwhile, many other clients are complaining about receiving a useless flood of confirmation slips along with increased problems scheduling audiovisual equipment. Some call this syndrome "winning the battle but losing the war" or "throwing the baby out with the bath water." In media management we might say, "throwing the lamp out with the projector" or "solving the problem but destroying the service." Whatever adage seems appropriate, we have lost more than we have gained. In learning from your mistakes you must be able to differentiate between a problem that will continue and a unique infrequent problem. If the problem is based on human error rather than a flaw in procedure, major changes are probably not necessary. Procedural changes may be needed if the problem continues.

Anticipate Possible Problems

Unless you are gifted with intuition on how people and media technology will integrate, predicting problem areas can be difficult. Ability to anticipate problems accurately is developed by experience. The only problem with experience is you have to grow old acquiring it. Of course there are those who would contend managing a media center makes you grow old rather quickly! However, experience gained through the school of hard knocks often creates the crusty stereotype who will reject a suggestion because "we tried it 45 years ago; it didn't work then and it won't work now!" One wonders what might have happened if Henry Ford and the Wright Brothers had listened to such skeptics? Circumstances change, making yesterday's impossibility today's possibility and tomorrow's inevitability. A lack of experience is not necessarily a hindrance and might provide fresh new ideas for tired old problems. Try to establish a nice blend, remembering the worthwhile lessons of experience while not losing the ability to risk new ideas.

Anticipating problems can be learned through experience but can also be acquired through practice. Managers of instructional media centers must develop the ability to construct accurate scenarios of how new services or procedures might work. Often managers do not realistically think through the possible implications of a new service or procedure. The key word is realistic. You must be realistic, pragmatic, and objective. Be honest in your accessment of human nature, staff expertise, service volume, and equipment capability. Probably a keen sense of human nature is most important. Clients will only patronize convenient, easy to use services. Training and experience will set limits on staff capability. Clients favor services with immediate results. Media equipment will break down. The more sophisticated the equipment is, the more often breakdowns will occur. These are just a few of the realities a media manager must consider. Anticipating problems means to contemplate objectively how new service concepts might survive the brutal test of reality. If new service concepts pass the reality test, chances of success are high; if new services fail, do not implement because no amount of wishful thinking will help unless the realities change.

Remember that many times a lemon can be turned into lemonade! A complaint can offer you the opportunity to generate additional client respect and use of the media center. Often people are more impressed by how a media center staff solved a problem than by the performance of regular services. You have probably heard people say they shop at a particular store because if there is a problem clerks are very responsive and courteous. Quick action and courtesy can help to solve a problem and possibly generate increased client loyalty.

SUMMARY

Anyone who manages an instructional media center will also have to handle complaints. Hopefully, complaints and problems can be kept to a minimum. But there are too many human and technological chances for error to leave even the best manager totally untouched by complaints. Simply stated: to some large or small degree client complaints are inevitable in media center management. The best course of action is to handle complaints effectively using the following techniques: be courteous; be concerned; put yourself in the client's shoes; take responsibility; be in control; get the facts; act quickly; learn from your mistakes; and anticipate possible problems. The entire media center staff, not just management, must learn to handle complaints effectively.

There is some bad news and some good news regarding complaints. The bad news is that complaints and media center management go hand in hand. The good news is that learning to effectively handle complaints can yield increased client trust and use of your services. Hopefully, the good news will be a source of inspiration so you can meet those inevitable complaints head-on, and yield some positive results!

SERVICE FORMS

W ELL DESIGNED service forms can save time and operating budget while contributing to faster more dependable services. Examples of service forms that have been tested and proven effective are included in this resource section for five media center departments: graphic production, television production, audio production, media distribution, and a learning resource center. A short explanation is provided on how each form can be used. Service forms in this section should be reviewed in terms of general concepts rather than specific layout and terminology. For example, many of the forms presented in the graphic production section, with minor revisions, could also be used in a photo production department. Use these service form examples as a foundation to help you develop or revise service forms for your own department.

White Copy –
Monthly File
Yellow Copy –
Dept.

Pink Copy –
Client

media services

Graphics
Production
Unit
436–5461

Production Request

Date In	Requested	Completed	Accepted By	Job #

Requested By

Department   **TAT**

Phone   **Artist**

Job Description   Notes:

- Slides ☐
- Transparencies ☐
- Tv Cards ☐
- Tv Slides ☐
- Prints ☐
- Misc ☐
- Orig. on File ☐
- Neg. on File ☐
- No Original ☐
- No Negative ☐

	Estimate	Actual
Labor		
Material		
Process		
Total		

We are interested in knowing how you liked the service and/or materials
provided by Media Services. If you have comments, please indicate below.

Quality of materials

☐   ☐   ☐   ☐   ☐
very good   good   average   poor   very poor

Comments: Send to:
Director of Media Services
436–5461

GRAPHIC PRODUCTION FORMS

Production Request

The "Production Request" is completed for each graphic production request. Basic production categories are listed along with space under "Notes" for additional information. The "Estimate" cost column is completed when the job is received and the "Actual" is completed after the job is finished. Ideally, estimated and actual costs should be very close. Use of the "Estimate" and "Actual" cost data helps keep staff on target regarding production deadlines and resulting costs. A job number is assigned from a master list, the "Monthly Job-In Record," described below. "TAT" or turnaround time indicates the time needed to finish a job from the dat of submission to completion. A pressure sensitive multiple copy form is suggested so when filling in the top sheet all copies are completed simultaneously. The following routing is suggested for color coded copies: (1) white is filed by month for utilization; (2) yellow is filed by department requesting production; and (3) pink goes to the client when the job is picked up. A comments section is included to elicit opinions regarding the quality of services.

Monthly Job-In Record

Each job coming into the graphic production area is logged on the "Monthly Job-In Record" by the artist accepting the request. Job numbers are started sequentially each month and assigned using the "Monthly Job-In Record." The job number is important since it is the means of identifying the job on several different forms in the graphics production area. A "Monthly Job-In Record" also provides a master list of all jobs coming in during the month and serves as a double-check to make sure all jobs were recorded.

Monthly Job-In Record
GRAPHICS REQUESTS FOR_____

JOB	NAME	DEPARTMENT	TYPE OF MEDIA	QUANT.	DATE IN	DEADLINE	DATE COMPLETED

GRAPHIC ARTIST
TIME RECORD

Name_____ Week of_____

Job Numbers	Creative	Conference	Supervision	Total
MONDAY				
*Unassigned				
TUESDAY				**Daily Total**
*Unassigned				
WEDNESDAY				**Daily Total**
*Unassigned				
THURSDAY				**Daily Total**
*Unassigned				
FRIDAY				**Daily Total**
*Unassigned				

*Specify which of the following: **Daily Total**

    Personal   **Weekly Total:**
    Illness
    Vacation/Holiday
    Administration

Graphic Artist Time Record

The ''Graphic Artist Time Record'' is completed by the artist each day. The artist must account for all the time spent, even unassigned time, in order to record labor cost information on the ''Graphics Working Record,'' page 181, and, ultimately, on the ''Production Request'' form, page 178.

Graphics
Working Record

<table>
<tr><td>Job Number</td></tr>
</table>

Date In   _____   **Shelf Time** _____

Date Requested   _____   **Actual TAT** _____

Date Started   _____   **Overall TAT** _____

Date Finished   _____

Materials Used   **Cost**

Total Material _____

Labor _____

Grand Total

Graphics Working Record

The "Graphics Working Record" is a work sheet used by the artist to record all materials costs. "Shelf time" refers to the length of time before the job is started. "Overall TAT" is the total time between date of submission and completion of a job. This is the time frame of most interest to the client since it represents the total time before a job was completed. "Actual TAT" is the amount of time the artist actually worked on the job. The "Shelf Time" and "Actual TAT" equal the "Overall TAT." When a job is completed the total hours spent on the job are transferred from the "Graphic Artist Time Record," page 180, to the "Graphics Working Record" to compute the total job cost. This form is a working record so that the final cost information can be transferred in a neat, orderly fashion to the "Production Request" form, page 178.

Graphics In-House Report

JOB #	DEPARTMENT	CLIENT	TYPE	UNITS COMPLETED	UNITS NOT COMPLETED	$ LABOR	$ MATERIAL	ARTIST

Graphics In-House Report

The "Graphics In-House Report" is completed by the artist and is used at the end of the month by the graphics manager to obtain a status report on unfinished jobs. "Type" refers to media produced such as slides, overhead transparencies, or prints. Work volume is shown in units completed. A unit is one piece of finished artwork. A job requiring 35 slides or units of finished artwork might show 20 "Units Completed" and 15 "Units Not Completed" for a given month.

Graphics Departmental Summary Sheet

The "Graphics Departmental Summary Sheet", page 184, is completed by the manager of the graphics area and provides a monthly status report of work for a specific client department. One agency or department may have many people using the graphic production area. Names of individuals from a department or agency using the graphic area are listed on the left side of the form. Information for the "Graphic Departmental Summary Sheet" is pulled from the "Production Request" for completed jobs, page 178; the "Graphics In-House Report" for jobs in progress, page 182; and the "Monthly Job-In Record" for jobs not started, page 179. The "Graphic Departmental Summary Sheet" also serves as a work sheet for transfer of final figures to the "Graphic Production Monthly Report" form, page 185.

Graphic Production Monthly Report

The "Graphic Production Monthly Report", page 185, is completed by the manager of the graphic production area and provides a summary of all work during a given month. Information for this form is pulled from the "Graphics Departmental Summary Sheet" on page 184. This form helps solve a perplexing problem in media production departments. Just showing jobs completed can be misleading for two reasons: (1) jobs can vary greatly in size so completion of two large jobs in a month may represent more work volume than completion

GRAPHICS Departmental
Summary Sheet

MONTH _____

DEPARTMENT _____

NAME	Job number.	this month	previous month	finished	started	not started	SLIDES done	SLIDES not done	TRANSPARENCIES done	TRANSPARENCIES not done	TV SLIDES done	TV SLIDES not done	TV CARDS done	TV CARDS not done	MISC. done	MISC. not done	hours spent	TAT	labor cost	material cost	photo requests	photo cost	TOTAL COST

APHIC
ODUCTION

ONTHLY
EPORT

	JOBS	JOBS COMPLETED	Units Completed	JOBS in PROGRESS	Units Completed	UNITS not COMPLETED	JOBS not STARTED	UNITS not COMPLETED	JOBS COMPLETED	Units Completed	JOBS in PROGRESS	Units Completed	UNITS not COMPLETED	LABOR	MATERIAL

OTALS

⌊ GRAPHIC PRODUCTION _____ ⌋⌊ CARRY OVER ____ ⌋
THIS MONTH

ES   ___
NS.   ___
TS   ___
CARDS   ___
.   ___

   TOTALS _____

TURNAROUND TIME
Longest   Shortest   Average
___   ___   ___

of 20 small jobs; and (2) just listing jobs completed in a month can result in erratic comparisons, with one month showing five jobs being completed and the next month 35 jobs being completed. Work volume can be more accurately expressed through completed units. In the case of graphic production, a unit is a piece of finished artwork. A job requiring 20 transparencies or units of finished artwork might show 15 "Units Completed" and 5 "Units Not Completed" for a given month. Using units as a form of measurement the "Graphic Production Monthly Report" can more accurately show actual work volume rather than just completed jobs.

Work volume is divided into two major categories: "Graphic Production This Month" and "Carry Over." "Graphic Production This Month" covers what has happened to all jobs received during the reporting month. Information is further subdivided into: (1) jobs received, and of these jobs, the number completed and the number of units completed; (2) jobs in progress and the number of units completed along with units not completed; (3) jobs not started and the units not completed. "Carry Over" refers to jobs started in previous months and is subdivided into: (1) jobs completed and resulting units completed; and (2) jobs in progress and the number of units completed along with units not completed. The "Grahic Production Monthly Report" gives a running total of actual work completed and resulting labor and materials costs for the month. This form also has a breakout for the number of units of a given type of media produced such as slides, transparencies, and prints. A monthly average for turnaround time, amount of time between submission and completion of a job, is included to give the manager an overall idea of how long it takes to complete jobs.

There are features in the "Graphic Production Monthly Report" that have application in other media center departments. For example, the same unit concept can be used in other production areas such as television, audio, and photography. Television and audio might use a production hour as the unit of measurement since some programs can be completed in a couple of hours while others may take weeks. A photographic area might use the unit concept for a slide or print.

TELEVISION PRODUCTION FORMS

Production Service Order

The "Production Service Order" is used to schedule television studio time and appropriate equipment. A pressure sensitive multiple copy form is suggested so when filling in the top sheet all copies are completed simultaneously. The following routing is suggested for color coded copies: (1) white is retained by the television production coordinator for utilization; (2) yellow goes to the program director; and (3) pink goes to the client and may be returned with the "client comments" section completed to elicit opinions regarding the quality of services.

REC

media services

TELEVISION UNIT
436-5461
White - Coordinator
Yellow - Producer
Pink - Client

PRODUCTION SERVICE ORDER

Date _____ Day _____ Dept. _____ Studio Time: from: _____ to: _____

Client _____ Phone _____

Tentative Title _____ Producer _____

☐ Camera Production   VTR Time: from: _____ to: _____

☐ Editing   Record on tape no. _____

☐ Remote   Length of Tape: 30 min. ☐ 60 min. ☐

Other Instructions: _____

_____

_____

_____

Client Comments:

very good ☐   good ☐   average ☐   poor ☐   very poor ☐

Send to: Director of Media Services 436-5461

187

DUB

DUBBING SERVICE ORDER

ms media services

TELEVISION UNIT
436-5461
White - Coordinator
Yellow - Studio
Pink - Client

Client_____ Dept._____ Phone_____ Date_____

DUB (Master) — To (Copy)

Title	Format	Length	Format	No. of Copies

Date Completed & Notified_____ Date of Pick-up_____ By_____

Comments:_____

Client Comments:

□ very good □ good □ average □ poor □ very poor

Send to: Director of Media Services 436-5461

188

Dubbing Service Order

The "Dubbing Service Order" form is used for any type of videotape transfer work. A pressure sensitive multiple copy form is suggested so when filling in the top sheet all copies are completed simultaneously. The following routing is suggested for color coded copies: (1) white is retained by the television production coordinator for utilization; (2) yellow and pink are sent to the television studio with the videotape or 16mm film to be duplicated; and (3) pink is attached to the finished copy given to the client. "Client comments" is included to elicit opinions regarding the quality of services. This form is designed primarily for duplication of in-house programs produced by the media center where copyright clearance might not be a problem. Any copyrighted program would require obtaining appropriate clearance before duplication.

Playback Order

The "Playback Order", page 190, form is designed primarily to schedule the transmission of videotapes over a closed-circuit cable system. A pressure sensitive multiple copy form is suggested so when filling in the top sheet all copies are completed simultaneously. The following routing is suggested for color coded copies: (1) white is retained by the television production coordinator for utilization; and, (2) yellow goes to the client confirming the specific playback information. "Client comments" is included to elicit opinions regarding the quality of services.

PB

media services

Television Unit
436-5461
White-Coordinator
Yellow-Client

Playback Order

Tape No. _____ Tape Title _____ Length _____

Play Date _____ Day _____ Time _____

Channel 2 4 5 6   Building _____ Room _____

Person Requesting PB _____ Department _____

Office Phone _____ Department Phone _____

Course Name & No. _____ Approx. No. Students Viewing _____

_____ Comments and/or Additional Titles _____

THANK YOU! This is a conformation of your request. Please check date and time. NOTE CHANNEL

Send to:
Director of Media Services 436-5461

Client Comments:

☐ ☐ ☐ ☐ ☐
very good good average poor very poor

190

Television Production Monthly Report

The "Television Production Monthly Report", pages 192–193, provides a summary of all work completed during a given month. All information for this form is pulled from the "Production Service Order, "page 187, the "Dubbing Service Order," page 188; and the "Playback Order," page 190.

Under "Part I," a program is split into preproduction, studio/field, and post production hours. Preproduction hours covers all conferences, script writing, and planning, up to the beginning of actual production. Studio/field hours represents the actual videotaping of all program segments. Post production hours covers all editing and followup activities needed for implementing and evaluating the program. Most production time should be spent in the pre/post stages rather than in the studio/field stage where the expense is much higher.

Parts I and II cover productions and tape duplication respectively and are summarized in Part III. The number of times a program is used and the resulting students served is tabulated in Part IV. Labor cost refers to the personnel expense required to provide the playback service. All information on the "Television Production Monthly Report" is arranged according to the department or agency making the service request.

TELEVISION PRODUCTION MONTHLY REPORT

Part I. PRODUCTIONS

Department	Pre-production Hours	Studio/Field Production Hours	Post Production Hours	Total Production Hours	Labor	Materials	Total Cost
Sub total							

Part II. TAPE DUPLICATION

Department	Number of Tapes	Production Hours	Labor	Materials	Total Cost

Part III. **PRODUCTION UTILIZATION SUMMARY**

	Pre-production Hours	Studio/Field Production Hours	Post Production Hours	Total Production Hours	Labor	Materials	Total Cost
PRODUCTIONS (sub total)							
DUPLICATIONS (sub total)							
GRAND TOTAL							

Part IV. **VIDEOTAPE PLAYBACKS**

Department	Number of Program Uses	Students Served	Labor
Total			

193

A

TV LOG

Date _____

Time	Channel	Tape #	PGM Time	Length	Distribution
8:00	2				
	4				
	5				
	6				
	Studio				
9:00	2				
	4				
	5				
	6				
	Studio				
10:00	2				
	4				
	5				
	6				
	Studio				
11:00	2				
	4				
	5				
	6				
	Studio				
12:00	2				
	4				
	5				
	6				
1:00	2				
	4				
	5				
	6				
	Studio				
2:00	2				
	4				
	5				
	6				
	Studio				

Television Log

The "TV Log" is used to record all scheduled productions, videotape duplications, and playbacks. A scheduling log is essential in a busy television studio to coordinate different production and service activities. Pertinent scheduling information is transferred to the log from the "Production Service Order," page 187, "Dubbing Service Order," page 188, and "Playback

B

TV LOG

Date ______________________

Time	Channel	Tape # PGM Time	Length	Distribution
3:00	2			
	4			
	5			
	6			
	Studio			
4:00	2			
	4			
	5			
	6			
	Studio			
5:00	2			
	4			
	5			
	6			
	Studio			
6:00	2			
	4			
	5			
	6			
	Studio			
7:00	2			
	4			
	5			
	6			
	Studio			
8:00	2			
	4			
	5			
	6			
	Studio			

Order,'' page 190. The person scheduling the studio must first check the ''TV Log'' before confirming any request. Television production and engineering people use the ''TV Log'' as a planning guide for activities in the studio. Television productions and videotape duplication requests are booked in the ''studio'' slot for the number of hours required. Videotape playbacks are booked by putting the program number, title, length, and viewing location next to an available channel number. One set of log sheets, ''A'' and ''B,'' is used for each day. Legal size, 8-½ × 14″, is suggested for the log to allow plenty of room to write in information.

▮▮▮ EDITING LOG

media services

INDEX #		TIME		Title	
				Description	

NOTES:

Editing Log

The "Editing Log" provides a breakdown of all segments on a videotape. "Index #" refers to the numbers that appear on the videotape recorder counter at the beginning and end of each tape segment. "Time" covers the actual running time for a segment. A two-and-a-half minute segment would be shown as starting at 0:00 and ending at 2:30. Several key words can be used to describe each segment. The last column can be used to rate each segment using abbreviations such as "G" for good, and "NU" for not useable. The "Editing Log" can be completed during production or at a post production conference with the client. Once editing starts, the "Editing Log" can be invaluable in helping the director quickly find the right videotape segments for the final program. The "Editing Log" concept can also be used in photo and audio production departments.

AUDIO PRODUCTION FORMS

Audio Production Request

Increased use of tape/slide programs, dual sound tracks on videocassettes, sophisticated multi-image presentations, and duplication from one audiotape format to another, has prompted many media centers to set up a separate audio production facility. The "Audio Production Request", page 198, covers basic productions and duplication jobs.

The "Audio Production Request" includes original production and duplication jobs on one form. A pressure sensitive multiple copy form is suggested so when filling in the top sheet all copies are completed simultaneously. The following routing is suggested for color coded copies: (1) white is filed alphabetically by client for monthly utilization; and (2) yellow goes to the client with the completed production or duplication. "Date Recv'd," "Date Completed," and "Date Requested" are used to establish accurate turnaround time figures, the time between submission and completion of a job. "Estimate" and "Actual" columns are provided for labor and materials charges. The "Estimate" column is completed upon submission of the job and the "Actual" is completed from a work log after the job is finished. Ideally, these figures should be very close, demonstrating the staff can accurately judge the cost of labor and materials. Writing space under "Job Description" is used for special instructions. Most of the "Audio Production Request" deals with describing the tape format, recording track configuration, and number of copies. Duplication of tapes refers primarily to in-house programs produced by the media center where copyright clearance might not be a problem. Any copyrighted program would require obtaining appropriate clearance before duplication. A "Client Comment" section is also included to elicit opinions regarding the quality of services.

Audio Production Log

Many production areas find it helpful to log requests as they are received. The "Audio Production Log", page 199, provides a quick visual check of jobs received and eliminates the need to go through numerous request forms to track down basic data. Each month starts with a new series of job numbers making the total number of requests received for the month easy to determine. The "Audio Production Log" also serves as an index since the job number in the left hand column of the log is also on the "Audio Production Request," page 198.

Audio Production Request

AUDIO PRODUCTION UNIT

JOB # _____

NAME _____
DEPT. _____
PHONE _____
TITLE _____

☐ PRODUCTION
☐ SYNC-SLIDE
☐ AUDIBLE ☐ IN-AUD.
☐ REAL-TIME
☐ HIGH SPEED DUB

☐ REMOTE RECORDING
WHERE _____
WHEN _____

DATE RECV'D _____
DATE COMPLETED _____
DATE REQUESTED _____

	Estimate	Actual
Labor		
Material		
TOTAL		

TIME STUDENT / PROFESSIONAL

AUDIO TAPE	TOTAL UNITS	600'	1200'	1800'	C-30	C-60	C-90

JOB DESCRIPTION (ie, SPECIAL INSTRUCTIONS, SCRIPT, NARR., MUSIC, ETC.)

MASTER

REEL ☐
SPEED _____ LP ☐
MONO ☐ STEREO ☐ MONO ☐ STEREO ☐
F-TR ☐
½-TR ☐
¼-TR ☐ L ☐ R ☐ BOTH ☐
CASSETTE ☐
MONO ☐ STEREO ☐
I SIDE ☐ BOTH SIDES ☐

DUPLICATIONS QUANTITY-

REEL ☐
SPEED _____
MONO ☐ STEREO ☐
F-TR ☐
½-TR ☐
¼-TR ☐ L ☐ R ☐ BOTH ☐
CASSETTE ☐
MONO ☐ STEREO ☐
I SIDE ☐ BOTH SIDES ☐
CHECKED BY _____

CLIENT COMMENT

VERY GOOD ☐
GOOD ☐
AVERAGE ☐
POOR ☐
VERY POOR ☐
STUDENTS SERVED _____

SEND TO DIRECTOR OF
MEDIA SERVICES 436-5461

Audio Production Log

Job#	Client	Dept.	Description	Sync Slide	Date Rec'd	Date Compl.	Master #	Units: Masters & Copies	Hours: Full-time Part-time

Audio Production Monthly Report

The "Audio Production Monthly Report", pages 201–203, has three sections: (1) "Production Load Analysis)" (2) "Audio Production Utilization by Department;" and (3) "Average Cost Analysis by Type of Request." Recording and dubbing are terms used in all three sections. A recording represents the production of an original sound track that may include one or more of the following: music; sound effects; narration; and sync tones for slides. The original sound track is often called the master. Dubbing involves duplicating or making copies of the master tape. "Production Load Analysis" shows the number of completed audiotape recordings and dubbing requests as well as the number of jobs carried forward, jobs started but not completed in a given month. By subtracting requests carried forward from requests received, the total requests completed for the month can be determined. "Units" refers to the number of audiotapes generated by completed requests. One job request could require producing a master audiotape and five copies for a total of six units. Average turnaround time, the time between submission and completion of a job, is shown for recordings and duplications. "Audio Production Utilization by Department," shows the number of completed recordings and dubbings along with units generated by departments submitting requests. "Average Cost Analysis by Type of Request" tabulates all direct charges to provide an average per hour cost for recording and dubbing requests completed during the month. Typically the per hour cost for dubbing should be much lower than for recording since the latter involves more preproduction and post production time. The average per hour cost for each type of production also allows the manager to monitor basic operational costs.

Audio Production Monthly Report

. Production Load Analysis

Total Recording Requests Received For Current Month		Requests Carried Forward to Next Month	
Previous Requests Brought Forward		Requests Started but not Completed	
New Requests Received		Requests Not Started	

Total Recording Requests Completed
Units

Total Dubbing Requests Received For Current Month		Requests Carried Forward to Next Month	
Previous Requests Brought Forward		Requests Started but not Completed	
New Requests Received		Requests Not Started	

Total Dubbing Requests Completed
Units

Average Turnaround Time	
Recording	Dubbing

II. Audio Production Utilization
By Department

Department	Recording		Dubbing	
	Requests	Units	Requests	Units
Total				

I. Average Cost Analysis by Type of Request

Recording Requests

Cost Factors	Expenditures
Commodities	
Contractual	
Student Help	
Personnel	

Total Completed
Production Hrs.
- Full-time ☐
- Part-time ☐
- Total ☐

$\div$ | Total Completed Production Hrs. | — | Cost/Completed Production Hr. |

Dubbing Requests

Cost Factors	Expenditures
Commodities	
Contractual	
Student Help	
Personnel	

Total Completed
Production Hrs.
- Full-time ☐
- Part-time ☐
- Total ☐

$\div$ | Total Completed Production Hrs. | — | Cost/Completed Production Hr. |

MEDIA DISTRIBUTION FORMS

Media Distribution Service Request

The "Media Distribution Service Request" form is used to record all information needed to facilitate a request for media equipment or program material. The general design of the form is ultimately for key punch conversion so utilization tabulation can be done by computer. "Stud. Served" refers to the number of students served by the equipment requested which can be more accurate when figuring cost effectiveness than just requests filled. "Del./P.U. Pt." indicates the delivery and pick up point or location for requested items. "NF" stands for "not filled code" which allows the equipment booker to indicate by a code number the reason an order could not be filled. The reasons why a request cannot be filled usually fall into several predictable categories so the coding process is not difficult. A "1" could mean all equipment is booked while a "2" could indicate equipment is being repaired. By tabulating what cannot be done the media manager is in a much better position to recommend changes in service procedures or request additional budget. "Dist. Pt." allows the person booking the equipment to code whether the equipment is coming from the main media center or a smaller satellite center. "Usage" allows the equipment booker to indicate the number of times the equipment will be used. For example, someone may order a 16mm projector for a training session held Monday through Friday. Instead of writing up five separate orders, a "5" is inserted next to "Usage" to indicate the same order will be used five times. "Router Only" refers to the delivery or pickup run on which the equipment order will be placed. Abbreviations are used for most items such as "OH" for overhead projector. Numerical codes are included to indicate type of equipment such as "008" for all overhead projectors. A numerical code is not printed if more than one type of equipment is available. For example, manual thread and auto thread are two types of 16mm projectors, each with a separate code. Use of numerical codes is especially important if any kind of computer tabulation is used. Ample space is provided for "Notes" to accommodate additional instructions for special orders. A pressure sensitive multiple copy form is recommended so when filling in the top sheet all copies are completed simultaneously. Suggested routing for color coded copies of this form is the following: (1) white filed alphabetically by client; (2) yellow attached to the equipment for delivery; (3) pink filed by pickup date; and (4) gold filed by delivery date.

Media Distribution
Service Request

NAME |_____| 6   DEPT. _____ |___| 24   Phone |___| 27   Stud Served |___| 34

Del./P.U. Pt. _____   Use Date |___| 38   Time |___| 44   Return Date |___| 65   Time |___| 71   Bldg |___| 48   ROOM |___| 51

Course |_____| 57   Sec. |___| 62   Dist. Pt |___| 76   N.F. Code |___| 75   Usage |___| 86

Router Only:

DEL RUN				PICK UP RUN				RUN			
Quan	Equipt.	Type	Dist. Code	Quan	Equipt.	Type	Dist. Code	Quan	Equipt.	Type	Dist. Code
	16 MM				Film strip	0 0 5			Opaque	0 0 7	
	O H	0 0 8			CART	0 1 0			Dual 8m	0 1 5	
	S 8 So	0 1 7			Rec PlayMS				Screen,Prt	0 2 1	
	CRSL.	0 2 5			Cass S Sync				Tpe Rcr MS		
	CASS	0 3 5			VCR 3/4	0 8 1			TV I/2 RR	0 8 3	
	Monitor MC				TV RR Ens	1 2 2			Audiotape	1 2 9	
	Fm strp cass	1 3 2			Fm strp R/F	1 3 3			R 8 LOOP	1 0 2	
	S 8 LOOP	1 4 1			3 1/2x 4	1 4 5			Ext. Cord	1 4 9	
	ADAPTER	1 5 0			Ptch. Crd.	1 5 4			OPERATOR	1 5 9	
	TV VCR Ens	1 7 8			OTHER				OTHER		

MATERIALS

SHELF NO.   NOTES:

| ― | ' | ― | ' | ― |

TITLE _____

_____
_____
_____
_____   Booked by _____

205

Media Distribution Monthly Report

The "Media Distribution Monthly Report" gives a monthly breakdown of service volume by type of equipment. Computerized tabulation is possible through use of equipment code numbers. Utilization volume is shown by the number of "requests filled" and "students served." Additional information calls for the number of "requests not filled," "students not served," and a "requests not filled code." By tabulating what cannot be done the media manager is in a much better position to recommend changes in service procedures or request additional budget. Reasons why a request cannot be filled usually fall into several predictable categories, so the coding process is not difficult. The "requests not filled code" is first determined from the "Media Distribution Service Request," shown on page 205. Cancellations are added to complete transactions in order to determine total transactions since a cancellation can take up valuable booking time.

Rental Film Order

The "Rental Film Order", page 208, is used for renting 16mm films. Although designed for film rental, this form could be used for any kind of program rental agreement. Since there are several steps involved in renting a film, the objective is to complete as many steps as possible when typing the initial order. A pressure sensitive multiple copy form is recommended so when filling in the top sheet all copies are completed simultaneously. Suggested routing for color coded copies of this form is the following: (1) white goes to the vendor as a request to rent the film; (2) green is filed alphabetically by film title; (3) yellow is placed in a master file by sequential order number with the remaining copies still attached until there is a response from the vendor; (4) gold is sent to the client if film is not available and the rest of the copies are thrown away; (5) pink is sent to the client if the film is confirmed by the vendor; (6) gold is sent to the client when film arrives indicating where and when it will be delivered; and (7) blue is sent to the film library where the film is received, circulated, and mailed back.

Equipment Check-In Form

The "Equipment Check-In Form", page 209, organizes the process of checking in new equipment. When new equipment arrives, numerous problems can cause costly mistakes and confusion. Damaged, incomplete, and incorrect shipments represent just a few typical problems.

All important purchasing information is listed such as purchase order number, dealer, and requisition number. Information to the left of the double lines

Media Distribution
Monthly Report

TYPE Filmstrips	Requests Filled	Students Served	Requests Not Filled	Students Not Served	Requests Not Filled Code*
Films					
6mm Projectors					
Filmstrip Projectors					
Opaque Projectors					
Overhead Projectors					
Projection Carts					
Dissolve Unit					
8mm Projector (regular)					
8mm Projector (super)					
8mm Projector (super/sound)					
Record Player Monaural					
Record Player Stereo					
Screens					
Slide Projector					
Audio Cassette Slide/Sync (player)					
Audio Cassette Slide/Sync (recorder)					
Audio reel-to-reel Monaural Recorder					
Audio reel-to-reel Stereo Recorder					
Audio Cassette Record/Play					
Super 8mm Camera					
TV Camera					
TV Tripod					
Video Cassette Record/Play					
TV VTR 3600					
TV Monitors (black & white)					
TV Monitors (color)					
TV VTR Rover					
TV Systems Ensemble					
Filmstrip/Sound Cassette					
Filmstrip Sound Record/Play					
Super 8mm Loop Projector					
Lantern Slide Projector					
Rental Film					
6mm Projector Ensemble					
Operator					
Projection Bulbs					
Totals					

Cancellations _____

Transactions + _____

TRANSACTIONS _____

*Code for Requests Not Filled:
1 Equipment and/or material checked out and not available
2 Student help not available
3 Equipment down

RENTAL FILM ORDER

VENDOR

SHIP FILM & COMPLETED INVOICE

VOUCHER TO: **Media Services**
University
Anywhere, USA

Catalog No.	Title	Use Date	Price	Order Date	No.

Film Length _____ Alternate Dates _____

Instructor _____ Dept. _____

Your Film: ☐ Has been confirmed ☐ Is not available

☐ Has arrived and will be delivered _____ to _____ on _____ run

Film must be returned _____ at _____

NOTE:

DATE ARRIVED _____ CHECKED BY _____ INSURANCE VALUE _____

REQ. # _____

DESCRIPTION	SERIAL #	DESCRIBE MISSING PART	BACK ORDERED	NOT FUNCTIONING	DATE RETURNED	WARRANTY COMPLETED	COMPLETELY OK	TAG #	CODE #	MS #

CHECKED BY _____ DATE _____ DELIVERED TO _____

By signing, I affirm order is complete. SIGNATURE _____

WHITE COPY - MEDIA SERVICES OFFICE   YELLOW COPY - MAINTENANCE

PINK COPY - DEPARTMENT

209

indicates the status of equipment items in the purchase order including missing parts and whether a portion of the purchase order has been back-ordered from the manufacturer for later delivery. Only when each item is totally satisfactory should the equipment coding information to the right of the double lines be completed. Equipment coding can include stenciling numbers on each item for identification and circulation. In this case "Tag #" refers to a thin metal tag with an inventory number which is affixed to each equipment item. The "Code #" and "MS #" are brightly colored numbers stenciled on each item indicating equipment type and circulation number respectively. For example, 025-10 could mean slide projector number 10.

There are spaces provided at the bottom for important signatures such as the staff member checking in the equipment and the department representative receiving the equipment. A pressure sensitive multiple copy form is recommended so when filling in the top sheet all copies are completed simultaneously. Suggested routing for color coded copies of this form is the following: (1) white goes to the media center office; (2) yellow goes to the maintenance or repair department; and (3) pink goes to the department receiving the equipment. You might want to combine the "Equipment Check-In Form" and the "Equipment History," page 212, so all important data regarding a specific piece of equipment is on one form.

EQUIPMENT REPAIR

DATE SENT OUT _____ DATE RETURNED _____

EQUIPMENT _____ MS # _____

DIFFICULTY REPORTED   COST

PARTS _____

_____

_____

_____

_____ [

_____

LABOR _____

_____ [

TOTAL _____ [

Equipment Repair

The "Equipment Repair" form provides a place to describe problems and record resulting repair costs. A pressure sensitive multiple copy form is recommended so when filling in the top sheet all copies are completed simultaneously. One copy of the form can be attached to the equipment item going to repair while another copy is kept on file with the department requesting maintenance. Length of time required for repair and resulting cost are important pieces of information on this form. Once the equipment is fixed, all important cost information can be transferred to the "Equipment History" form, page 212.

Equipment History

The "Equipment History", page 212, form brings together all important cost information for a piece of equipment. Purchase and check-in information is located across the top. The account number from which the equipment item was purchased along with requisition and purchase order numbers can be very helpful if there is a need to check back on original paper work. "Location Code" is a number designating where the equipment is assigned. "Code #" and "MS #" are numbers used for identification and circulation. See the "Equipment Check-In Form," pages 206 and 210, for a full discussion of "Code #" and "MS #."

A place is provided to record all maintenance costs for the equipment item. Frequency of repair, length of time in repair, and resulting repair costs are all useful sources of information. The "Equipment History" can be a valuable resource when deciding whether to purchase more of a particular brand and model of equipment. There are many cases where the total maintenance cost can be much more than the original purchase price for a piece of equipment. You might want to combine the "Equipment History" and "Equipment Check-In Form," page 209, so all important data regarding a specific piece of equipment is located on one form.

EQUIPMENT HISTORY

Acct.# _____ Req.# _____ P.O.# _____ Dealer _____ Purchase Price _____

DESCRIPTION	SERIAL #	LOCATION CODE	INVENTORY #	CODE #	M S #

MAINTENANCE RECORD

DATE		Repairs	Parts	Labor	Total
OUT	IN				

LEARNING RESOURCE CENTER FORMS

Circulation Card

A circulation card, page 214, is completed for each software or program item placed in a learning resource center. Each card is completed in numerical order by "Call Number." "Date" indicates when the item was placed in the materials collection. One card is completed for each item. Multiple copies of an item can be noted on the card. A place is also provided for special instructions such as restricted circulation in the "Notes" space. Each time an item is checked out the date, individual's social security number, and course number are noted on the card. Information can be transferred from these cards to the "Learning Resource Center Monthly Utilization" on page 215.

Learning Resource Center Monthly Utilization

A learning resource center typically houses mediated instructional programs which students check out and use on a self-paced basis. The typical learning resource center has branched out and accepted responsibility for services other than just checking out mediated programs. Simulation units, basic production facilities, and audiovisual equipment practice areas have also become service aspects of a learning resource center. The "Learning Resource Center Monthly Utilization", page 215, expresses utilization by students served for the major service functions of graphic production, audio production, audiovisual equipment practice, lesson playback, and special workshops. Utilization is also shown by departments that have students using the learning resource center services. "Learning Resource Center Cost Analysis" includes all direct operational costs divided by the number of students served to determine the cost per student. Dividing direct operational costs by students served provides a quick easy cost effectiveness figure for the whole area. A more refined cost analysis technique could figure cost on the basis of contact hours, the actual time a student worked in a specific learning resource area. Although cost analysis based on contact hours is much more accurate, it is also more difficult to tabulate.

Call Number	Date	Card#
Title:		

Copies		Notes	
Date	Soc.Sec. #	Course	

Department	GRAPHICS			AUDIO PROD.	AV EQUIP. PRAC.	LESSONS				SPECIAL WORKSHOPS	Total
	Work-shops	Graphic Production	Material Sold			Audio	Tape/ Slide	Kits	Video-cassettes		
Total											

*Utilization is expressed in students served except materials sold column

LEARNING RESOURCE CENTER COST ANALYSIS

FACTORS	EXPENDITURE
Commodities	$ _____
Contractual	$ _____
Personnel	$ _____
Student Help	$ _____
TOTAL COST	$ _____ ÷ _____ Students Served = $ _____ Cost/Student

A SELECTED BIBLIOGRAPHY

THIS BIBLIOGRAPHY provides further information on many topics important to the field of media center management. Sources selected are grouped in broad subject areas. There are cases of overlap where, for example, a source might fit equally well under "Instructional Development" or "Materials Evaluation and Utilization." Therefore, check under several appropriate topic headings since the author did not multiple list publications. In most cases, annotations are directly quoted from the publications cited to ensure accuracy.

MANAGEMENT SKILLS

American Association of School Librarians (AASL), American Library Association (ALA), and the Association for Educational Communications and Technology (AECT). *Media Programs: District and School.* Washington, D.C.: American Library Association and the Association for Educational Communications and Technology, 1975.

This publication delineates guidelines and recommendations for media programs and resources essential for quality education. Major focus is on qualitative goals, offering criteria for district and school media programs that make exemplary educational experiences available to children and youth. Standards are provided for staff, collections, and facilities. All recommendations apply to public and parochial school systems and to independent schools. This publication replaces *Standards for School Media Programs,* published jointly in 1969 by AASL and the Department of Audiovisual Instruction of the National Education Association (since 1971, AECT).

Association for Educational Communications and Technology (AECT) and the Association of Media Producers. *Copyright and Educational Media: A Guide to Fair Use and Permissions Procedures.* Washington, D.C.: Association for Educational Communications and Technology and the Association of Media Producers, 1977.

This book discusses the fair use section of the new copyright law enacted January 1978 and includes examples of fair use applications. The guide also provides helpful information about the permissions process.

————. *Evaluative Checklist: An Instrument for Self-Evaluating an Educational Media Program in Colleges and Universities.* Washington, D.C.: Association for Educational Communications and Technology, 1979.

A checklist which facilitates an evaluation of educational media programs in higher education, allowing comparison of elements in media service programs.

————. *Evaluative Checklist: An Instrument for Self-Evaluating an Educational Media Program in School Systems.* Washington, D.C.: Association for Educational Communications and Technology, 1979.

A widely used, validated method designed to discriminate among the varying levels of quality in school system educational media programs.

————. *Guidelines for Certification of Media Specialists.* Washington, D.C.: Association for Educational Communications and Technology, 1978.

Updated materials on certification, including a status report on state certification and practices, competency-based model and task lists, background and supporting materials.

————. *Evaluating Media Programs: District and School.* Washington, D.C.: Association for Educational Communications and Technology, 1976.

A detailed comprehensive workbook for evaluating media programs at the school district level; based on another Association for Educational Communications and Technology publication, *Media Programs: District and School.*

————. *Planning and Operating Media Centers: Readings from Audiovisual Instruction-2.* Washington, D.C.: Association for Educational Communications and Technology, 1975.

A collection of articles from *Audiovisual Instruction* magazine, dealing with media centers in grades K–12 and media center case studies.

Brown, James W., ed. *Educational Media Yearbook.* New York: R. R. Bowker Co. Annually.

Published annually and designed as a source of information on developments in educational media that is frequently required by media specialists in schools, colleges and universities, libraries, industrial organizations involved with training, educational broadcasters, media designers-producers-distributors, and publishers, as well as by professors and students of instructional technology, audiovisual education, library science, information science, and telecommunications. Has directory of producers, distributors, and publishers.

Brown, James W.; Norberg, Kenneth D.; and Srygley, Sara K. *Administering Educational Media: Instructional Technology and Library Services.* 2nd ed. New York: McGraw-Hill, 1972.

The central concern of this book is the organization and administration of educational media services to support and extend opportunities for teaching and learning. The authors' interests, in these respects, range from elementary and secondary schools, school districts and counties, state departments of education, and colleges and universities through various units of government and industry, including the research and development centers that now seek to bridge the gap between research and practice in education. Includes bibliographies.

Brush, Douglas P. and Judith M. *Private Television Communications: An Awakening Giant*. New Providence, New Jersey: International Industrial Television Association, 1977.

The purpose of this study was to investigate the wide range of uses and applications of private television so the management of both present and future video user organizations could make more effective decisions on their own use of television. Results were based on responses from 273 organizations to a survey along with over 50 in-depth interviews. This follows up a 1974 study conducted by the same authors entitled *Private Television Communications: A Report to Management*. Includes a bibliography.

Bunyan, John; Crimmins, James; and Watson, N. Kyri. *Practical Video: The Manager's Guide to Applications*. White Plains, N.Y.: Knowledge Industry Publications, Inc., 1978.

At the heart of this book are dozens of case histories using television for specific applications to solve communication problems. Each case history usually includes a summary of the equipment used by the producing facility and basic personnel budget figures.

————. *Television and Management—The Manager's Guide to Video*. New York: Knowledge Industry Publications, 1977.

Major emphasis is placed on practical information on how television can be used effectively in corporations, non-profit institutions and government. The idea of this book is to bring together the manager and the video producer in order to teach the manager about video and help the video producer better solve management problems.

Educational Technology. Educational Technology Publications, 140 Sylvan Avenue, Englewood Cliffs, New Jersey, 07632. Monthly.

A magazine for managers dealing with technological change and innovation in education at all levels.

Erickson, Carlton W. H. *Administering Instructional Media Programs*. New York: The Macmillan Company, 1968.

The contents of this textbook are directed toward graduate students who are undertaking their preparation for leadership in the instructional media field, but the very nature of the purpose and arrangement of the content enhances its value as a handbook for school-building media-program coordinators and as a guide for planning by school superintendents, principals, and curriculum specialists. The book includes guidelines and principles, case studies of common practice, and examples of advanced media programs that should aid the prospective media director. Includes bibliographies.

Hannigan, Jane Anne, and Estes, Glenn E. *Media Center Facilities Design*. Chicago: American Library Association, 1978.

This publication looks at the many human, educational and physical factors that must be considered when planning media center facilities. Numerous experts in the field of media center facilities design have contributed articles in this publication.

Instructional Innovator (formerly *Audiovisual Instruction*). Association for Educational Communications and Technology, 1126 16th Street, N.W., Washington, D.C., 20036. Monthly (September–June).

The official publication of the Association for Educational Communications and Technology, *Instructional Innovator* includes articles and features on current topics in educational media and instructional technology.

Liesener, James W. *A Systematic Process for Planning Media Programs.* Chicago: American Library Association, 1976.

The process, techniques, and conceptual model described are the result of efforts, begun by the author in 1968, to conceptualize media programs more systematically and to develop more sophisticated management tools for improving the capability of media personnel to articulate and develop more responsive and effective programs of media services.

Merrill, Irving, and Drob, Harold. *Criteria for Planning the College and University Learning Resources Center.* Washington, D.C.: Association for Educational Communications and Technology, 1977.

Staff and space criteria for the development of a learning resources program for colleges and universities, covering media production, media services, instructional development, administration, and planning.

Tracey, William R. *Managing Training and Development Systems.* New York: AMACOM, a Division of American Management Associations, 1974.

This book is highly specific to training and development and focuses on the practical problems of training managers. Its aim is to describe critical elements of the training management process—the elements that are fundamental to the successful and profitable operation of training and development activities—in all types of enterprise, large and small, public and private, profit and nonprofit. Includes bibliographies.

LIBRARY SKILLS

Akers, Susan G. *Akers' Simple Library Cataloging.* 6th ed. Revised by Arthur Carley and Jana Varlejs. Metuchen, New Jersey: Scarecrow Press, 1977.

This book tries to give the librarian of a small public school, college or special library the basic required skills needed for cataloging. In attempting to adapt the complex body of established cataloging rules for effective use by small libraries, simplification has of course been a goal, but enabling the small library to achieve excellence in providing access to its resources has been the overriding objective of this manual. Precedes *Anglo-American Cataloging Rules,* 2nd ed. Includes bibliographies.

Bloomberg, Marty, and Evans, G. Edward. *Introduction to Technical Services for Library Technicians.* 3rd ed. Littleton, Colorado: Libraries Unlimited, 1976.

This text is meant to serve as a general introduction to technical services for library technicians and other non-professionals. The material covered should give the reader a foundation on which to develop library skills through practical work experience.

Cabeceiras, James. *The Multimedia Library: Materials Selection and Use.* New York: Academic Press, 1978.

This book is intended as a basic introduction to the selection and utilization of various information media in all types of libraries. The book analyzes the characteristics of each type of information medium with regard to uniqueness as well as similarity to other information media, providing a systematic general approach to their selection and utilization. The writing is concise and succinct, and the inclusion of history, theory, and complicated technical data has been intentionally held to a minimum. Includes bibliographies.

Carter, Mary Duncan; Bunk, Wallace John; and Magrill, Mary Rose. *Building Library Collections*. 4th ed. Metuchen, New Jersey: Scarecrow Press, 1974.

This book is divided into three parts: selection, acquisitions, and appendices. Emphasis is not placed on record keeping and management controls, but rather on developing sound procedures for building collections that will be beneficial to the community served by the library. Includes bibliographies.

Hicks, Warren B., and Tillian, Alma M. *Developing Multi-media Libraries*. New York: Bowker Co., 1970.

This book presents the concept of the modern library as a comprehensive resource center. The philosophy and objectives of the center are clarified, and desirable practices in the selection and acquisition of nonbook or audiovisual materials—interchangeably defined as those materials that communicate primarily through aural and visual stimuli—are recommended, along with information pertinent to facilitating these tasks. Includes bibliographies.

————. *Managing Multi-Media Libraries*. New York: R. R. Bowker Co., 1977.

This book deals with the problems and practices of selection, acquisition, cataloging, and administration of non-book or audiovisual materials.

Johnson, Jean Thornton; Franklin, Marietta Griffin; McCotter, Margaret Palmer; and Warner, Veronica Britt. *AV Cataloging and Processing Simplified*. Cincinnati, Ohio: Capozzolo Typesetting and Printing, 1971.

A manual divided into 20 sections, each dealing with different media types. Each section includes: definition, cataloging, accessioning, processing, storing, a work sheet sample of the media type, and sample catalog cards. Includes bibliography.

Piercy, Esther J. *Commonsense Cataloging*. 2nd ed. Revised by Marian Sanner. New York: H.W. Wilson Co., 1974.

This book is designed to be practical, to serve as a manual or handbook for the beginning cataloger, trained or untrained. The reviser has retained the arrangement of the first edition, proceeding from the general to the specific, from principles to practices. Precedes the *Anglo-American American Cataloging Rules, 2nd Edition*. Includes bibliography.

Tillin, Alma M., and Quinly, William J. *Standards for Cataloging Nonprint Materials*. 4th ed. Washington, D.C.: Association for Educational Communications and Technology, 1976.

This volume concerns itself solely with the cataloging of nonprint materials. This is not a manual on how to catalog. It is assumed that those who use it have a knowledge of cataloging, classification, and subject analysis. References to the *Anglo-American Cataloging Rules* are provided to assist those who wish to consult the full text of the original rule. Includes bibliography.

Wynar, Bohdan S., and Immroth, John Philip. *Introduction to Cataloging and Classification*. 5th ed. Littleton, CO: Libraries Unlimited, 1976.

This book is both an introductory text for the beginning student in library science and a handy companion volume for practicing catalogers. Any changes in the *Anglo-American Cataloging Rules* through 1975 have been incorporated in this fifth edition. Includes bibliography.

INSTRUCTIONAL DEVELOPMENT

Cavert, C. Edward. *An Approach to the Design of Mediated Instruction.* Washington, D.C.: Association for Educational Communications and Technology, 1974.

A reference text covering frame of reference, definition of target population, needs, goals, strategy, structure, mediation, and diagnosis.

Hug, William E. *Instructional Design and the Media Program.* Chicago: American Library Association, 1975.

The purpose of this book is to assist school and district media professionals, school administrators, and teachers to build media programs as an integral part of the school curriculum. The book supports a movement away from the limited perceptions of the school library, toward a more comprehensive view of the media program. This more comprehensive view stresses the value of instructional design.

Journal of Instructional Development (JID). Association for Educational Communications and Technology, 1126 16th Street, N.W., Washington, D.C., 20036. Quarterly.

A journal devoted exclusively to instructional development, JID contains articles on theories, techniques, reports, case studies, and critical reviews of instructional development projects and systems. Of particular interest to those involved with the design, implementation, and evaluation of courses or curricula.

Kemp, Jerrold E. *Instructional Design: A Plan for Unit and Course Development.* 2nd ed. Belmont, California: Fearon Publishers, 1977. (now Pitman Learning, Inc.)

Suggestions on methods for defining purpose, organizing content, selecting learning methods, and utilizing technological development. Includes bibliography.

Mager, Robert F. *Preparing Instructional Objectives.* 2nd ed. Belmont, California: Fearon Publishers, Inc., 1975. (now Pitman Learning, Inc.)

A clear statement of objectives will provide a sound basis for choosing methods and materials and for selecting the means for assessing whether the instruction has been successful. This book provides techniques on how to state such objectives.

Training. Lakewood Publications, 731 Hennepin Avenue, Minneapolis, Minnesota, 55403. Monthly.

A magazine covering solutions to training problems in business and industry. May, 1976, started special monthly feature, "Resource Center," covering advantages and disadvantages of media equipment along with a chart comparing specifications from different manufacturers.

Training and Development Journal. American Society for Training and Development, Box 5307, Madison, Wisconsin, 53705. Monthly.

A journal providing articles on training and human resource development.

MATERIALS EVALUATION AND UTILIZATION

Anderson, Ron H. *Selecting and Developing Media for Instruction.* New York: American Society for Training and Development and Van Nostrand Reinhold Company, 1976.

This book is intended as a reference guide for anyone involved with the process of selecting media and planning the development of media for instructional purposes. Although aimed primarily at course writers and instructors, it can also be a valuable tool for managers of training departments or supervisors of course development programs. Includes selected references.

Association for Educational Communications and Technology. *Selecting Media for Learning*. Washington, D.C.: Association for Educational Communications and Technology, 1976.

Thirty-one articles from *Audiovisual Instruction* magazine on selecting media for instruction. The articles are grouped under four major sections: selecting media in accordance with objectives of instruction; media evaluation procedures and guidelines; instructional development and the selection process; and external factors affecting materials selection.

Brown, James W.; Lewis, Richard B.; and Harcleroad, Fred F. *AV Instruction: Technology, Media and Methods*. 5th ed. New York: McGraw-Hill, 1977.

This book presents an overview of media used for instruction and communication and can be used as a text for pre-service and in-service teachers, media specialists, and librarians, and for curriculum and course developers from preschool through college and continuing education. Principles, practices and resources discussed are relevant for training programs in business, industry, government, and other organizations. Includes classified directory of sources for audiovisual materials, programs, services, and equipment.

Educational Communication and Technology Journal (formerly *AV Communication Review*). Association for Educational Communications and Technology, 1126 16th Street, N.W., Washington, D.C. 20036. Quarterly.

A research journal featuring indepth articles on communication, technology, and the teaching/learning process.

Educator's Purchasing Guide. 6th ed. North American Publishing Company, 134 North 13th Street, Philadelphia, Pennsylvania, 19107, 1974.

A reference source listing publishers, producers, and manufacturers of educational materials, equipment, and supplies for 12,000 product categories resulting in over 100,000 entries.

EPIEgram: Materials. Educational Products Information Exchange Institute, P.O. Box 620, Stony Brook, NY 11790. Bimonthly (October–June).

An educational consumer's newsletter providing information on problems and solutions regarding the use of instructional materials and programs.

EPIE Materials Report. Educational Products Information Exchange Institute, P.O. Box 620, Stony Brook, NY 11790. Quarterly.

Contains objective analyses of instructional materials in a given discipline, at times with reports from classroom users of materials.

Gerlach, Vernon S., and Ely, Donald P. *Teaching and Media: A Systematic Approach*. Englewood Cliffs, New Jersey: Prentice-Hall, Inc., 1971.

This book is an attempt to identify and to describe in detail several elements of teaching which have been useful to good teachers in the past and appear to be of continuing value. This book casts the teaching-learning process into a new scheme known as a *systematic approach to teaching learning*. It will provide the teacher with a framework for the design of instruction and give the learner a roadmap for his educational process. The content is a blend of the science of learning and the art of teaching that focuses on the learner, the definition of objectives, instructional design, the proper selection of media, and the teacher as a coordinator of the entire process. Includes bibliographies.

Media and Methods. North American Publishing Company, 401 North Broad Street, Philadelphia, Pennsylvania, 19108. Monthly (September–May).

Has articles dealing with the development and utilization of educational media materials with some articles on management of learning resource centers.

Previews. R. R. Bowker Company, 1180 Avenue of the Americas, New York, New York, 10036. Monthly (September–May).

Provides news and reviews of nonprint media.

Webster, William J. *The Evaluation of Instructional Materials.* Washington, D.C.: Association for Educational Communications and Technology, 1976.

This publication has three objectives: (1) to synthesize, through a selective review of the literature, a brief description of the state of the art of evaluation; (2) to present a working model demonstrating the functions of various forms of evaluation in assessing the relative merits of instructional materials; and (3) to provide an annotated bibliography of sources for readers seeking further information on evaluation. Includes bibliography.

EQUIPMENT EVALUATION AND UTILIZATION

Audio-Visual Equipment Directory, The. National Audio-Visual Association, Inc., 3150 Spring Street, Fairfax, Virginia, 22030. Annually.

A directory listing many types and brands of audiovisual equipment along with specifications and price information.

Bensinger, Charles. *The Video Guide.* 2nd ed. New York: Esselt Video Inc., 1979.

A "how to" book on the set up and use of basic video equipment. Topic areas covered include operation, maintenance, setting goals, and purchasing equipment.

EPIEgram: Equipment. Educational Products Information Exchange Institute, P.O. Box 620, Stony Brook, NY 11790. Bimonthly (October–June).

An educational consumer's newsletter providing information on problems and solutions regarding the use and operation of media hardware.

EPIE Equipment Report. Educational Products Information Exchange Institute, P.O. Box 620, Stony Brook, NY 11790. Quarterly.

In its fully equipped testing facility, EPIE tests audiovisual and other equipment used in schools and the findings are published in *EPIE Equipment Report.*

Laird, Dugan. *A-V Buyer's Guide: A User's Look at the Audio-Visual World.* 2nd ed. Fairfax, Virginia: National Audio-Visual Association, 1977.

Brief concise summary of rationale for selecting and purchasing audiovisual equipment along with basic descriptions of most commonly used audiovisual equipment. Includes bibliography.

Library Technology Reports. American Library Association, 50 East Huron St., Chicago, Illinois, 60611. Bimonthly.

Evaluative information on library systems, equipment and supplies.

Videofreex. *The Spaghetti City Video Manual.* New York: Praeger Publications, 1973.

A guide to use, repair, and maintenance of small system video equipment. Includes reference section.

Wallington, C. James, and Bruce, Carol. *Training Programs for Educational Media Technicians.* Washington, D.C.: Association for Educational Communications and Technology, 1972.

This publication is a directory to training programs for educational media technicians in junior, technical, and community colleges. With the increasing need to find qualified technicians for all types of media equipment, the media center manager might find this publication helpful when needing to hire technical personnel.

"Writing Equipment Specifications: A How-to Handbook." *EPIE Report 72* (Special Report), revised edition of *EPIE Report 28*. Educational Products Information Exchange Institute, P.O. Box 620, Stony Brook, NY 11790.

In this report, EPIE has attempted to provide information and guidance in the critically important area of specifying what to look for when purchasing specific types of instructional equipment or systems. Guidance is provided on writing specifications that clearly communicate the buyer's wishes.

Wyman, Raymond. *Mediaware: Selection, Operation and Maintenance.* 2nd ed. Dubuque, Iowa: William C. Brown Company, 1976.

A book for people who must understand, select, operate, and maintain audiovisual equipment, or train teachers and students in its operation. This book is written with the assumption that most readers have a very limited, or no, technical background. Includes reference section.

PRODUCTION

Educational and Industrial Television. C. S. Tepfer Publishing Company, Inc., 607 Main Street, Ridgefield, Connecticut, 06877. Monthly.

Has articles dealing with production and management of instructional television facilities in education and business.

Kemp, Jerrold E. *Planning and Producing Audiovisual Materials.* 4th ed. New York: Harper and Row, 1980.

Primarily a text book on the production and proper application of media materials for effective learning. Major emphasis is placed on the use of learning theory when planning audiovisual materials and selecting the most appropriate medium to serve specific instructional needs. Includes bibliography and sources for equipment, materials, and services.

Mattingly, Grayson, and Smith, Welby. *Introducing the Single-Camera VTR System.* New York: Charles Scribner's Sons, 1973.

A basic introductory book covering practical information required for the successful use of a single camera VTR system.

Minor, Ed., and Frye, Harvey R. *Techniques for Producing Visual Instructional Media.* New York: McGraw-Hill Book Company, 1970.

Provides techniques, methods, and processes for preparing modern visual instructional media. The book is concerned with simplified methods and it has been written both for the person without skills in art, graphic art, and photography, and for the professional seeking new approaches to production problems. Includes bibliography.

Quick, John, and Wolff, Herbert. *Small Studio Video Tape Production.* Reading, Massachusetts: Addison-Wesley Publishing, 1972.

A discussion of methods for selecting equipment, organizing the layout of a small studio, necessary personnel, and ways to produce video programming.

Video Systems. Intertec Publishing Corporation, 9221 Quivira Road, P.O. Box 12901, Overland Park, Kansas, 66212. Bimonthly.

Articles cover television production techniques and general areas of interest to people managing television production facilities.

Videography. United Business Publications, Inc., 750 Third Avenue, New York, New York, 10017. Monthly.

Articles dealing with the use of video in profit and non-profit organizations.

VU Marketplace. Knowledge Industry Publications, 2 Corporate Park Drive, White Plains, New York, 10604. Biweekly.

A newspaper for users and producers of video hardware, programs, and services.

COMPUTER TECHNOLOGY

Baker, Frank B. *Computer Managed Instruction: Theory and Practice.* Englewood Cliffs, NJ: Educational Technology Publications, 1978.

The book has two goals: (1) to provide the reader with the conceptual framework for computer managed instruction (CMI); and (2) to initiate a dialogue leading to a definition of instructional management. Major emphasis is to appeal to a general audience of persons in the field of education. Includes bibliography.

Interface Age. McPheters, Wolfe, and Jones, 13913 Artesia Blvd., Cerritos, California, 90701. Monthly.

Covers the broad spectrum of computer application, written for the person without a background in computer technology. Specific issues have dealt with the use of computers in education.

Levien, Roger E., and others. *The Emerging Technology: Instructional Uses of the Computer in Higher Education.* New York: McGraw-Hill, 1972.

A study for the nontechnical reader that examines the use of computers in higher education, the current state of the use of computers in general, and the future prospects of computer assisted instruction.

onComputing. onComputing, Inc., 70 Main Street, Peterbrough, NH, 03458. Quarterly.

A guide to personal computers to keep people informed on new developments in the field of personal mini computers.

Rothman, Stanley, and Mosemann, Charles. *Computers and Society.* 2nd ed. Chicago: Science Research Associates, 1976.

Written for people without a computer background. The book works its way from the technology through applications to social impact and the future. There are special sections covering the use of computers in education and administration. Includes bibliographies.

Sanders, Susan; Speedie, Stuart; Richardson, Duane and others. *The Computer in Educational Decision Making.* Hanover, NH: Time Share, 1978.

The purpose of this book is to provide the educational administrator with a working understanding of the most useful operations research techniques and experience in using computers to provide the background computations required by each. The emphasis throughout the text is on the practical application of the techniques to solve educational problems. Includes bibliographies.

ASSOCIATIONS AND ORGANIZATIONS

American Library Association (ALA), 50 Huron Street, Chicago, Illinois, 60611. (312) 944-6780.

Librarians, libraries, trustees, friends of libraries, and others interested in the responsibilities of libraries in the educational, social, and cultural needs of society.

To promote libraries and librarianship to assure the delivery of user-oriented library information service to all. Approximately 33,000 members.

American Society for Training and Development (ASTD), P.O. Box 5307, Madison, Wisconsin, 53705. (608) 274-3440.

Professional society of persons engaged in the training and development of business, industrial, and government personnel. Established Media Division in 1976. Approximately 14,500 members.

Association for Educational Communications and Technology (AECT), 1126 16th Street, N.W., Washington, D.C., 20036. (202) 833-4180.

Audiovisual and instructional materials specialists, educational technologists, audiovisual and television production personnel and teacher educators. To improve education through the systematic planning, application, and production of communications media for instruction. Approximately 9,000 members.

Association of Audio-Visual Technicians (AAVT), 236½ West 13th Avenue, Denver, Colorado, 80204. (303) 534-5671.

An international organization of audiovisual production and repair technicians and instructors in schools, industry, and service shops. The purpose of the organization is to exchange information within and about the audiovisual industry as it pertains to technicians. Approximately 800 members.

Educational Products Information Exchange Institute (EPIE), P.O. Box 620, Stony Brook, NY 11790. (516) 751-1457.

The EPIE Institute gathers and disseminates descriptive and analytical information—along with empirical information on performance and effects on learners—about instructional materials, equipment, and systems. EPIE is a not-for-profit, consumer-supported agency.

International Television Association, 26 South Street, New Providence, New Jersey, 07974. (201) 464-6747.

Persons engaged in communications needs analysis, script writing, producing, directing, consulting, and operations management in the videotape and non-broadcast television fields. Seeks to advance the arts and sciences in the field of non-broadcast industrial television as used in business training and corporate communications. Approximately 1,600 members.

INDEX

Accountability of employees, 18, 25
Acquisition of instructional materials, 108-09
Advanced training of personnel, 33, 36
Advertising for personnel, 26-27
Affective domain in learning, 98
American Airlines, training complex of, 77
Anderson, Ron H., 98, 102
Art director, 3, 4
Audio production forms, 197-203
Audiotapes: advantages and disadvantages of, 122, 127; operating environment for, 129; time commitments to, based on media characteristics, 163
Automatic presentation rate of media material, 121, 124
A-V Buyer's Guide: A User's Look at the Audio-Visual World (Laird), 126
Average cost analysis by type of request (audio), 200, 203
Average life depreciation in equipment cost accounting, 87, 89, 91, 92, 93

Awards for promoting media center services, 151

Bibliography, 216-26
Bid procedures for equipment purchase, 134-35
Brainstorming, 158
Broadcast Management and Engineering magazine, 131
Brochure, as promotion device, 149
Buyer's list for evaluating equipment, 134

Cataloging of instructional materials, 109
Centralized organization of media center, 10-16, 25
Check-in form, equipment, 206, 209, 210
Check-in procedure for new equipment, 140-44
Clients of media center: 3-4, 5, 9, 11, 17, 24; complaints by, effective handling of,

Clients of media center (*continued*) 169-76; developing constructive relationships with, 156-67; feedback sessions of, 153; needs of, and management needs, 169-71; and political relations, 153, 154, 155

Coding, distribution or circulation, and equipment purchase, 145-46

Cognitive domain in learning, 98

Commercial instructional programs: advantages of, 103-04; resistance to, 103; and tips for selecting commercial materials, 104-05

Complaints, effective handling of, 169-76

Computer technology, 109; in equipment depreciation, 89

Consistency of media center services, 18-19, 25

Consumer's Index to Product Evaluations and Information Sources, 134

Conversion table for regular and military time, 48

Cooperative acquisition plans for instructional materials, 109

Cost accounting, 62-95; equipment, *see* Equipment cost accounting; for television productions, 63-79 *passim; see also* Costs

Cost analysis: average, by type of request (audio), 200, 203; learning resource center, 213

Cost effectiveness, 77-79, 80, 83, 116, 213; in equipment cost accounting, 90-94

Costs: actual and estimated, 76-77; and comparisons, 76-83; determination of, 63, 84; direct, 63, 64-67, 71, 73, 74, 75, 76, 84; estimated and actual, 76-77; indirect, 63, 67, 84; of instructional programs, 80-83; maintenance, of equipment, 84; overhead, 63, 67-76 *passim;* tabulating, 63-76 *passim; see also* Cost accounting

"Creeping complexity," 112

Cross-training of personnel, 29, 33-34, 36

Dealer, selection of, 139-40

Decentralized organization, independent, of media center, 8-10, 25

Depreciation in equipment cost accounting, 84-90, 91

Design of service forms, 37-49

Direct costs, 63, 64-67, 71, 73, 74, 75, 76, 84

Direct learning experience, 98

Director: art, 3, 4; media center, *see* Media center director

Distribution monthly report (media), 206, 207

Distribution service request (media), 204, 205

Dubbing service order (television), 188, 189

Editing log, television, 196

Educational and Industrial Television magazine, 131

Educational Products Information Exchange (EPIE), 87, 90, 131, 134

Equipment: buyer's list for evaluating, 134; essential needs for, 126, 129; evaluation of, 126-34; operating environment for, 129-30; personal experience in evaluating, 130-31; purchase of, *see* Equipment purchase; safety of, 130

Equipment check-in form, 206, 209, 210

Equipment cost accounting, 84-94; computer program in, 89; and cost effectiveness, 90-94; depreciation in, 84-90, 91; purchase price in, 84

Equipment history form, 210, 211, 212

Equipment purchase, 112, 134-46; bid procedures for, 134-35; and check-in procedure, 140-44; coding for, 145-46; and dealer, selecting, 139-40; and inventory procedure, 144-45; requisitions for, *see* Requisitions

Equipment repair form, 210, 211

Equipment selection, 115-34; case study in, 118-19; cautions regarding, 111-15; and demand for equipment, projected, 116, 119; to fit function, 119-26; and function of equipment, determination of, 115-19; and money set aside for equipment incidentals, 117, 119; screening questions concerning, 115-19; and security provisions, 117, 119; and software packages, 117, 119; and units needed, 117, 119

Evaluation forms: for equipment, 131, 132; for instructional materials, 105, 106, 107; for promoting media center services, 152

Exhibits for promoting media center services, 149-50

External information from service form, 37, 38, 39

File, resource, and commercial instructional program, 104

Film order, rental, 206, 208

Filmstrips, 121, 124, 125, 126; advantages and disadvantages of, 120, 122, 127; and class size, 125; time commitments to, based on media characteristics, 163

Floor plans for media center, 13, 14, 15

Graphic artist time record, 180

Graphic production monthly report, 183, 185, 186

Graphic production request, 178, 179

Graphics departmental summary sheet, 183, 184

Graphics in-house report, 182, 183

Graphics working record, 181

Group, large, media material presented to, 120-21

Group interaction, small, as teaching-learning pattern, 98

Growth projections, 21-22

Hybrid organization of media center (centralization with decentralization), 16-18, 25

Independent decentralized organization of media center, 8-10, 25

Indirect costs, 63, 67, 84

Individual, media material presented to, 120

Individualized learning, as teaching-learning pattern, 98

Information from service forms: essential, 38, 49; external, 37, 38, 39; internal, 37, 38; logical sequencing of, 38, 40

Instruction: mediated, *see* Mediated instruction; traditional, costs of, 80, 81, 82, 83

Instructional development, 96, 97, 98, 160-61; and commercial programs, *see* Commercial instructional programs; evaluation of, 99; learned through practice, 102; and media selection, 98-99, 101, 103-08; model for, 97-99, 100, 101, 113, 114; practice and theory of, 99-102, 112-15; and program adjustments, 99; and selection of media, 98-99, 101, 103-08; theory and practice of, 99-102, 112-15; updating program for, 99

Instructional materials: acquisition of, 108-09; cataloging of, 109; evaluation forms for, 105, 106, 107; inspection of, before releasing payment, 109; maintenance budget for, 109; preview of, before purchase, 105; selection of, 103-05

Instructional problem, questions concerning, 116, 118

Instructor: compromise by, for good of program, 167; as content specialist, 157, 165; and director, 158, 160, 161, 164-65; essential content covered by, 165; objectives established by, 165; and open mind, 166-67; requirements for, 161-66, 167; and sources of control, 157; time commitments made by, 161, 162, 163, 164

Internal information from service forms, 37, 38

International Television Association, 131

International Television News, 131

Interviews of job applicants, 28, 36

Inventory depreciation schedule, total, 85-87, 88
Inventory procedure, and equipment purchase, 144-45

Kemp, Jerrold E., 97, 98, 102, 120

Laird, Dugan, 126
Learner motivation ratio, 159
Learning, basic kinds of, 98
Learning resource center forms, 213-15
Lease contracts for acquisition of instructional materials, 108, 109
Letters of commendation in promoting media center services, 151
Log: audio production, 197, 199; television, 194-96
Long form requisition, 137

Maintenance costs of equipment, 84
Media center, 1; budget for, 5, 7, 9, 11, 17, 24; centralized organization of, 10-16, 25; clients of, see Clients of media center; and complaints, effective handling of, 169-76; corporate, 3, 4; decentralized organization of, independent, 8-10, 25; definition of, 1; director of, see Media center director; and environmental influences, 3-7; equipment for, 5, 7, 9, 11, 17, 24 (see also Equipment); facilities for, 5, 7, 9, 11, 13, 17, 24; floor plans for, 13, 14, 15; hybrid organization of (centralization with decentralization), 16-18, 25; management of, 4, 5, 6, 9, 11, 17, 24; management tips for, 18-24; organizational approaches to, 7-18; and political relations, 153-55; politics in management of, 5, 6-7, 9, 11, 17, 24; promoting services of, 148-55; and public relations, 148-53; selection and purchase of equipment as responsibility of, 111; staff of, 5, 6, 9, 11, 17, 24; typical, 1, 3; university, 2, 3

Media center director, 3, 4, 6, 7, 116; compromise by, for good of program, 167; and instructor, 158, 160, 161, 164-65; as media specialist, 164, 165; and open mind, 166-67; requirements for, 157-61, 166-67; sample portfolio developed by, 161; and technology, attitude toward, 158-60
Media characteristics, 122-23, 127-28; and class size, 124-25; definitions of, 120-21, 124
Media distribution forms, 204-12
Mediated instruction, 161, 162, 213; costs of, 80, 81, 82, 83
Mediaware: Selection, Operation and Maintenance (Wyman), 131
Meter installation on equipment, 90
Mid-level training of personnel, 33, 36
Model, instructional development, 97-99, 100, 101, 113, 114
Monthly distribution report, media, 206, 207
Monthly graphic production report, 183, 185, 186
Monthly job-in record for graphic production area, 179
Monthly learning resource center utilization, 213, 215
Monthly production report, audio, 200, 201
Monthly production report, television, 191, 192-93
Motion pictures, advantages and disadvantages of, 123, 128

National Audio-Visual Association (NAVA), 140
News releases, 151
Newsletter, as promotional piece, 151-52

Orientation programs for personnel, 30-31, 36
Overcommitment, avoidance of, 22
Overhead costs, 63, 67-76 passim

Overhead projector, 124, 126, 133; evaluation form for, 132; features of, 129
Overhead transparencies, 125, 126, 161; advantages and disadvantages of, 123, 124, 126, 128; and class size, 125; time commitments to, based on media characteristics, 163

Personnel: accountability of, 18, 25; advertising for, 26-27; hiring, 28-29, 36; interviewing, 28, 36; orientation of, 30-31, 36; and performance review, 34-35, 36; references of, checking, 27-28; screening applications of, 27-28, 36; selection of, 26-29, 36; termination of, 35, 36; training of, *see* Training of personnel
Photography, 3, 4, 10, 63
Playback order (television), 189, 190
Presentation, as teaching-learning pattern, 98
Presentation rate of media material: automatic, 121, 124; instructor's control of, 121, 124
Preview of educational materials before purchase, 105
Previews magazine, 131
Printed word abstractions, as category of learning experience, 98
Production monthly report: audio, 200, 201; television, 191, 192-93
Production request: audio, 197, 198; graphic, 178, 179
Production service order, television, 186, 187
Production utilization by department, audio, 200, 202
Program length, and student/trainer attention span, 166
Projector, overhead: *see* Overhead projector
Prototype service form, 41, 42, 49
Psychomotor domain in learning, 98
Public relations, and media center, 148-53
Purchase: of equipment, *see* Equipment

purchase; of instructional materials, 108, 109
Purchase price in equipment cost accounting, 84

Rental film order, 206, 208
Rent-to-own contracts for acquisition of instructional materials, 108, 109
Repair form, equipment, 210, 211
Requisitions, 135-39; long form, 137; short form, 136; writing tips for, 137-39
Resource file, and commercial instructional program, 104
Resumés of personnel, 27
Review panel, and commercial instructional program, 104-05

Satellite centers in hybrid organization of media center, 16, 17, 18
Sensory learning experience, vicarious, 98
Service forms, 177-215; audio production, 197-203; completion time for, 44; design of, 37-49; easy use of, 38; final revisions of, 41, 43-44; graphic production, 179-86; information from, *see* Information from service forms; learning resource center, 213-15; media distribution, 204-12; prototype, 41, 42, 49; revisions of, final, 41, 43-44; staff recommendations for, 40, 49; television production, 186-96
Short form requisition, 136
Slides, 125, 126; advantages and disadvantages of, 122, 124, 127; and class size, 125; time commitments to, based on media characteristics, 163
Small group interaction, as teaching-learning pattern, 98
Staff productivity formula, 19
Staff recommendations for service forms, 40, 49
Staff speakers' bureau for promoting media center services, 150

Staff volume, analysis of, 19-20

Standardization of operational procedures, 23-24, 25, 44, 45

Student evaluation form for instructional materials, 107

Student/trainer attention span, and program length, 166

Superintendent of AV services, 3, 4

Systematic developmental format, 124

Target audience in instructional development model, 97, 99, 113, 114

Television, 8, 10, 13, 19, 51, 117, 124-25, 161, 164; and cost accounting techniques for productions, 63-79 *passim;* and "creeping complexity," 112

Television production forms, 186-96

Time, regular and military, conversion table for, 48

Total inventory depreciation schedule, 85-87, 88

Tours in promoting media center services, 150-51

Traditional instruction, costs of, 80, 81, 82, 83

Training magazine, 131

Training of personnel, 30, 31-34, 36; advanced, 33, 36; beginning, 31-32, 36; cross-, 29, 33-34, 36; mid-level, 33, 36

Transparencies, overhead: *see* Overhead transparencies

Turnaround time, 20, 21, 22, 23, 25, 38

U-matic videocassette machines, 125

United Laboratories (UL), 130

Utilization: audio production, by department, 200, 202; and conciseness of information, 57; and contact hours measurement, 52-53; and deciding what to count, 50-53; expressed in understandable terms, 57; and instructional effectiveness, 53; key concepts in, 50-61 *passim;* learning resource center, 213, 215; making it work for you, 57-58, 61; negative and positive, documentation of, 58, 61; and numerical information, 50-53; positive and negative, documentation of, 58, 61; requests-filled category of, 51; and selection of time frame for comparison, 53-57; students-served category of, 52, 57; and trends, general, 54; units-produced category of, 51-52

Verbal word abstractions, as category of learning experience, 98

Vicarious sensory learning experience, 98

Videocassette recorder, easy operation of, 124, 125

Videography magazine, 131

Videotapes: advantages and disadvantages of, 123, 128; operating environment for, 129; time commitments to, based on media characteristics, 163

Word abstractions, verbal or printed, as category of learning experience, 98

Workshop groups, 31, 33

Wyman, Raymond, 131

DATE DUE